THE PUBLIC'S RIGHT TO KNOW

THE PUBLIC'S RIGHT TO KNOW

The Supreme Court
and the
First Amendment

David M. O'Brien

PRAEGER SPECIAL STUDIES • PRAEGER SCIENTIFIC

Library of Congress Cataloging in Publication Data

O'Brien, David M.
  The public's right to know.

  Bibliography: p.
  Includes indexes.
  1. Government information—United States.
2. Public records—Law and legislation—United
States. I. Title.
KF5753.024   342.73′0853   81-988
ISBN 0-03-062612-9 (pbk.)   AACR2
ISBN 0-03-058029-3 (hb)

Published in 1981 (hb) and 1982 (pb) by Praeger Publishers
CBS Educational and Professional Publishing
A Division of CBS, Inc.
521 Fifth Avenue, New York, New York 10175 U.S.A.

© 1981 by Praeger Publishers

23456789   145   987654321

Printed in the United States of America

For
J. R. O.

"Give me the liberty to know, to utter,
and to argue freely according to
conscience, above all liberties."

John Milton, *Areopagitica*

PREFACE

Prominent in U.S. politics are two perennial controversies: reconciling bureaucratic secrecy with democratic governance, and the equally vexing problem of accommodating judicial review with representative democracy under a written Constitution. The salience of the political ideal of the public's right to know arises precisely because it so intimately touches both of these controversies. In the post-World War II era the public's right to know was championed by the press and in Congress when combating syndromes of administrative secrecy, and was registered in an impressive amount of legislation designed to ensure governmental openness and accountability. The public's right to know also emerged within the grammar of constitutional interpretation. In the 1970s perhaps the most significant First Amendment litigation involved members of the press claiming special privileges and affirmative constitutional rights of access to government information and facilities so as to vindicate the public's right to know.

This book examines the public's right to know in terms of constitutional politics; that is, the politics of constitutional rights as interpreted and enforced by the Supreme Court.. Chapter 1 considers the symbolic appeal and ambiguity of claims to the public's right to know as well as to the basis for asserting a constitutionally enforceable right to know against the government. Chapter 2 examines the public's right to know with respect to the founding period and, in particular, the debates over adopting and ratifying the Constitution and the First Amendment. The remaining chapters explore the Court's interpretation of the First Amendment and the public's right to know in view of competing judicial philosophies, developing constitutional principles, and considerations of public policy. Chapter 3 shows that the Court's predominant treatment of the First Amendment manifested neither complete self-restraint nor uninhibited judicial activism but, rather, modest intervention. In articulating constitutional principles designed to ensure First Amendment interests, the Court gradually elaborated a broad functionalist approach to First Amendment protection, while adhering to the constitutional redundancy of the speech and press clauses and rebuffing claims for press exceptionalism as the guardian of the public's right to know. Chapter 4 turns to constitutional adjudication over First Amendment affirmative rights to acquire access to government information and facilities. The final chapter considers the Court's policy against prior restraints and the problems of reconciling the First Amendment with competing interests in national security. The book concludes that within the constitutional and political system the political ideal of the public's right to know has been enhanced by the Supreme Court's broad interpretation of the First Amendment as securing the conditions for an informed public and electorate. The First Amendment, however, only indirectly, derivatively ensures the public's right to know. The promise and performance of the Supreme Court in addressing the dilemma of governmental secrecy versus democratic governance is essentially limited, constrained by the constitutional and political limitations of judicial review within a representative republic.

As always, I am indebted to my colleagues and students. I am particularly grateful to Kenneth Thompson and the University of Virginia Committee on Summer Grants and to the Earhart Foundation for their generous support. An award from Project '87, sponsored by the American Political Science Association and the American Historical Association, embarked my inquiry and permitted the writing of two preliminary pieces on the First Amendment, appearing the *Hastings Constitutional Law Quarterly* and the *Villanova Law Review*. During 1979–80 it was also my good fortune to have two reliable research assistants, Michael Guest and Tracy Reid. Finally, I have special gratitude and appreciation for my colleague, Henry J. Abraham, and for my former teachers, C. Herman Pritchett and Gordon E. Baker.

Charlottesville, Virginia   D.M.O.
August 30, 1980

CONTENTS

THE PUBLIC'S RIGHT TO KNOW

CHAPTER 1

THE POLITICAL IDEAL OF THE PUBLIC'S RIGHT TO KNOW

> Freedom to speak and write about public questions is as important to the life of our government as is the heart to the human body. In fact, this privilege is the heart of our government. If that heart be weakened, the result is death.
>
> Justice Hugo Black, *Milk Wagon Drivers Union* v. *Meadowmoor Dairies* (1940)

> Because freedom of public expression alone assures the unfolding of truth, it is indispensible to the democratic process.
>
> Justice Felix Frankfurter, *Bridges* v. *California* (1941)

The public's right to know has become increasingly salient in the wake of Cold War secrecy and, later, Watergate.[1] Sensitive to growing political pressures for governmental openness, Congress and state legislatures enacted legislation—in particular, freedom of information laws—to further the public's right to know by granting access to governmental documents, records, and meetings. In contrast, the Supreme Court appeared particularly unsympathetic to the rising number of claims that the First Amendment guarantees the public a right to know and grants the press special privileges. Notably, the Burger Court's First Amendment rulings in the 1970s were assailed as establishing "a dangerous pattern" that "for all practical purposes [constitutes a] war against the press" and diminishes the constitutional significance of the public's right to know.[2]

Neither the Constitution nor the Bill of Rights expressly guarantees the public a right to know, yet an impressive amount of litigation aims at vindicating that right as implicit in the First Amendment. The controversy over *The Progressive* magazine article, "The H-Bomb Secret: How We Got It, Why We're Telling It," epitomizes much of the symbolic appeal of claims to the public's right to know. In *United States* v. *The Progressive, Inc.*, District Court Judge Robert W. Warren granted a preliminary injunction against publication of the article. Acknowledging that the injunction "will infringe upon [the public's] right to know and to be informed," Judge Warren concluded that "this Court can find no plausible reason why the public needs to know the technical details about hydrogen bomb construction to carry on an informed debate on this issue."[3] Subsequently, because a similar article was printed by another Madison, Wisconsin, periodical, the Department of Justice withdrew its motion for an injunction. *The Progressive* case, like the earlier *Pentagon Papers* case in *New York Times Co.* v. *United States*,[4] nevertheless focused public attention on a basic dilemma in constitutional politics: reconciling governmental restrictions on freedom of information with the First Amendment. The political and legal salience of the controversy persists precisely because vexatious problems remain in determining the scope of the First Amendment and the legitimacy of a directly enforceable constitutional right to know.

POLITICS, THE PRESS, AND THE RIGHT TO KNOW

The origins and evolution of the idea that the public has an enforceable right to know have less to do with constitutional history than with the public's and, especially, news publishers' and broadcasters' understanding of the role of the First Amendment within the polity. Although during the founding period the public's right to know was debated in the federal and state constitutional conventions, not until the middle of the twentieth century did the idea become politically potent, registered by legislation designed to ensure governmental openness and by claims that a right to know is constitutionally enforceable against the government.

According to Kent Cooper, executive director of the Associated Press in the 1940s, popular approval of the phrase "the right to know" arose with a speech on January 23, 1945, in which he argued: "The citizen is entitled to have access to news, fully and accurately presented. There cannot be political freedom in one country, or in the world, without respect for 'the right to know.'" Eleven years later, in *The Right to Know*, he urged adoption of a constitutional amendment to clarify the First Amendment guarantees and to specifically ensure a right to know. For Cooper the right signified "that the government may not, and the newspapers and broadcasters should not, by *any method whatever* curb delivery of any information essential to the public welfare and enlightenment." He furthermore suggested that the First Amendment should be rewritten to read: "Congress shall make no law . . . abridging the Right to Know through the oral or printed word or any other means of communicating ideas or intelligence."[5]

With the ensuing decades, Cooper's turn of the phrase proved prophetic for the politics of the press, public policy making, and constitutional adjudication. In the 1950s the public's right to know was championed by the press in combating syndromes of bureaucratic secrecy—secrecy prompted as much by governmental practices following World War II as by what Max Weber identified as the bureaucratic phenomenon of "official secrets"—that is, the tendency of "every bureaucracy [to] seek [] to increase the superiority of the professionally informed by keeping their knowledge and intentions secret."[6] In particular, James Russell Wiggins, executive editor of the *Washington Post* and *Times Herald* and chairman of the Committee on Freedom of Information of the American Society of Newspaper Editors, wrote a series of articles celebrating both the legitimacy of a right to know and the role of the press in safeguarding that right. In 1956 in *Freedom or Secrecy* Wiggins, unlike Cooper, sought to clarify this symbolically appealing but as yet undefined right. The public's right to know, Wiggins argued, actually refers to a composite of several rights:

> It has at least five broad, discernible components: (1) the right to get information; (2) the right to print without prior restraint; (3) the right to print without fear of reprisal not under due process; (4) the right of access to facilities and material essential to communication; and (5) the right to distribute information without interference by government acting under law or by citizens acting in defiance of the law.[7]

These subsidiary rights indicate the broad contours and appeal of the public's right to know, but also the confusion and controversy invited by demands for such a directly enforceable right. The idea of the public's right to know actually covers several different, although interrelated, rights. Moreover, those more specific rights are disparate and not equally meritorious in their legal and political justifications. For instance, whereas claiming the right to print and distribute information without prior restraint might prove defensible under the First Amendment, claims to a "right to get information" and a "right of access" have no apparent constitutional basis and ostensibly depend on statutory recognition or developments in common law. The public's right to know engenders political controversy not only because the right appears elliptical for more specific, albeit diverse, rights, but also because claims to a right to know appear unconditional, unqualified, and, therefore, unacceptable.

The public's right to know was nevertheless proclaimed in "A Declaration of Principles" adopted by the American Society of Newspaper Editors (ASNE) on July 12, 1957 (reprinted in this chapter). The declaration at once embodied the more specific rights associated with the public's right to know and foreshadowed the political and constitutional conflicts inevitably to arise with the press's efforts to vindicate the right.

A DECLARATION OF PRINCIPLES

by the
American Society
of Newspaper Editors

The American people have the right to know, as the heirs of Magna Charta, the inheritors of the privileges and immunities of the English Common Law and the beneficiaries of the freedoms and liberties guaranteed them by the Constitution and the Bill of Rights of the United States.

To exercise this right citizens must be able to gather information at home or abroad, except where military necessity plainly prevents; they must find it possible to publish or relate otherwise the information thus acquired without prior restraint or censorship by government; they must be free to declare or print it without fear of punishment not in accord with due process; they must possess the means of using or acquiring implements of publication; they should have freedom to distribute and disseminate without obstruction by government or by their fellow citizens.

The members of the American Society of Newspaper Editors, as citizens, partake of and share in this right to know in their own names, and, as editors, reporters and writers they act, besides, as agents and servants of other citizens whose right to knowledge they invoke. They are therefore twice-concerned and doubly alarmed by measures that threaten the right to know, whether they involve restrictions on the movement of the press to sources of news and information at home or abroad, withholding of information at local, state or federal levels, or proposals to bring within the purview of the criminal statutes those who do not place security of the nation in jeopardy, but whose only offense is to disagree with government officials on what may be safely published.

The officers and directors of the American Society of Newspaper Editors are authorized and instructed by the members of the Society to resist by all appropriate means every encroachment upon the right so indispensable to the exercise of their profession, so essential to the liberties of every free people and so inseparable from all the other rights essential to self-government.

The American Society of Newspaper Editors commissioned Harold Cross, counsel for the New York *Herald Tribune* and professor at the Columbia University School of Law, to prepare a report on federal, state, and municipal information procedures, policies, and practices. When published in 1953, Cross's report, *The People's Right to Know*, proved highly influential because of both the systematic nature of the study and his conclusions about the status of public access to government information. His study confirmed the American Society of Newspaper Editors' own conclusions about the inadequacy of legal provisions for freedom of information. Under federal information law and policy, for example, he found that,

> Records of the Executive Department are indeed "quasi-confidential", "privileged communications", commonly beyond the reach of the public, press, or courts, as if they actually were the memorials of a government administering its own affairs except when the heads thereof, acting in the exercise of broad, practically unrestrained powers of discretionary character, choose to make them available.[8]

In documenting the legal and political obstacles for public access to government materials and proceedings, Cross's study provided an impetus for new legislation. He attributed "the fountainhead of [government] secrecy" to the ambiguous provisions of the Administrative Procedure Act of 1946.[9] The Administrative Procedure Act was the initial congressional attempt to establish a comprehensive regulatory system, including information management procedures, for federal agencies. Previously, departments of the federal government were empowered by the Housekeeping Statute, dating back with minor amendments to 1789,[10] to establish their own procedures for disseminating information. The Administrative Procedure Act appeared to have had little effect on agency information practices and to have negligible benefits for the public and the press.

In the late 1950s Cross's work served as the basis for the press's campaign for the enactment of state and federal freedom of information laws. In a more direct fashion Cross was influential in the development of freedom-of-information laws. In 1955 Cross met and convinced Congressman John Moss of California of the problems in achieving governmental openness under the Administrative Procedure Act and of the necessity for further federal legislation guaranteeing the public a right of access to government documents and records.

Moss, as chairman of the Government Information Subcommittee of the House Committee on Government Operations, initiated hearings on government secrecy that by 1960 produced no less than 17 volumes of hearings transcripts and 14 volumes of reports.[11] Like Cross's study, the congressional investigations found that the Administrative Procedure Act was used by agencies to deny access to information that could be made available to the public. Under the Administrative Procedure Act federal agencies denied requests for information on an evaluation of the need to know, and agencies thereby effectively thwarted the public's right to know by denying legitimate requests for information. Agencies, for instance, denied requests for materials such as a textbook of George Washington's intelligence methods, the memoirs of a Confederate Army general, a report on the use of shark repellents—detailing 69 cases of shark attacks, 55 between 1907 and 1940—and a list of military installations that sold packaged liquor to military personnel. [12] Frequently information was "withheld in order to cover up embarrassing mistakes or irregularities and the withholding justified by such phrases in Section 3 of the Administrative Procedure Act as—'requiring secrecy in the public interest,' or 'required for good cause to be held confidential.'" Even when no good cause could be found for withholding information, agencies released information selectively and to only those individuals "legitimately and properly concerned." [13] Consequently the public's right to know about government activities, as Louis Henkin observed, was more often "reduced by the 'right—or duty, or responsibility—of the Government to withhold' in the public interest." [14]

In 1960 the Moss subcommittee agreed that the ambiguous provisions of the Administrative Procedure Act must be eliminated and that the only way to check against the abuse of administrative discretion in granting or denying access to information was an omnibus federal disclosure bill. Instead of reforming the Administrative Procedure Act, Jacob Scher, researcher for the Moss subcommittee and professor at the Northwestern University School of Journalism, recommended legislation conferring the right on *any* individual to request access to government information (subject to certain exemptions for national security materials) and guaranteeing, when access was denied, the right of appeal to the judiciary. This innovative proposal for an omnibus federal disclosure law was embraced by Missouri Senator Thomas Hennings, Jr., a long-time advocate of governmental openness. [15] More successful in 1963, Senator Henning's successor, Senator Edward Long, and Senate Republican leader Everett Dirksen cosponsored and agressively pushed enactment of a freedom-of-information act. As Senator Long declared: "Free people are, of necessity, informed; uninformed people can never be free." [16] The Long-Dirksen bill, however, encountered the hostility of federal agencies because it failed to entertain legitimate agency demands for confidentiality in such areas as routine internal agency correspondence and concerns related to foreign affairs but not clearly in the interests of national defense. Hearings continued through 1964 and only after political compromises over extending the number of exemptions from disclosure requirements did the Senate eventually pass the bill (S. 1666) on July 28, 1964.

The 89th Congress edged toward enacting the first comprehensive freedom-of-information act in the nation's history. In the Senate, S. 1666 was again amended and reintroduced in February 1965, and subsequently passed as S. 1160. In the House of Representatives, Moss proceeded with a similar bill (H. R. 5012), adopting the Senate's extensive exemptions from the disclosure provisions of the bill. The House Committee on Government Operations refused to consider S. 1160 until 1966, but finally approved the bill on June 20th, 1966. There was no little irony when President Lyndon Johnson signed the Freedom of Information Act into law on July 4th, 1966, just one day before the bill would have died from pocket veto. When a powerful Senate leader in 1960, Johnson had shown no interest in the public's right to know, and, when signing the bill, he emphasized that "this bill in no way impairs the President's power under our Constitution to provide for confidentiality when the national interest so requires." Yet on Independence Day he proclaimed: "I have always believed that freedom of information is so vital that only the national security, not the desire of public officials or private citizens, should determine when it must be restricted."[17]

The Freedom of Information Act of 1966 eliminated the ambiguous provisions of the Administrative Procedure Act and aimed at "confining, structuring, and checking"[18] federal agencies' discretion in disclosing or withholding information. The purpose of the act, as a Senate committee report states, was to establish "a general philosophy of full agency disclosure unless information is exempt under delineated language and to provide a court procedure by which citizens and the press may obtain information wrongly withheld."[19] Individuals' access to government information under the Freedom of Information Act, unlike under the old provisions of the Administrative Procedure Act, is not limited to those persons with particular reasons for seeking disclosure. Instead, material is available to *any* person. Moreover, courts are precluded from considering the needs of the party seeking relief unless the information sought falls within one of the nine statutory exemptions from the Act. Consequently, agencies may legally withhold only those materials specifically authorized to be kept secret and relating to matters of national security or foreign policy covered by an Executive Order; or specifically exempted from disclosure by another statute; or concerning "trade secrets" or personal, medical, or other records, the disclosure of which would "constitute a clearly unwarranted invasion of personal privacy." Also exempt are law enforcement investigatory records and certain materials concerning financial institutions and geological or geophysical information pertaining to wells.[20]

Initial administrative compliance with the Freedom of Information Act was not particularly impressive. In 1972 the House Government Operations Subcommittee on Foreign Operations and Government Information found that the act "had been hindered by five years of foot-dragging by the federal bureaucracy," and recommended further legislative and administrative reforms.[21] Two years later, after overriding President Gerald Ford's veto, Congress reiterated support for the public's right to know by strengthening provisions of the act with amendments. In particular, Congress responded to the Supreme Court's holding in *Environmental Protec-*

tion Agency v. *Mink* [22], that courts could not examine materials withheld by an agency under one of the act's nine exemptions, by authorizing *in camera* judicial review of materials, thereby ensuring that agencies deny access only to materials legitimately and properly exempt from disclosure under the act. The 1974 amendments to the Freedom of Information Act, along with other legislation in the late 1970s, significantly confined, structured, and checked agency discretion in permitting or denying access by members of the public to government information and proceedings. [23]

After over a decade of political struggles in Congress and against the background of administrative and executive officials' opposition, enactment of the Freedom of Information Act (reprinted, as amended in 1974, in Appendix A) remains the basic legislative mandate for ensuring governmental openness and the political ideal of the public's right to know. [24]

Passage of the Freedom of Information Act registers in important ways the political role of the press in vindicating the public's right to know. Members of the press, especially the American Society of Newspaper Editors, aggressively persued enactment of statutory rights of access to give tangibility to the political ideal of the public's right to know and to combat abusive governmental secrecy. With studies such as that by Cross and testimony before Congress and state legislatures, the press contributed to the formulation and passage of freedom of information laws. In the decade preceding enactment of the federal Freedom of Information Act, no less than 16 states adopted open-records laws, and in the following decade 46 states enacted or revised similar statutes (see Appendix B for a compilation of state open-records and open-meetings laws). By 1980 only one state had not enacted a freedom of information law. [25]

"Publicity through the press," as James T. O'Reilly emphasized, "played an important role in the passage of the [federal Freedom of Information] Act." [26] The press prompted and widely publicized congressional hearings, which in turn encouraged reform efforts. As a former staff member of the Moss subcommittee observed, the Freedom of Information Act "itself is proof that publicity about government secrecy is a powerful weapon." [27] Primarily because of the political pressures of the press and its alliances with members of Congress and state legislatures, the political ideal of the public's right to know was translated into specific statutory rights of access to government documents and records.

In the 1970s members of the press pushed not merely for statutory recognition of the public's right to know but also for a constitutional right to know. Reliance on First Amendment litigation and the judicial forum as an arena for articulating national information policies was perhaps inevitable; indeed, much of constitutional history bears out the veracity of Alexis de Tocqueville's astute comment that, "[s]carcely any political question arises in the United States that is not resolved, sooner or later, into a judicial question." [28] In his 1953 study Cross eloquently anticipated the role of the press in the political and constitutional controversies over the public's right to know.

> The public business is the public's business. The people have a right to know. Freedom of information about public records and proceedings is their just heritage. Citizens must have the legal right to investigate and examine the conduct of their affairs. They must have a simple, speedy means of enforcement. These rights must be raised to the highest sanction. The time is ripe. The First Amendment points the way. The function of the press is to carry the torch.[29]

THE PRACTICE OF RIGHTS AND THE SYMBOLIC USES OF RIGHTS

Perhaps it is a measure of the fascination of the public's right to know that the growing literature often declines or neglects to either define the nature and scope of the right or to analyze the role and responsibility of the press in vindicating the public's interests in governmental openness. Insistence on constitutional denomination of an enforceable right to know, unlike the statutory acknowledgement, raises a plethora of vexing questions. What does the public have a "right" to know and what is the constitutional status of the press in informing the public about governmental affairs? Does the public and the press possess an affirmative First Amendment right of access, and on what occasions and to what kinds of government facilities and materials? Under the Constitution, furthermore, what is the responsibility of the Supreme Court, as compared to that of the Congress and the president, for ensuring freedom of information? May the Court legitimately articulate an independent, directly enforceable right to know against the government? If so, on what basis?

That the public possesses an enforceable constitutional right to know, instead of simply an abstract political claim to information about governmental affairs, also presupposes crucial issues of legal and political theory that are independent of, albeit interrelated with, the questions posed by the dynamics of judicial interpretation that would give the public's right to know constitutional status.[30] These issues concern the propriety of members of the press claiming for the public an enforceable right to know, and thus bear examining before considering the controversies raised in constitutional adjudication.

On Claiming Rights and their Symbolic Uses

The symbolic appeal of the public's right to know has not been lost on journalists and jurists. Some commentators find claims by the press to a right to know self-serving and pernicious. "Defenders of press freedom have appropriated the expression," argues John C. Merrill, professor of journalism at the University of Missouri, "because it sounds more democratic than the simple term 'freedom of the press' and shifts the theoretical emphasis from a private and restricted institution (the press) to a much broader and popular base (the citizenry)."[31] Less sanguine, the Court of Common Pleas of Ohio observed:

> The so-called "right of the public to know" is a rationalization developed by the fourth estate [the press] to gain rights not shared by others . . . to improve its private ability to acquire information which is a raw asset of its business. . . . The constitution does not appoint the fourth estate the spokesmen [sic] of the people. The people speak through the elective process and through the individuals it elects to positions created for that purpose. The press has no right that exceeds that of other citizens.[32]

There are serious problems with the press claiming that the public has a right to know and that the right conveys special privileges to the press so it may vindicate interests in governmental openness. In a 1947 report for the Commission on Freedom of the Press, William Hocking succinctly noted: "We [members of the press] say recklessly that [readers] have 'a right to know'; yet it is a right which they are helpless to claim, for they do not know that they have the right to know what as yet they do not know."[33] The problems attendent to litigation over the public's right to know require examining the nature of claims to the public's right to know within the context of the practice of rights.

The claim that the public possesses a directly enforceable right to know presupposes concerns over who is the public and what, and on what basis, has the public a right to know. Frequently, members of the press fail to appreciate that in a large republic and pluralistic society, discussion of *the* public, although symbolically appealing, is a misleading reification.[34] The issue, moreover, is not circumvented by the alternative argument that "the American system of freedom of expression . . . seem[s] to call for principles which locate the right to know in various social groups—economic, cultural, religious, and the like."[35] Regardless of whether the right to know is claimed by members of the press for the entire body politic or for particular special interest groups, the press frequently confuses rights with interests. Rights and interests are different; and to see how different they are requires examination of the politics of the practice of rights.

The symbolic and tangible import for politics of legal rights, including the right to know, arises from the character of the practice of rights in a society. The practice of rights is a sociopolitical phenmenon. It involves a certain kind of interaction among people; namely, the activity of formally claiming entitlements to do or to have something. "By conferring a right on an individual," John R. Lucas observes, "we enable him to know what he is entitled to do and what others are not, at least without his consent, entitled to do."[36] In adjudication, legal rights are in a strict and narrow sense claim-rights. That is, "legal claim rights are necessarily the grounds of people's duties toward the right-holder. A legal right is a claim to performance, either action or forbearance as the case may be."[37] Rights have an affinity with claims. Claims are often assertions of rights since, in claiming, individuals exercise their rights by showing that they are entitled legally, morally, or politically, despite the objections of others, to do or to have something. Yet rights are not the same as claims, because rights may be possessed, exercised, or enjoyed, whereas individuals make claims but do not possess, exercise, or enjoy them. Similarly, Joel Feinberg explains that

> [h]aving a claim to X is not (yet) the same as having a right to X, but is rather having a case, consisting of relevant reasons or at least minimal plausibility, that one has a right to X. The case establishes a right, not to X, but a fair hearing and consideration. Claims, so conceived, differ in degree: some are stronger than others. Rights, on the other hand, do not differ in degree; no one right is more of a right than another.[38]

The activity of claiming consists in having a case for doing or for having something; it involves the assertion of a right, or entitlement, to be at liberty to do or to have something without interference. An individual who has a right may then, as Richard Flathman concisely states, "decide whether, when, and how to exercise it, whether to alienate it, how vigorously to defend it, and so forth."[39]

The import of viewing rights as constituting a practice lies in clarifying both the processes by which interests are adjudicated and raised to the status of legally recognized rights and, simultaneously, the legal boundaries of rights—that is, the occasions when and with regard to what other legal, moral, and political considerations individuals may legitimately claim a right. Within the practice of rights a fundamental distinction must be drawn between *making a claim to* a right and *claiming that* an individual or a group has some right. In *making a claim* to a right individuals are claiming in a "performative sense". That is, they are asserting their own interests as entitlements or rights to something, which if reasonable and not overridden by some other legal, moral, or political consideration they may successfully vindicate. In contrast, when individuals *claim that* there is a right to something they are claiming in a "propositional sense". They are making statements about interests that are or should be recognized in the practice of rights. As Feinberg points out:

> One important difference then between *making legal claim to* and *claiming that* is that the former is a legal performance with direct legal consequences whereas the latter is often a mere piece of descriptive

commentary with no legal force. Legally speaking, *making claim to* can itself make things happen.[40]

For the discussion here, a more significant difference between *making a claim to* and *claiming that* is that an individual in the position of claiming a right (in a performative sense) asserts personal interests, whereas an individual claiming (in a propositional sense) that some interest is or should be legally acknowledged may assert the interest of a third party and therefore an interest about which the individual may be wrong. In other words, individuals are in different positions relative to their assertions of interests and claims of rights. On the one hand, by *making a claim* to a right individuals assert their own, or what they believe to be their own, interests. On the other hand, in *claiming that* a right does or should exist individuals are asserting the existence of interests that they deem, but perhaps wrongly, to be the interests of some third party. The import of this distinction for understanding claims by the press to the public's right to know is evident on further considering the relationship between interests and the activity of claiming rights in judicial forums.

Interests and rights differ inasmuch as rights, in a sense, qualify or condition interests. If a right is legally recognized, then an individual may enjoy that right, assured that it will not be overridden by the interests of others unless those interests are also raised to the status of rights and in certain crucial circumstances the interests *qua* rights of others outweigh and override the individual's asserted interests and legally claimed right. Rights, however, are not simply specifically legally protected interests. Both rights and interests are assignable, but only rights are personal—first personal—whereas interests may be either personal or third personal. When individuals claim a right they do so because they believe their interests to be sufficiently meritorious to entitle legal protection. Other people may claim that an individual does not know what is in the individual's best interests, and so, too, judicial and legislative bodies may decide that the individual's claim of a right is simply wrongheaded or overridden by other legal, moral, or political considerations. Yet when people claim that interests of some third party are or are not worthy of legal protection, they may be wrong about whether those interests are in fact the interests of that third party. In sum, individuals may not make claims to represent the rights of third parties, since rights are personal, and they are first-personal because only the individual concerned is in a position to determine on what occasions to claim entitlement to legal representation of personal interests.

When members of the press claim that the public has a right to know, they are making propositional claims about the interests of a third party. Members of the press cannot make a claim (in the performative sense) to the public's right to know, since they may not permissibly assert and irrebuttably demonstrate the interests of the public, or publics, by their claim. This is so because members of the press cannot show that acknowledgement of the public's right to know will vindicate the interests of the public or guarantee an informed public. Peter Bathory and Wilson Carey McWilliams eloquently express this underlying dilemma of members of the press who claim the public's right to know. "There is more than a semantic difference," they note, "between an 'informed public' and a 'public informed,' for an 'informed public' has presumably heard and learned what a 'public informed' was merely *told* [by the press]."[41] In claiming the public's right to know, members of the press cannot demonstrate that the public has interests in knowing about some particular item or issue.* An individual's interests in knowing about particular issues neither entitles the press to claim the public's right to know and to demand access to everything pertinent to the issues nor guarantees that an individual informed of such matters will be an informed individual. As Bathory and McWilliams apprehend, claims to the public's right to know are misleading:

> The case for democracy does not require that the citizen be familiar with all the bits and pieces of expert knowledge. He cannot be, in any case, and we do him individually and the people collectively no credit if we believe that the political claims of democracy can be maintained only by telling lies that exaggerate the ability of the citizen. . . . Vindicating the "public's right to know" does not require that all specialized, private, and relatively inaccessible information be "made public." It demands, rather, that the public have access to those facts necessary for public judgment about public things, and, more important, that it have the *greatest possible opportunity to learn and master the art of political judgment.*[43]

Likewise, as Chapter 2 shows, the Founding Fathers—particularly James Madison and Thomas Jefferson—understood that the republic depended on popular and accessible information not as secured by a right to know vicariously asserted by members of the press, but, instead, as secured by the freedom of speech and press and as reinforced by public education and citizen participation in the affairs of governance.

At best, members of the press may claim that the public's right to know should be legally recognized so *any* member of the public, including the press, might make a claim to know and assert a right of access to governmental information, as under the Freedom of Information Act.

Pluralism and the Individual's "Right to Know"

Although claims to the public's right to know are symbolically appeal-

---

*Ironically, the press and broadcast media have been criticized for their actual or potential manipulation of public opinion.[42]

ing, within the practice of rights, recognition of a right does not entail that an individual has the right to exercise that right on every occasion. When individuals claim the right to know, there remains the further task of determining the legitimacy of those claims with regard to competing legal, moral, and political considerations.

As Chief Justice Warren Burger notes, "interest alone does not create a constitutional right."[44] Nor does the fact that certain members of the public or the press merely want or desire access to government facilities or materials appear particularly meritorious. Edward Levi poignantly argues:

> The people's right to know cannot mean that every individual or interest group may compel disclosure of the papers and effects of government officials whenever they bear on public business. Under our Constitution, the people are the sovereign, but they do not govern by the random and self-selective interposition of private citizens.[45]

Claims to a right to know must be linked to the individual's *need* to know about the affairs and operations of government, but in a more specific way than the general claim that an informed citizenry is essential to a representative democracy. Joseph Tussman correctly comments: "We cannot demand answers to our questions. We are entitled to know by virtue of some functional status; the right to know is tied to the need to know."[46] An individual's interests in knowing, or need to know, entitles that person to claim a right to know when governmental disclosure is vital to that person's self-governance. An individual's need to know is sufficiently meritorious only when demonstrated by a personal or proprietary interest in claiming access to government information.[47]

Most commentators on the public's right to know overlook perhaps the most significant occasion for claiming a right to know: when individuals are confronted by the government with criminal or administrative sanctions. Still, as Justice Robert Jackson, dissenting in a decision permitting the exclusion of an alien without a hearing or even disclosure of the basis for exclusion, observed: "The most scrupulous observance of due process, including *the right to know* a charge, to be confronted with the accuser, to cross-examine informers and to produce evidence in one's behalf, is especially necessary when the occasion of detention is fear of future misconduct, rather than crimes committed."[48]

Actually, the Supreme Court initially acknowledged a right to know not as an emanation of the First Amendment but as implicit within the requirements of due process imposed on adversary proceedings and administrative investigations.[49] Justice William Douglas, for example, found "[*t*]*he right to know* the claims asserted against one and to contest them—to be heard—to conduct a cross-examination—these are all implicit in our concept of 'a full and fair hearing' before any administrative agency."[50]

An individual's right to know is meritorious within adversary proceedings for two reasons: first, because the accusatorial relationship between the individual and the government presupposes a "fair state-individual balance";[51] second, because the individual asserts a personal and proprietary interest in a particular kind of information, namely, the nature and basis for a criminal charge.

Individuals' claims to a right to know in other contexts may not be equally meritorious. Claims to know about Central Intelligence Agency (CIA) funding, agents, or secret operations, for instance, are not as compelling as claims to government information to present an adequate defense against a criminal prosecution. Furthermore, without a standing requirement that individuals demonstrate a personal or proprietary interest, claims to the right to know prove to be open-ended and unacceptable. In *Zemel* v. *Rusk* Chief Justice Earl Warren pointed to the absurdities of broadly construing the right to know:

> There are few restrictions on action which could not be clothed by ingenious argument in the garb of decreased data flow. For example, the prohibition of unauthorized entry into the White House diminishes the citizen's opportunities to gather information he might find relevant to his opinion of the way the country is being run, but that does not make entry into the White House a First Amendment right. The right to speak and publish does not carry with it the unrestrained right to gather information.[52]

The legitimacy of an individual's claim to the right to know depends on the merits of demonstrating the need, not merely desire, to know relative to other moral, legal, and political considerations for withholding government information.

The import of this discussion is underscored by recognizing that when courts legitimate claims to legal rights they provide more than a tangible means by which individuals may vindicate their interests. Judicial enforcement of legal rights has significant consequences for other policy-making institutions and at times may pose fundamental dilemmas for the body politic. Further consideration of judicial articulation of a right to know illustrates in a preliminary way the broad political consequences of the practice of rights and the necessity of attending to the nature and scope of any right to know.

The repercussions for the administration of justice and legislation designed to safeguard national security information were largely unanticipated in the 1950s when the Supreme Court acknowledged that due process guarantees individuals a right to know in adversary and administrative proceedings. In 1953 a unanimous Court in *Gordon* v. *United States* held that an individual has the right to inspect documents possessed by the government that pertain to the government witnesses' testimony.[53] The petitioner, Gordon, demanded access to a government witness's prior written statements that ostensibly contradicted his trial testimony and that therefore would be useful for impeachment purposes. Four years later the Court was bitterly divided over a similar claim in *Jencks* v. *United States.* Here, Jencks, the president of a labor union, was convicted under the National Labor Relations Act for having falsely stated that he was neither a member of nor affiliated with the Communist Party. The crucial testimony against him came from two undercover agents of the Federal Bureau of Investigation (FBI) who infiltrated the Communist Party and had made regular reports to the FBI on the activities of Jencks and the party. Jencks claimed a right to the production of those reports with a view to impeaching the testimony of the undercover agents. Justice William Brennan, for the majority, held that justice requires no less than that individuals have the right to inspect such documents and that the government possesses no absolute evidentiary privilege to withhold such documents. Justice Brennan claimed that even when disclosure diminishes vital national interests:

> [T]he Government can invoke its evidentiary privileges only at the price of letting the defendant go free. The rationale of the criminal cases is that, since the Government which prosecutes an accused also has the duty to see that justice is done, it is unconscionable to allow it to undertake prosecution and then invoke its governmental privileges to deprive the accused of anything which might be material to his defense.[54]

In *Jencks* the sole dissenter, Justice Thomas Clark, foresaw the broader implications for reconciling competing interests in national security and governmental openness. As a result of the Court's ruling, he warned, "those intelligence agencies of our Government engaged in law enforcement may well close up shop, for the Court has opened their files to the criminal and thus afforded him a Roman holiday for rummaging through confidential information as well as vital national secrets."

Justice Clark's apprehension of "a veritable Pandora's box of troubles" was indeed borne out: Enforcement of laws against espionage, perjury, bribery, and narcotics violations often required the Department of Justice to choose between disclosing confidential information in a prosecution, at the request of the defendant, or letting the individual go unpunished and thereby withholding and safeguarding confidential information. Individuals engage in a sort of "graymail" insofar as they are granted *de facto* immunity from prosecution because the Department of Justice refuses to prosecute where the potential exists for revealing sensitive information in the course of a trial.[55] The dilemma caused by the development of gray mail necessitated legislation, more effective administrative sanctions for the disclosure of classified information and greater cooperation between the Department of

Justice and intelligence agencies.* The import of considering the Court's articulation of a right to know within adversary proceedings here, lies in underscoring that judicial creation of a right to know has wide-ranging political consequences as well as the necessity of assessing the relative merits of claims to the right to know in different kinds of cases and controversies.

Judicial enforcement of the right to know with respect to adversary proceedings prompted governmental openness at the cost of frustrating enforcement of laws designed to ensure the confidentiality of sensitive government information. In other circumstances, judicial articulation of the right to know may nevertheless diminish, rather than enhance, freedom of information. Within the practice of rights, claims to a directly enforceable right to know are inevitably qualified because of the necessity of accommodating competing moral, legal, and political considerations. When members of the press claim a First Amendment right to know, as they did in the Pentagon Papers and *The Progressive* cases, courts may be forced to determine what the public has or has not a right to know, and determination of what the public does not have a right to know may well entail restrictions on speech and press. James Goodale, executive vice president of The New York Times Company, thus cautions against demanding judicial elaboration of an enforceable right to know independent of specific First Amendment guarantees. "[T]he problem with the right to know," he points out, "is that it invariably involves prior restraint. Since the right is not self-executing, a court must decide what the public is permitted to know or not to know."[56] Litigation over the public's right to know therefore might actually prove pernicious because judges must balance the public's need to know against governmental demands for confidentiality in the conduct of its operations.

The potential for prior restraints that attends judicial determination of what the public is entitled to know indicates the deleterious political consequences of judicial articulation of a public's right to know. Judicial delimitation of the public's right to know would be substituted for evaluations by the people's elected representatives of what the public legitimately needs to know about the details of governmental affairs. The judiciary having fashioned a broadly enforceable right to know inexorably assumes the role of a super-legislature in determining the wisdom, need, and propriety of permitting public access to governmental materials or policy-making processes and institutions.

PRINCIPLES AND POLICIES IN CONSTITUTIONAL ADJUDICATION

Rights are systematically ambiguous. Individuals make claims to a

*On October 15, 1980, President James Carter signed into law the Classified Information Procedures Act of 1980. The act is designed to facilitate the use of classified information in federal criminal prosecutions and to eliminate the problem of gray mail.

variety of rights. They may claim moral, legal, political, and natural rights, but when they do their claim to one kind of right is not coterminous with claims to other kinds of rights. An individual might claim a legal right to do something for which there is no moral right. Citizens also may claim political rights to something to which they concede they have, at the moment, no legal right. Article 19 of the Universal Declaration of Human Rights adopted by the United Nations General Assembly in 1948, for example, recognizes "freedom of information" as a universal human right that includes "the right to speak, receive and impart information and ideas through any media and regardless of frontiers." Although individuals might claim the right as a moral or political right against the government, only claims to a corresponding right as found in statutory, constitutional, or common law provisions are legally enforceable. Moreover, legal rights differ, for individuals might claim the right to know under a state or federal statute and still not be able to claim the right under the Constitution.

Distinguishing different kinds of rights permits a more perspicuous view of the public's right to know. The right to know might be claimed as a moral, legal, or political right, but that is also to notice that the basis for establishing such claims diverges according to the kind of right that is asserted. Prior to enactment of state and federal freedom of information laws, individuals could claim the right to know as a political, but not a legal, right. Political claims to the public's right to know were sufficiently persuasive that state legislatures and Congress enacted freedom of information laws recognizing the public's right to know. These important developments in statutory law, however, did not thereby legitimate claims to a constitutional right to know. To the contrary, since the Constitution is silent on the public's right to know, compelling arguments must be found for justifying individuals' claims to a constitutional right to know.

The failure to distinguish between different kinds of rights fosters considerable confusion over the public's right to know. Some commentators, for instance, argue that the constitutional right of privacy limits the scope of any constitutional right of the public to know, as do regulations that protect individuals from having information or materials forced upon them.[57] To be sure, interests in the public's right to know and personal privacy might clash. Considerable confusion exists over reconciling the statutory right of access to government information granted by the Freedom of Information Act and individuals' informational privacy interests in government records, as recognized by the Privacy Act of 1974.[58] The Acts confront administrative agencies and courts with what the Court has described as "a 'split-personality' legislative reaction, by the conflict between a seeming passion for privacy and a comparable passion for needless invasions of privacy."[59] Here, the problem of balancing claims to the right to know with privacy interests requires further legislation, not constitutional adjudication, to achieve greater statutory parity between the Freedom of Information and Privacy Acts.

Consider now, the competing interests in the public's right to know, and personal privacy at the level of constitutional adjudication. The Bill of Rights protects individuals against unwarranted governmental intrusions and abuses of governmental power. The Fourth Amendment prohibition against unreasonable searches and seizures thus applies to only searches and seizures by the government, not to those by private individuals.[60] Accordingly, a directly enforceable constitutional right to know would apply to only governmental facilities or materials and not entitle public access to private homes or personal effects. (In addition, the moral and political basis for claiming the public's right to know about the intimate details of an individual's life appears untenable and indefensible.) Therefore, constitutional controversies over the right to know and competing interests in personal privacy would arise in rare circumstances—circumstances where members of the public claim access to government facilities or materials to which other individuals also make claims of personal privacy—and only after the denomination of a constitutional right to know.

In 1970, for example, Justices John Harlan, Jr., William Douglas, and William Brennan were prepared to treat such conflicting interests as posing a constitutional controversy. They dissented from the denial of a writ of *certiorari* to hear a challenge to a state supreme court enjoining the commercial distribution of the film *Titticut Follies*. The film was a documentary portraying the inhumane treatment and condition of inmates at the Bridgewater State Hospital for the criminally insane. Six justices did not deem the case "certworthy," perhaps partially because the public's right to know had not attained constitutional legitimacy, but the dissenters thought the Court should achieve a "balance between these two interests, that of the individual's privacy and the public's right to know about conditions in public institutions."[61]

The political and constitutional controversies over the public's right to know largely arise from the failure to attend to the foundations for claiming a constitutional right to know. Members of the press and constitutional scholars advocating the public's right to know fundamentally err by failing to distinguish the public's right to know as an abstract political right—a bulwark, as it were, for freedom of information—from the concrete rights embodied in the First Amendment. Ronald Dworkin explains the difference between abstract and concrete rights:

> An abstract right is a general political aim the statement of which does not indicate how that general aim is to be weighted or compromised in particular circumstances against other political aims. Concrete rights . . . are political aims that are more precisely defined so as to express more definitely the weight they may have against other political aims on particular occasions. . . . Abstract rights . . . provide arguments for concrete rights, but the claim of a concrete right is more definite than any claim of abstract right that supports it.[62]

Abstract rights are, in a sense, unconditional and unqualified, whereas concrete rights are qualified by competing moral, legal, or political considerations. Abstract rights, therefore, may serve as important arguments for the legitimacy of concrete rights as against other moral, legal, or political considerations.

The significance of the public's right to know as an abstract political right is that it provides powerful arguments for extending concrete rights guaranteed by the First Amendment. As an abstract right the public's right to know at once under: sores the import of the enumerated guarantees for freedom of speech and press, but does not itself mandate a concrete constitutional right to know. As later chapters show, when adjudicating First Amendment claims the Supreme Court has acknowledged the need for freedom of information and treated the public's right to know as an abstract political right or constitutional background right. The political ideal of the public's right to know is invoked to underline the importance of broadly interpreting specific rights guaranteed by the First Amendment. Thus, Walter Gellhorn's observation that "the 'right to know' principle is itself so broad and vaguely phrased that it cannot decide cases"[63] correctly criticizes the insistence on claiming a concrete constitutional right to know, but fails to appreciate how a broad principle or abstract political right may provide powerful arguments for the protection of free speech and press.

Members of the press and some constitutional scholars, nevertheless, argue that the public's right to know is a concrete and directly enforceable constitutional right against the government.[64] Notably, Thomas I. Emerson, a distinguished First Amendment scholar, insists that, "The Supreme Court has recognized in a number of cases that the first amendment embodies a constitutional guarantee of the right to know." He is quick, however, to note that the Court "has never clarified the right or pressed it toward its logical borders."[65] For Emerson, delineation of a First Amendment right to know presents no major theoretical or practical problems in constitutional interpretation. The right to know simply "focuses on the affirmative aspects of the first amendment and the system of freedom of expression."[66] He reasons that,

> In a number of areas the development of a constitutional right to know would play a significant role in the system of freedom of expression. In some situations the government attempts to interfere directly with the right to know, as when it imposes sanctions on reading or receiving certain materials. Here the right to know should be afforded full protection. In other situations . . . the right to know may give standing to the recipients or potential recipients of the communication. . . . The most significant application of the right to know, however, lies in its potential role in increasing the amount of information available to citizenry from the government. . . . Government secrecy is essentially in conflict with the underlying premises of the first amendment.[67]

Ostensibly, much would be gained by acknowledging a First Amendment "penumbra"[68] embodying the public's right to know. The Supreme Court has recognized other penumbral rights as being constitutionally guaranteed. The due process clause of the Fourteenth Amendment was construed in the early twentieth century to safeguard the "liberty of contract"[69] and, more recently, a right of privacy and a right to travel.[70] The First Amendment has been interpreted to safeguard such penumbral rights as the right to receive information, the right of association, and associational privacy.[71] Hence, Emerson urges the Supreme Court to articulate a constitutional right to know by refining and embellishing other previously recognized First Amendment penumbral rights, as the Court analogously delineated an independent constitutional right of privacy by elaborating prior judicial recognition of protected privacy interests under the First, Fourth, and Fifth Amendments.[72] Like Cooper, Cross, and Wiggins, Emerson thus insists on judicial denomination of a concrete constitutional right to know as a composite right derived from other First Amendment penumbral rights—for example, the right to receive and gather information and the right of access to governmental facilities and materials.

Because the public's right to know is deemed political beneficial, Emerson and members of the press underestimate the potential costs for both the Court and the republic of proclaiming an independent, concrete constitutional right to know. At the turn of the century the Court was widely criticized for acting like a super-legislature in striking down progressive economic legislation as an infringement of individuals' liberty of contract under the Fourteenth Amendment. The dangers of infidelity to the parchment guarantees of the Constitution appeared once again with the proclamation in *Griswold* v. *Connecticut* of a constitutional right of privacy. Dissenting in *Griswold*, Justice Black cautioned: "One of the most effective ways of diluting or expanding a constitutionally guaranteed right is to substitute for the crucial word or words of a constitutional guarantee another word or words, more or less flexible and more or less restricted in meaning."[73] As was judicial development of a constitutional right of privacy, judicial elaboration of a right to know would be tantamount to "constitutional common law."[74] The costs of the Court's enforcement of penumbral rights bear not only upon judicial craftsmanship and extraconstitutional decision making but on the basic structure of our constitutional democracy. Again, Justice Black warned, "unbounded judicial authority would make of this Court's members a day-to-day constitutional convention."[75]

Elevation of the public's right to know to constitutional status therefore raises fundamental issues about the limits of constitutional interpretation and about the role of judicial review in a constitutional democracy. It is not necessary to rehearse the debates over the permissible scope of judicial creativity in constitutional interpretation. Instead, controversies over the public's right to know may best be addressed by attending to the foundations for the Supreme Court's delineation of a concrete constitutional right to know.

The transformation of the public's right to know from an abstract political right into a concrete constitutional right under the First Amendment ostensibly is permissible upon establishing one or more of three basic justifications for the constitutional legitimacy of such a right. First, a historical argument: The right to know expresses an underlying tenet of constitutionally limited government evident and endorsed during the founding period in debates over the ratification of the Constitution and the adoption of the First Amendment. Second, a policy argument: Regardless of constitutional history, the public's right to know attains legitimacy solely on policy considerations of the desirability of governmental openness. Third, an argument based on constitutional common law: The public's right to know may be legitimately judicially created upon showing that prior *dicta* (statements of judicial philosophy) and holdings on the First Amendment acknowledged, albeit in a more limited fashion, the interests of the public in knowing about governmental operations.

The strongest justification for the Supreme Court's construction of a constitutional right to know entails showing that all three arguments are meritorious. That is to say, the public's right to know has some basis in constitutional history, attains support from previous rulings on the First Amendment, and would likely prove auspicious for the polity. Weaker justifications might be accepted by activist members of the Court, demanding only that two of the three rationales appear demonstrable. Indeed, a radical realist or purely result-oriented justice might maintain that the anticipated beneficent policy of governmental openness per se provides an adequate basis for establishing a directly enforceable constitutional right to know. However, all three rationales—the historical, the policy, and the constitutional common law arguments—are unpersuasive for members of the laity and the Supreme Court who subscribe to a theory of strict construction or literal interpretation of the First Amendment.

THE PUBLIC'S RIGHT TO KNOW AND THE FIRST AMENDMENT

In the 1970s perhaps the most significant First Amendment litigation involved members of the press claiming the public's right to know and special privileges in order to obtain access to information that ostensibly serves the interests of an informed public. These developments signify new directions in First Amendment litigation and raise the fundamental issue of whether the public's right to know has constitutional legitimacy. Inexorably these constitutional controversies challenge the Supreme Court and the public to comprehend the meaning of the First Amendment and the proper role of judicial review as much as the legitimacy and political ramifications of the public's right to know. The following chapters explore the legitimacy of the public's right to know as a concrete constitutional right under the First Amendment in terms of constitutional history, judicial politics, and developing constitutional law as well as considerations of public policy.

NOTES

1. See Francis E. Rourke, *Secrecy & Publicity: Dilemmas of Democracy* (Baltimore: Johns Hopkins Press, 1966); Norman Dorsen and Stephen Gillers, eds., *None of Your Business: Government Secrecy in America* (New York: Viking Press, 1974); Miles Beardsley Johnson, *The Government Secrecy Controversy* (New York: Vantage Press, 1967); David Wise, *The Politics of Lying* (New York: Random House, 1976); and David Wise and Thomas B. Ross, *The Invisible Government* (New York: Random House, 1964).

2. See David M. Alpern and Diane Camper, "The Court and the Press," *Newsweek,* June 26, 1978, at 12; Jonathan Kwitny, "A Judicial War on the Press?" *Wall Street Journal,* August 23, 1978 at 12; and Editors, "High Court No Friend of the Media," *Broadcasting,* July 10, 1978, at 22–23.

3. *United States* v. *The Progressive, Inc.,* 467 F. Supp. 990, 994, 996 (1979).

4. *New York Times Co.* v. *United States*, 403 U.S. 713 (1971), discussed in Chapter 5.

5. Kent Cooper, *The Right to Know* (New York: Farrar, Straus and Cudahy, 1956) iv, 16 (emphasis added).

6. Max Weber, "Bureaucracy," in *From Max Weber: Essays in Sociology*, ed. H. H. Gerth and C. Wright Mills (New York: Oxford University Press, 1946) 232–35.

7. James R. Wiggins, *Freedom or Secrecy* New York: Oxford University Press, 1956) 3–4. See also James R. Wiggins, "The Role of the Press in Safeguarding The People's Right to Know Government Business," 40 *Marquette Law Review* 74 (1956).

8. Harold L. Cross, *The People's Right to Know* (Morningside Heights, N.Y.: Columbia University Press, 1953) 198.

9. Administrative Procedure Act, 5 USC § 1002 (1964), 60 Stat. 238 (1946).

10. Housekeeping Statute, 5 USC § 301, 1 Stat. 28, 49, 65, 68 (1789).

11. See, for example, U.S., Congress, House, Committee on Government Operations, *Availability of Information from Federal Departments and Agencies*, Hearings, 84th Cong., 1st Sess.–86th Cong., 2d Sess. (1958); U.S., Congress, Senate, Committee on the Judiciary, Subcommittee on Constitutional Rights, *Freedom of Information and Secrecy in Government*, Hearings, 85th Cong., 2d Sess. (1958); U.S., Congress, Senate, Committee on the Judiciary, *Amending Section 161 of Revised Statutes With Respect to Authority of Federal Officers and Agencies to Withhold Information and Limit Availability of Records*, Senate Report 85-1621, 85th Cong., 2d Sess. (1958); U.S., Congress, House, Committee on Government Operations, *Availability of Information from Federal Departments and Agencies*, Department of Defense. 27th Report. House Report 85-1884, 85th Cong., 2d Sess. (1958); U.S., Congress, Senate, Committee on the Judiciary, Subcommittee on Constitutional Rights, *Freedom of Information and Secrecy in Government*, Hearings, 86th Cong., 1st Sess (1959); U.S., Congress, House, Committee on Government Operations, *Availability of Information from Federal Departments and Agencies* (Progress of Study, August 1958–July 1959). 12th Report. House Report 86-1137, 86th Cong., 1st Sess. (1959); U.S., Congress, House, Committee on Government Operations, *Availability of Information from Federal Departments and Agencies (the First Five Years and Progress of Study, August 1959–July 1960)*, 24th Report. House Report 86-2084, 86th Cong., 2d Sess. (1960).

12. Department of Defense, *Availability of Information from Federal Departments and Agencies*, House Report 85-1884, 5, 10, 45, 125.

13. U.S., Congress, Senate, Committee on the Judiciary, Senate Report 89-813, 89th Cong., 1st Sess. 3 (1965); and U.S., Congress, House, Committee on Government Operations, Subcommittee on Government Information and Individual Rights, *Freedom of Information Act and Amendments of 1974—Sourcebook: Legislative History, Texts and Other Documents*, Committee Print, 94th Cong., 1st Sess. (1975).

14. Louis Henkin, "The Right to Know and The Duty to Withhold: The Case of The Pentagon Papers," 120 *University of Pennsylvania Law Review* 271, 275 (1971).

15. See Thomas C. Hennings, Jr., "The People's Right to Know," 45 *American Bar Association Journal* 667 (1959) and "The Executive Privilege and The Public's Right to Know," 19 *Federal Bar Journal* 1 (1959).

16. U.S., Congress, Senate, Committee on the Judiciary, Subcommittee on Administrative Practice and Procedure, *Freedom of Information*, Hearings on S. 1666 and S. 1663, 88th Cong., 1st Sess. (1964).

17. Lyndon Baines Johnson, *Availability of Government Records and Information*, Statement by the president on signing bill revising the public information provisions of the Administrative Procedure Act (July 4, 1966) in 2 *Weekly Compilation of Presidential Documents* 895–896 (1966).

18. See, generally, Kenneth Culp Davis, *Discretionary Justice* (Urbana, Ill.: University of Southern Illinois Press, 1969).

19. U.S., Congress, Senate, S. 1663, *Freedom of Information* 3.

20. Freedom of Information Act, 5 USC § 552 (b) (1)-(9) (1974).

21. U.S., Congress, House, Committee on Government Operations, Subcommittee on Foreign Operations and Government Information, *Administration of the Freedom of Information Act*, House Report 92-1419, 92d Cong., 2d Sess. 8 (1972).

22. *Environmental Protection Agency* v. *Mink*, 410 U.S. 73 (1973).

23. See, for example, Government in the Sunshine Act, 5 USC § 552b (1976); and Federal Advisory Committee Act, 5 USC App. 1 (1973).

24. See, for example, Symposium, "The Freedom of Information Act a Decade Later," 39 *Public Administration Review* 310 (1979); "Developments Under the Freedom of Information Act—1978," 1979 *Duke Law Journal* 327; "Developments Under the Freedom of Information Act—1976," 1977 *Duke Law Journal* 532; "Developments Under the Freedom of Information Act—1974," 1975 *Duke Law Journal* 416; "Developments Under the Freedom of Information Act—1973," 1974 *Duke Law Journal* 251; "Developments Under the Freedom of Information Act—1972," 1973 *Duke Law Journal* 178; "Project: Federal Administrative Law Developments—1971, Freedom of Information," 1972 *Duke Law Journal* 136; "Project: Federal Administrative Law Developments—1970," 1971 *Duke Law Journal* 149.

25. See William R. Henrick, "Public Inspection of State and Municipal Executive Documents: 'Everybody, Practically Everything, Anytime, Except . . . " 45 *Fordham Law Review* 1105 (1977); Lucille Amico, *State Open Records Laws: An Update* (Columbia, Missouri: Freedom of Information Center, 1976); and Wallis C. McClain, ed., *A Summary of Freedom of Information and Privacy Laws of the 50 States, Access Reports*, Report No. 3 (Washington, D.C.: Access Reports, October, 1978).

26. James T. O'Reilly, *Federal Information Disclosure: Procedures, Forms and the Law* (Colorado Springs: Shepard's, 1979) 2–13.

27. Ibid.

28. Alexis de Tocqueville, *Democracy in America*, ed. Phillips Bradley (New York: Vintage, 1945) vol. I, 156–157.

29. Cross, *People's Right* 132.

30. See, for example, Thomas I. Emerson, "Legal Foundations of the Right to Know," 1976 *Washington University Law Quarterly* 1; David M. Ivester, "The Constitutional Right to Know," 4 *Hastings Constitutional Law Review* 109 (1977); Lawrence K. Rockwell, "The

Public's Right to Know: *Pell* v. *Procuiner* and *Saxbe* v. *Washington Post Co.*," 2 *Hastings Constitutional Law Review* 829 (1975); Robert A. Liston, *The Right to Know* (New York: Beacon, 1973); William H. Marnell, *The Right to Know* (New York: Franklin Watts, 1970); Frank Horton, "The Public's Right to Know," 1972 *North Carolina Central Law Review* 123; Luis Kutner, "Freedom of Information: Due Process of the Right to Know," 18 *Catholic Lawyer* 50 (1972); O. John Rogge, "The Right to Know," 41 *American Scholar* 648 (1972); Symposium, "The People's Right to Know," 8 *Trial* 12–16, 18–33 (March/April 1972); Irving Brant, "The Constitution and the Right to Know," in *Mass Media and the Law*, ed. David G. Clark and Earl Hutchison (New York: Wiley Interscience, 1970); J. Skelly Wright, "Defamation, Privacy, and the Public's Right to Know," 46 *Texas Law Review* 630 (1968); Wallace Parks, "The Open Government Principle: Applying the Right to Know Under the Constitution," 26 *George Washington Law Review* 1 (1957); and Leon Yankwich, "Legal Implications of, and Barriers to, The Right to Know," 40 *Marquette Law Review* 3 (1956).

31. John C. Merrill, "The 'People's Right to Know' Myth," 45 *New York State Bar Journal* 461, 461 (1973).

32. *Dayton Newspapers, Inc.* v. *City of Dayton*, 259 N.E.2d 522 (1970), aff'd, 274 N.E.2d 766 (1971).

33. William Hocking, *Freedom of the Press: A Framework of Principle* (Chicago: University of Chicago Press, 1947) 170–71.

34. See, generally, David Truman, *The Governmental Process* (New York: A. A. Knopf, 1951); and Robert Dahl, *A Preface to Democratic Theory* (Chicago: University of Chicago Press, 1956).

35. Emerson, "Legal Foundations of the Right to Know," at 9.

36. John R. Lucas, *On Justice* (Oxford: Clarendon Press, 1980) 27.

37. Joel Feinberg, *Social Philosophy* (Englewood Cliffs, N.J.: Prentice-Hall, 1973) 58.

38. Ibid. at 66.

39. Flathman, *The Practice of Rights* (Cambridge: At the University Press, 1976) 1–2.

40. Joel Feinberg, "The Nature and Value of Rights," in *Rights*, ed. David Lyons (Belmont, Calif.: Wadsworth, 1979) 86.

41. Peter D. Bathory and Wilson Carey McWilliams, "Political Theory and the People's Right to Know," in *Government Secrecy in Democracies*, ed. Itzhak Galnoor (New York: New York University Press, 1977) 3, 8.

42. See, for example, Jermone Barron, *Freedom of the Press for Whom?* (Bloomington: Indiana University Press, 1973); and Comment, "Freedom to Hear: A Political Justification of the First Amendment," 46 *Washington Law Review* 311 (1971).

43. Bathory and McWilliams, "Political Theory and the People's Right to Know."

44. *Gannett* v. *DePasquale*, 99 S.Ct. 2898, 2913 (1979) (Burger, C.J., con. op.).

45. Edward H. Levi, "Confidentiality and Democratic Government," 30 *Record of the Association of the Bar of the City of New York* (1975) 323, 327.

46. Joseph Tussman, *Government and the Mind* (New York: Oxford University Press, 1977) 118. See also Bill Moyers, "The Right and the Need to Know," 38 *Social Action* 3, 6–7 (1972); and William Colby, "Intelligence Secrecy and Security in A Free Society," 1 *International Security* 3 (1976).

47. That is, in some instances the need to know may provide an individual with standing as a traditional "Hohfeldian plaintiff." See Wesley H. Hohfeld, *Fundamental Legal Conceptions* (New Haven: Yale University Press, 1919).

48. *Shaughnessy* v. *United States ex rel. Mezei*, 345 U.S. 206, 225 (1953) (Jackson, J., dis. op.). (emphasis added).

49. See *United States* v. *Cruikshank*, 92 U.S. 542, 559 (1876); *Gompers* v. *Bucks Stove & R. Co.*, 221 U.S. 418, 446 (1911); *Bowles* v. *United States*, 319 U.S. 33, 37 (1943) (per curiam) (Jackson, J., dis. op.); *Davis* v. *United States*, 328 U.S. 582, 611 (1946) (Frankfurter, J., dis. op.); *United States* v. *Mine Workers of America*, 330 U.S. 358, 370–71 (1947) (Rutledge, J., dis. op.); *Maryland* v. *Baltimore Radio Show*, 338 U.S. 912, 920 (1950); *Shenker* v. *Washington*,

369 U.S. 541, 580 (1962) (Douglas, J., dis. op.); *International Longshoremen's Assn.* v. *Philadelphia Marine Trade Assn.*, 389 U.S. 64, 71 (1967); *In re Ruffalo*, 390 U.S. 544 (1968); and *Smith* v. *Illinois*, 390 U.S. 129, 130 (1968).

50. *Hannah* v. *Larche*, 363 U.S. 420, 502 (Douglas, J., dis. op.) (emphasis supplied). See also *Morgan* v. *United States*, 304 U.S. 1, 18 (1938); and *Greene* v. *McElroy*, 360 U.S. 474, 496–97 (1959).

51. See David M. O'Brien, "The Fifth Amendment: Fox Hunters, Old Women, Hermits, and the Burger Court," 54 *Notre Dame Lawyer* 26, 35–41 (1978).

52. *Zemel* v. *Rusk*, 381 U.S. 1, 16–17 (1965).

53. *Gordon* v. *United States*, 344 U.S. 414 (1953).

54. *Jencks* v. *United States*, 353 U.S. 657, 671 (1957), quoting *United States* v. *Reynolds*, 345 U.S. 1, 12 (1952). See also *Jay* v. *Boyd*, 351 U.S. 345 (1956); *Greene* v. *McElroy*, 360 U.S. 474 (1959); *Alderman* v. *United States*, 394 U.S. 165 (1969); *McLucas* v. *DeChamplain*, 421 U.S. 21 (1975). After *Jencks* Congress limited and codified the decision with the Jencks Act, 18 U.S.C. 3500 (1976). See U.S., Congress, Senate, *Senate Report No. 981*, 85th Cong., 1st Sess. (1957).

55. See Allan Adler, "The Graymail Tale: How Prosecutions Fail," 4 *First Principles* 1 (March 1979); U.S., Congress, Senate, Senate Select Committee on Intelligence, Subcommittee on Secrecy and Disclosure, *National Security Secrets and the Administration of Justice*, 95th Cong., 2d Sess. (1978); and U.S., Congress, House, Committee on Government Operations, *Justice Department Handling of Cases Involving Classified Data and Claims of National Security*, House Report 96-280, 96th Cong., 1st Sess. (1979).

56. James Goodale, "Legal Pitfalls in The Right to Know," 1976 *Washington University Law Quarterly* 25, 33. See also George A. Benson, "The Essence of Our Freedom," 2 *American Editor* 24 (1958).

57. See Emerson, "Legal Foundations of the Right to Know," at 19–23.

58. Privacy Act, 5 USC § 552 (a) (1974). See also David M. O'Brien, *Privacy, Law, and Public Policy* (New York: Praeger, 1979), Chapter 6.

59. *Department of the Air Force* v. *Rose*, 96 S.Ct. 1592, 1610 (1976) (Burger, C.J., dis. op.). See also David M. O'Brien, "Freedom of Information, Privacy, and Information Control: A Contemporary Administrative Dilemma," 39 *Public Administration* Review 323 (1979) and "Privacy and the Right of Access: Purposes and Paradoxes of Information Control," 30 *Administrative Law Review* 45 (1978). Also see *Whalen* v. *Roe*, 97 S.Ct. 869 (1977).

60. See *Burdeau* v. *McDowell*, 256 U.S. 465, 475 (1921), and O'Brien, *Privacy, Law, and Public Policy* at 35–88.

61. *Wiseman* v. *Massachusetts*, 398 U.S. 960, 961 (1970) (denial of cert.) (Harlan, J., dis. op.).

62. Ronald Dworkin, "Hard Cases," 88 *Harvard Law Review* 1057, 1070 (1975).

63. Walter Gellhorn, "The Right to Know: First Amendment Overbreadth?" 1976 *Washington University Law Review* 25, 26.

64. See, for example, *New York Times Co.* v. *United States*, 403 U.S. 711, 749 (1971) (Burger, C. J., dis. op.); *Branzburg* v. *Hayes*, 408 U.S. 665, 684–85 (1972) (Douglas, J., dis. op.); *Gravel* v. *United States*, 408 U.S. 606, 643 (1972) (Douglas, J., dis. op.); *Miller* v. *California*, 413 U.S. 15, 44 (1973) (Douglas, J., dis. op.); *Columbia Broadcasting System, Inc.* v. *Democratic National Committee*, 412 U.S. 94, 165 (1973) (Douglas, J., dis. op.); *United States* v. *Richardson*, 418 U.S. 87, 141 (1974) (Brennan, J., dis. op.); *Hamling* v. *United States*, 418 U.S. 87, 141 (1974) (Brennan, J., dis. op.); *Saxbe* v. *Washington Post*, 417 U.S. 843, 857 (1974) (Powell, J., dis. op.); *Pell* v. *Procuiner*, 417 U.S. 817, 840–41 (1974) (Douglas, J., dis. op.); *Virginia State Board of Pharmacy* v. *Virginia Citizens Consumer Council*, 425 U.S. 748, 785 (1976) (Rehnquist, J., dis. op.); *Buckley* v. *Valeo*, 424 U.S. 1, 237–38 (1976) (Burger, C.J., con. and dis. op.); *Houchins* v. *KQED*, 438 1, 35 (1978) (Stevens, J., dis. op.).

65. Thomas I. Emerson, "Colonial Intentions and Current Realities of the First Amendment," 125 *University of Pennsylvania Law Review* 737, 755 (1977).

66. Emerson, "Legal Foundations of the Right to Know," at 2.

67. Emerson, "Colonial Intentions and Current Realities of the First Amendment," at 755. See also Thomas I. Emerson, *The System of Freedom of Expression* (New York: Vintage Books, 1970) 94–95, 152, 463–65, 613–14, 649–50, 671–72.

68. Justice Douglas, in *Griswold* v. *Connecticut*, 381 U.S. 479, 482 (1965), stated that "specific guarantees in the Bill of Rights have penumbras formed by emanations from those guarantees that help give them life and substance."

69. The Fourteenth Amendment provides in part that "No state shall . . . deprive any person of life, liberty, or property, without due process of law." U.S. Constitution, Amendment XIV. See, for example, *Lockner* v. *New York*, 198 U.S. 45 (1905).

70. See *Griswold* v. *Connecticut*, 381 U.S. 479 (1965) and *Roe* v. *Wade*, 410 U.S. 113 (1973) (right of privacy). Also *Kent* v. *Dulles*, 357 U.S. 116 (1941); *United States* v. *Guest*, 383 U.S. 745 (1966); *Shapiro* v. *Thompson*, 394 U.S. 618 (1969); *Dunn* v. *Blumstein*, 405 U.S. 330 (1972); and *Memorial Hospital* v. *Maricopa County*, 415 U.S. 250 (1974) (recognizing the right to travel).

71. See *Niemotko* v. *Maryland*, 340 U.S. 268 (1951) and *West Virginia State Board of Education* v. *Barnette*, 319 U.S. 624 (1943) (recognizing religious associations); *Smith* v. *Allwright*, 321 U.S. 649 (1944) and *Terry* v. *Adams*, 345 U.S. 461 (1953) (recognizing political associations); and *NAACP* v. *Alabama*, 357 U.S. 449, 462 (1958) (recognizing a First Amendment right of associational privacy).

72. For a more extensive discussion see O'Brien, *Privacy, Law, and Public Policy*, Chapters 2–6.

73. *Griswold* v. *Connecticut*, 381 U.S. 479, at 508 (Black, J., dis. op.). See also *Roe* v. *Wade*, 410 U.S. 113, 172–73 (1973) (Rehnquist, J., dis. op.).

74. See, generally, Harry Wellington, "Common Law Rules and Constitutional Double Standards," 83 *Yale Law Journal* 222 (1973); Henry Monaghan, "Constitutional Common Law," 84 *Harvard Law Review* 1 (1975); and Thomas S. Schrock and Robert C. Welsh, "Reconsidering The Constitutional Common Law," 91 *Harvard Law Review* 1117 (1978).

75. *Griswold* v. *Connecticut*, 381 U.S. 479, 508 (1965) (Black, J., dis. op.).

CHAPTER 2

THE FOUNDING AND
FREEDOM OF INFORMATION

Like the course of the heavenly bodies, harmony in national life is a resultant of the struggle between contending forces. In frank expression of conflicting opinion lies the greatest promise of wisdom in governmental action; and in suppression lies ordinarily the greatest peril.
Justice Louis Brandeis, *Gilbert* v. *Minnesota* (1919)

The principle of "consent of the governed" would have no meaning if public discussion were banned.
William O. Douglas, *We the Judges* (1956)

Does the public's right to know attain constitutional legitimacy in historical perspective? Is an enforceable constitutional right to know defensible in terms of the debates over adopting and ratifying the Constitution and, subsequently, over enacting the First Amendment?

The dilemma of claiming that a right to know is constitutionally implied disposes the press and some students of the Constitution to argue that "the founding fathers intended to guarantee the right to know per se, that is, that the First Amendment was specifically intended to extend to the people a directly enforceable right to know about governmental affairs." Lexical and psychohistorical difficulties in determining the framers' intent on any matter, however, suggest the more qualified claim that "the freedom of speech and press clauses were intended at least as instrumental means of securing and protecting the right to know. In other words, assuming the framers had no intent to create a directly enforceable right to know, they expected that the guarantee of freedom of speech and press would effectively secure the right of the people to know about their government."[1]

An often cited testimonial by members of the press, constitutional scholars, and legislators is James Madison's eloquent statement: "A popular

Government, without popular information, or the means of acquiring it, is but a Prologue to a Farce or a Tragedy; or perhaps both. Knowledge will forever govern ignorance: And a people who mean to be their own Governors, must arm themselves with the power which knowledge gives."[2] Commentators thus argue that as much as government censorship of the press is politically and constitutionally objectionable, an affirmative right of access to government information is politically and constitutionally legitimate in historical perspective.[3] Senator Thomas Hennings, for instance, reasons:

> By 1787, the year the Constitution was written, there had developed in England the concept of a right in the people to know what their Government was doing. There can be no doubt that the framers of our Government recognized the existence of such a right and were strongly influenced by it in writing both the original Constitution and the Bill of Rights. . . . [But] no explicit provision was made concerning the people's "right to know." The explanation for this seems to be that the right to know, like many other fundamental rights, was taken so much for granted that it was deemed unnecessary to include it.[4]

The continuity between the founders' understanding of freedom of information and contemporary commentators' understanding of a constitutional right to know is merely apparent and actually distorts the founders' vision of representative government. Madison's testimonial, for example, was made not in defense of First Amendment freedoms. Rather, he made it in a letter applauding the liberal appropriations by Kentucky for a system of public education. Madison, like Thomas Jefferson, believed "that a well-instructed people alone can be permanently a free people."[5] Yet, there is no evidence that Madison or any other members of the constitutional conventions or the first Congress supported the view that the people have a directly enforceable constitutional right to know against the government.

The absence of an expressly guaranteed right to know is because, although the availability of information to the public was deemed essential to free government, the view that the people enjoy an enforceable right to demand access to government information was premature in terms of the historical struggle for freedom of speech and press. The most that may be claimed is that the founders envisioned the public's right to know as an abstract political right, at once underscoring and attaining significance from the freedoms of speech and press.[6] In other words, the public's right to know was secured indirectly, derivatively by the First Amendment. That the founders envisioned the public's right to know in this less ambitious, though no less important, way is evident from the common law background of, and the political struggles over, adopting and ratifying the Constitution and the First Amendment.

THE ENGLISH HERITAGE AND THE ARTICLES OF CONFEDERATION

There is little doubt that colonists and, later, members of the Continental Congress acknowledged an intimate connection between freedom of information and the exigencies of a free government. The seventeenth and eighteenth century understanding of freedom of speech and press, however, was considerably more circumscribed than the contemporary understanding, reflecting the protracted battle for freedom of the press in England that dates back to the Middle Ages.

Governmental censorship of speech and press to preserve the public realm, instead of to redress private wrongs, stems from the 1275 enactment of *De Scandalis Magnatum*, imposing penalties for any false talk about the king and, subsequently, as reenacted in 1378 punishing such talk about all government officials.[7] The law punished what a later amendment in 1559 termed "seditious words" because they constitute a public mischief, contributing to public disorder and lawlessness. In the sixteenth and seventeenth centuries censorship expanded and the law against seditious libel— defamation of the government—emerged from the administration of *Scandalum Magnatum* by the King's Council, which sat in the "starred chambre" at Westminster and became infamously known as the Star Chamber. During the reign of Queen Elizabeth I, the Star Chamber effectively and severely punished libel and exercised almost complete control over printing with a 1585 Act requiring publishers to obtain a printing licence.

De Libellis Famosis illustrates the principles of libel law that the Star Chamber enunciated and that eventually dominated English and early colonial common law. Here, the court explained the seriousness of defamation and the fundamental difference between libel of private individuals and seditious libel:

> *If it be against a private man it deserves a severe punishment*, for although the libel be made against one, yet it incites all those of the same family, kindred, or society to revenge, and so tends *per consequens* to quarrels and breach of the peace, and may be the cause of shedding of blood, and of great inconvenience: *if it be against a magistrate, or other public person, it is a greater offence*; for it concerns not only the breach of the peace, but also the scandal of government; for what greater scandal of government can there be than to have corrupt or wicked magistrates to be appointed and constituted by the King to govern his subjects under him? And greater imputation to the state cannot be, than to suffer such corrupt men to sit in the sacred seat of justice, or to have any meddling in or concerning the administration of justice.[8]

Because seditious libel was particularly egregious and judicial complicity an even greater evil, the Star Chamber was especially merciless in cases such as that of the *Trial of William Prynn*.[9] The defendant had published a book expressing disdain for actors and acting, and the Star Chamber viewed the book as an attack on the queen, who had recently appeared in a play, and, therefore, as seditious libel against the government. Prynn was fined £10,000 and sentenced to life imprisonment, as well as suffered branding on the forehead and having his nose slit and ears cut off!

The abusive treatment of individuals by the Star Chamber left a legacy of human tragedy, but also an indelible imprint on the English heritage from which the drafters of the Constitution and Bill of Rights drew their principles for free government.[10] In England, not until 1641 was the Star Chamber abolished by the Long Parliament and, then, for two years it continued issuing licenses for publishers. Even after the Star Chamber was abolished, the principles articulated in cases such as *De Libellis Famosis* were applied by common law courts, which gradually assumed the role of *custos moram* of the realm. Criminal liability for libel remained a question of law, not of fact for juries to decide, and the truth or falsity of a publication was immaterial. Furthermore, although censorship declined by comparison to that wielded by the Star Chamber, partisan political publications were discouraged by both the Licensing Act of 1662 and the additional burden of a tax on all newspapers and advertisements imposed by the Stamp and Advertising Act of 1711.[11]

By 1776 and the American Revolution, speech and press was deemed free, but not unconditionally so. In England the freedom of speech and press was restricted by the law of seditious libel and the irrelevance of truth as a defense in such prosecutions as well as by the taxation of publications. Freedom of speech and press basically meant freedom from prior censorship. As Sir William Blackstone observed:

> The liberty of the press is indeed essential to the nature of a free state; but this consists in laying no *previous* restraints upon publications, and not in freedom from censure for criminal matter when published. Every freeman has an undoubted right to lay what sentiments he pleases before the public; but if he publishes what is improper, mischievous, or illegal, he must take the consequences of his own temerity.[12]

No less poignantly, in 1770, Lord Mansfield in *H. S. Woodfall* commented: "As for the liberty of the press, I will tell you what it is; the liberty of the press is, that a man may print what he pleases without a licenser: so long as it remains so, the liberty of the press is not restrained."[13]

At common law, freedom of speech and press even in the absence of prior restraints was not unqualified or permitted what Blackstone and Mansfield termed the "licentiousness of the press." Denying Sir Thomas Erskine's argument for a new trial in 1783 in the case of *Dean of St. Asaph*, for example, Lord Mansfield reiterated the common law understanding that "[t]he *liberty of the press* consists in printing without any previous licence, subject to the consequences of the law. The *licentiousness* of the press is *Pandora's* box, the source of every evil."[14] In England and in the colonies, differences in opinion over what constitutes liberty and licentiousness, truth and falsehood, and good motives and criminal intent perpetuated the struggle for freedom of speech and press. In 1792, with the enactment of the Fox Libel Act, English juries were finally given the power to determine the culpability of alleged libelous publications, rather than to simply decide the question of whether an individual in fact published the materials.[15] Still, even after the Fox Libel Act a jury convicted Thomas Paine for publishing *The Rights of Man* on hearing only a brief defense and without asking for a reply or either attorneys' summation.[16] By the late eighteenth century the turbulent struggle in England had established only that liberty of speech and press meant the absence of prior restraints, prior censorship. Not until the enactment of Lord Campbell's Act in 1843 was truth accepted as a defense against libel indictments, and only after 1855 was the stamp and Advertising Act abandoned.[17] These developments broadened the freedom of publication, but by no means provided a foundation for a right of access to government information. Indeed, until 1771 the government not only supervised all reporting on government affairs but also prohibited any publication of Parliamentary proceedings.[18]

The libertarian impulse for freedom of speech and press achieved somewhat earlier, albeit mixed, success in the colonies. That is not to say that early colonial governments were any less suppressive than were the Crown and Parliament. To the contrary, the restrictions and constraints on speech and press articulated in English common law were largely incorporated into colonial common law, reinforced both by Puritans and by royalist judges.[19] "Colonial America was an open society dotted with closed enclaves," John P. Roche perceptively notes, "and one could generally settle in with his co-believers in safety and comfort and exercise the right of oppression."[20]

Censorship and licensing accompanied the introduction of printing presses in the colonies, with the General Court of Massachusetts appointing two licensers for the press as early as 1662.[21] In Massachusetts, licenses were required for publications until 1719—24 years later than in England. The censorship inherent in the licensing of publishers was prevalent in other northern and southern colonies. In 1671, Virginia Governor Berkeley applauded the absence of printing presses in his colony: "I thank God, we have no free schools nor printing; and I hope we shall not have these [for a] hundred years; for learning has brought disobedience and heresy and sects into the world; and printing has devulged them, and libels against the government. God keep us from both."[22] Eleven years later the colony went so far as to punish an individual for printing the laws of Virginia without a license and thereafter printing was not allowed until 1729, when a single press controlled by the governor served the colony until 1765.

Throughout the seventeenth and eighteenth centuries colonial courts embraced common law principles permitting the punishment of licentious speech and press. When reflecting on the evolution of English and colonial common law, the chief justice of Massachusetts in 1768 registered the prevailing understanding of free speech and press:

> Formerly, no Man could print his Thoughts ever so modestly and calmly, or with ever so much Candour and Ingenuousness, upon any subject whatever, without a License. When this restraint was taken off, then was the true Liberty of the Press. Every Man who prints, prints at his Peril; as every Man speaks, speaks at his Peril. It was in this Manner I treated this Subject at the last Term, yet the Liberty of the Press and the Danger of an *Imprimatur* was canted about, as if the Press was going under some new and illegal Restraint. No Gentleman of the Bar, I am sure, could have so misunderstood me. This Restraint of the Press, in the Prevention of Libels, is the only Thing which will preserve your Liberty. To suffer the licentious Abuse of Government is the most likely Way to destroy its Freedom.[23]

While objecting to prior censorship of the press, even seventeenth and eighteenth century English and colonial libertarians did not seriously question the propriety of punishing seditious libel and licentious publications. Thus, although John Milton exalted freedom of speech and press in *Areopagitica*, he refused to recognize such freedom for Protestants and deplored royalist libel against the Parliament.[24] So too, John Locke, whose writings were so influential for the Founding Fathers and who wrote a document for the House of Commons condemning governmental censorship, was rather intolerant of what he deemed seditious libel. In *A Letter Concerning Toleration*, Locke urged that "no opinions contrary to human society, or to those moral rules which are necessary to the preservation of civil society, are to be tolerated by the magistrate."[25] Perhaps even more widely read in the colonies than John Locke's works were the letters of two English Whig political journalists, John Trenchard and Thomas Gordon, who wrote under the pseudonym of Cato.

Published in England in 1720 and numbering no less than 138 essays, *Cato's Letters* were collected in four volumes and underwent several editions as well as individual republication in colonial newspapers. In 1721 and 1722 Benjamin Franklin first published Cato's important essays "Of Freedom of Speech" and "Reflections on Libell." His own "Apology for Printers" printed on June 10, 1731, rehearsed Cato's principles.[26] In proclaiming freedom of speech and press as "the great bulwark of Liberty," Cato observed:

> The Administration of Government, is nothing else but the Attendance of the Trustees of the People upon the Interest, and Affairs of the People. And it is the Part and Business of the People, for whose sake

alone all publick Matters are or ought to be transacted, to see whether
they be well or ill transacted; so it is the Interest, and ought to be the
Ambition of all honest Magistrates, to have their Deeds openly examined and publickly scanned.

Freedom of Speech is ever the Symptom as well as the Effect of
good Government.[27]

Although giving popular expression to early eighteenth century libertarian
visions of freedom of speech and press, Cato challenged only the common
law rejection of truth as a defense in libel actions. Like Milton, Locke, and
other libertarians, Cato did not challenge the common law proscription of
seditious libel. Significantly, even Cato's colonial proteges John Peter
Zenger and James Alexander failed to repudiate the common law of
seditious libel per se.

Undoubtedly, the *cause celebre* of colonial prosecutions was the trial
of John Peter Zenger, publisher of *The New York Weekly Journal*. The
Journal, like other colonial newspapers, was a partisan publication, and
Zenger, poorly educated and neither editor nor writer for his paper, was part
of a political faction that lost power when William Cosby became Governor
of New York. In 1734 Zenger and Alexander published along with several of
Cato's essays a series of satirical ballads attacking Governor Cosby. Zenger
was tried a year later for printing "many things tending to raise factions and
tumults among the people of this province, inflaming their minds with
contempt for his majesty's government, and greatly disturbing the peace
thereof."[28] In the penultimate trial before royal judges,[29] Zenger's initial
lawyers, James Alexander and William Smith, sought to use the trial to
further discredit Cosby's administration and went so far as to attack the
chief justice for presiding at the trial. They were promptly disbarred from
practicing law in the colony. An acclaimed Quaker attorney, Andrew
Hamilton, came unsolicited from Philadelphia to defend Zenger with an
unprecedented challenge of the common law principles—deriving from *De
Libellis Famosis*. Hamilton, however, did not challenge seditious libel per se;
rather, he contended that Zenger's publications were true and that if he was
not permitted to demonstrate their truth as a defense, then the jury should
acquit Zenger. The jury, already critical of Cosby's administration and the
chief justice, found Zenger not guilty.

The Zenger trial popularized for colonists the struggle against governmental censorship in the form of prosecutions for sedition. Significantly,
Zenger's defenders and detractors agreed that freedom of speech and press
was essential to the public and popular government and also that that
freedom did not permit licentiousness. That both sides of the Zenger
controversy accepted this basic principle of common law and disagreed only
on when and where to draw a line between permissible political commentary
and licentious criticism is illustrated by the exchange following Zenger's trial

between James Alexander and Andrew Bradford. In the *Pennsylvania Gazette* Alexander reasoned: "THE FREEDOM OF SPEECH is a *principal pillar* in a free Government: when this support is taken away the Constitution is dissolved, and tyranny is erected on its ruins. Republics and limited monarchies derive their strength and vigor from a *popular examination* into the actions of the Magistrates. This privilege in all ages has been and always will be abused." Andrew Bradford was no less libertarian and eloquent in depicting the relationship between freedom of the press and popular government: "This is the *Liberty of the Press*, the great *Palladium* of all our other *Liberties*, which I hope the good People of this Province, will forever enjoy; and that every *Pennsylvanian*, will resent with *Scorn and Indignation*, the least Attempt to weaken or subvert it." What disturbed Bradford and other commentators on the common law was the unpardonable licentiousness of the press in criticizing government officials:

> Nor, by the *Liberty of the Press*, do I understand a *License* of traducing the Conduct, of those Gentlemen who appointed our Lawful Governors: When they behave themselves well, they ought to be treated with all the Respect and Gratitude, that's due from an obliged People; should they behave themselves ill, their Measures are to be remonstrated against in Terms of *Decency*, and Moderation not of Fury and Scurrility.[30]

The struggle for freedom of speech and press during the colonial period typically was over the application of accepted common law principles. Libertarians accepted the common law principle of punishing seditious and licentious communications, although disabused of the idea that truth was immaterial in such prosecutions. They quarreled about what publications were to be deemed licentious.

Seventeenth and eighteenth century libertarians thus differentiated between mere political commentary *cum* criticism and licentiousness or seditious libel. The former was considered a natural and political right with auspicious consequences for society; the latter, they agreed, might prove pernicious and be legally punished. The potential salutory affects of political commentaries and criticism did not absolve editors of their responsibilities to adhere to common law principles. William Livingston observed in the August 30, 1753, *Independent Reflector*:

> A Printer ought not to publish every Thing that is offered to him; what is conducive of general Utility, he should not refuse, be the Author a Christian, Jew, Turk or Infidel. Such Refusal is an immediate Abridgement of the Freedom of the Press. When on the other hand, he prostitutes his Art by the Publication of any Thing injurious to his Country, it is criminal—It is high Treason against the State. The usual Alarm rung upon the LIBERTY OF THE PRESS, is groundless and trifling, and whenever it is assumed the Printer should be punished.[31]

Likewise, in 1766 William Bollan, a Massachusetts lawyer and "faithful friend of America," as John Adams called him, refined Zengerian principles to emphasize the crucial role of a free press in promoting popular government. In his treatise on freedom of speech and press, Bollan observed:

> [T]he free examination of public measures, with a proper representation by speech or writing of the sense resulting from that examination, is the right of the members of a free state, and requisite for the preservation of their other rights; and that all things published by persons for the sake of giving due information to their fellow subjects, in points immediately affecting the public welfare, are worthy of commendation.[32]

In the late eighteenth century, controversies arose when publishers were deemed to have abused their press freedom, and legislative assemblies, like royalist judges and governors earlier, enforced the law against seditious libel as a matter of parliamentary privilege, punishing speakers or writers who impeached their authority.[33] The New York Assembly, for example, resolved that "it is the undoubted right of the people of this Colony to know the proceedings of their representatives in General Assembly and that any attempt to prevent their proceedings being printed or punished is a violation of the rights and liberties of the People of this Colony."[34] Nevertheless, even after the Revolutionary War the New York Assembly, like other state assemblies, exercised a parliamentary privilege to censure and imprision individuals for political commentaries and criticisms deemed to constitute sedition.

Exhortations of the auspiciousness of freedom of speech and press for popular government therefore must be comprehended within the context of the common law and colonial practices. The Continental Congress in a letter to the inhabitants of Quebec, for example, proclaimed:

> [T]he first grand right is that of the people having a share in their own government, by their representatives chosen by themselves, and in consequences of being ruled by laws which they themselves approve, not by edicts of men, over whom they have no controul. . . .
>
> The last right we shall mention, regards the freedom of the press. The importance of this consists, besides the advancement of truth, science, morality, and arts in general, in its diffusion of liberal sentiments on the administration of government, its ready communication of union among them, whereby oppressive officers are shamed or intimidated, into more honorable and just modes of conducting affairs.[35]

Still, prosecutions for seditious libel were permissible and the libertarian argument that truth is a defense against libel actions remained unaccepted.[36]

The struggle for free speech and press prior to the founding period and constitutional conventions, moreover, provides no foundation for an affirmative right of the public to demand access to government information. Article IX of the Articles of Confederation did provide that,

> The Congress of the United States . . . shall publish the Journal of their proceedings monthly, except such parts thereof relating to treaties, alliances or military operations, as in their judgment require secrecy; and the yeas and nays of the delegates of each state, or any of them, at his or their request shall be furnished with a transcript of the said Journal, except such parts as are above excepted, to lay before the legislatures of the several states.[37]

Yet under the Articles of Confederation the people had no direct access to congressional proceedings. Only their representatives could obtain materials relating to the proceedings of the Continental Congress and even the representatives had access to only those materials not deemed to require secrecy. While the necessity for popular information about the government was understood, it was always balanced against, if not usually sacrificed because of, the simultaneous need for confidentiality in negotiating financial transactions, foreign affairs, and military operations. Thus, libertarians, including Thomas Jefferson, unsuccessfully insisted on the import of public access to information concerning governmental operations even when confronted with such incidents of domestic violence as Shay's Rebellion: "The way to prevent these irregular interpositions of the people, is to give them full information of their affairs thro' the channel of the public papers, and to contrive that those papers should penetrate the whole mass of the people."[38] The notes and reports of the proceedings of the Continental Congress remained inaccessible to the public and were not collected and published, as the *Rough and Secret Journals*, until 1821—more than 30 years after the adoption and ratification of the Constitution.[39]

THE CONSTITUTIONAL CONVENTIONS AND CONGRESSIONAL JOURNALS

Libertarians like Thomas Jefferson protested against the secrecy of the Constitutional Convention. During the summer of 1787 in a letter to John Adams, Jefferson wrote: "I am sorry they began their deliberations by so abominable a precedent as that of tying up the tongues of their members. Nothing can justify this example but the innocence of their intentions, and ignorance of the value of public discussions."[40] Politically neither naive nor ignorant, James Madison, who as a delegate to the convention unofficially took voluminous notes throughout the debates, would not permit their publication during his lifetime and they were not published until 1840, four years after his death. The necessity for secrecy and confidentiality remains undisputed. "No body can say what sort of constitution would have emerged if the convention had been open to the public," Irving Brant perceptively observes," [but had] Madison's notes been published before the states held their ratifying conventions, the Constitution would never had been adopted. The dialogue contained far too much that would have been seized upon by demogogues."[41]

During the federal and state conventions on the adoption of the Constitution, the issue of the public's right to know was directly confronted in connection with the publication of congressional proceedings. On August 11, 1787, James Madison and John Rutledge moved the adoption of the following provision: "[T]hat each House shall keep a Journal of its proceedings, and shall publish the same from time to time; except such part of the of the proceedings of the Senate, when acting not in its legislative capacity, as may be judged by that House to require secrecy."[42] The proposal differed from the analogous provision in the Articles of Confederation in how often the proceedings would be published as well as in its granting direct public access to the printed records except where the Senate withheld information concerning its proceedings—proceedings apparently relating to the negotiation of treaties and to military operations.

During debate on the proposal, Oliver Ellsworth argued that the clause was superfluous because "[t]he legislature will not fail to publish their proceedings from time to time." James Wilson thought the clause prudent: "The people have a *right to know* what their agents are doing or have done, and it should not be in the option of the legislature to conceal their proceedings. Besides, as this is a clause in the existing Confederation, the not retaining it would furnish the adversaries of the reform with a pretext by which weak and suspicious minds may be easily misled." Similarly, George Mason found the clause necessary because "it would give a just alarm to the people, to make a conclave of their legislature." The convention subsequently adopted as Article I, Section 5, Clause 3 of the Constitution the following provision: "Each House shall keep a Journal of its Proceedings, and from time to time publish the same, excepting such Parts as may in their Judgment require Secrecy; and the Yeas and Nays of the Members of either House on any question shall, at the Desire of one fifth of those Present, be entered on the Journal."

Concern over this provision and the public's interests in information about legislative proceedings, emerged again during the debates in the state conventions on the ratification of the Constitution. In particular, during the Virginia convention Patrick Henry impassionately warned that "[u]nder the abominable veil of political secrecy and contrivance, your most valuable rights may be sacrificed by a most corrupt faction, without having the satisfaction of knowing who injured you. . . . [Legislative representatives] are bound by honor and conscience to act with integrity, but they are under no constitutional constraint." In his animated appeals "to take off the veil of secrecy," Henry further lamented:

Give us at least a plausible apology why Congress should keep their proceedings in secret. They have the power of keeping them secret as long as they please [in Article I, Section 2, Clause 3], for the provision for a periodical publication is too inexplicit and ambiguous to avail anything. The expression from *time to time*, as I have more than once observed, admits of any schemes under the dark veil of secrecy. The liberties of a people never were, nor ever will be, secure, when the transactions of their rulers may be concealed from them. The most iniquitous plots may be carried on against their liberty and happiness.[43]

Once again George Mason objected to the ambiguity of the provision: "Under this veil they may conceal any thing and every thing."

But neither Patrick Henry nor George Mason advocated "divulging indiscriminately all the operations of government." Henry, the ardent libertarian, acknowledged that "[s]uch transactions as relate to military operations or affairs of great consequence, the immediate promulgation of which might defeat the interests of the community, I would not wish to be published, till the end which required their secrecy should have been effected." Mason further explained:

The reason urged in favor of this ambiguous expression was, that there might be some matters which require secrecy. In matters relative to military operations and foreign negotiations, secrecy was necessary sometimes; but [I do] . . . not conceive that the receipts and expenditures of the public money ought ever to be concealed. The people . . . had a right to know the expenditures of their money.[44]

Hence, even the two most vociferous advocates of the public's right to know did not entertain the notion that the public's interest in access to governmental information was unconditional or unqualified. Notably there was no claim that individuals have a directly enforceable constitutional right to know.

The sentiments of other delegates to the Virginia Convention were more restrained; they were, perhaps, epitomized by James Madison's observation that "[t]here never was any legislative assembly without a discretionary power of concealing important transactions, the publication of which might be detrimental to the community." Madison concluded that "by giving [both Houses of Congress] an opportunity of publishing [their Journals] from time to time, as might be found easy and convenient, they would be . . . sufficiently frequent." He thought, "after all, that this provision went farther than the constitution of any state in the Union, or perhaps in the world."[45]

Delegates to the federal and state constitutional conventions recognized the need to balance the public's interests in information about governmental affairs with the competing exigencies of informed, efficient decision making by their representatives. The delegates unanimously agreed that it was both necessary and legitimate for the government to withhold from the public information concerning the negotiation of foreign affairs, treaties, and military operations as well as on particular occasions information relating to domestic governance. Early congressional practice adhered to the principle that representative government requires an informed citizenry but not unlimited disclosure or publication of governmental affairs. Although the House of Representatives permitted the public to attend its deliberations on May 4, 1789, the Senate did not do so until 1794, and the right of the press to attend proceedings of both Houses was not secured until 1801.[46]

The public therefore enjoys no specific constitutional right to know, nor does Congress have an obligation to disclose or permit unlimited access to its materials or processes. Materials that in Congress's judgment require secrecy may be constitutionally withheld from the public. Congress, for example, has no obligation under the Constitution to disclose its appropriations for the intelligence operations of the Central Intelligence Agency, and the House of Representatives has consistently rejected attempts to impose such a requirement.[47]

Despite express constitutional limitations, some commentators and jurists maintain an expansive notion of the right to know. In 1974 the Supreme Court considered a federal taxpayer's suit seeking a declaration that the section of the Central Intelligence Agency Act permitting the CIA to account for its expenditures "solely on the certificate of the Director" was unconstitutional. The Court held that the taxpayer had no standing to bring the challenge. Dissenting Justice Douglas asserted that the public has a right to know as evidenced by the Constitutional Convention debates. That right, he said, both imposes a general obligation on the government to disclose such secret funding and entitles individuals to demand access to government materials withheld from the public.[48] Justice Douglas, however, interpreted the convention debates so broadly that he significantly departed from, and thereby distorted, the political ideal of the public's right to know embedded in the parchment guarantees of the Constitution.

The principles of governmental openness and an informed citizenry were debated and deemed politically essential to the republic. Yet during the founding period those principles comprehended only the view that "[t]o cover with the veil of secrecy the common routine of [government] business is an abomination in the eyes of every intelligent man and every friend of his country."[49] The public has no enforceable right to know under the Constitution. Rather, the necessity for and the occasions deemed to require governmental openness are political issues to be decided by the public's elected representatives. The public's interest in openness about governmental activities was until the mid-twentieth century thought to be adequately satisfied by the publication of congressional records, by communications from representatives in public speeches and print, and, most important, by the guarantees for freedom of speech and press.

LIBERTY, LICENTIOUSNESS, AND A
DECLARATION OF RIGHTS

After the Federal Convention completed drafting the Constitution, political intrigue centered around the state ratifying conventions. In the initial half-dozen conventions—held in Delaware, Pennsylvania, New Jersey, Georgia, Connecticut, and Maryland—ratification came without further recommendations or amendments, although Luther Martin opposed Maryland's ratification because of the absence of a declaration of rights. The omission of a declaration of rights was an almost insurmountable source of controversy in the later conventions. Following the convening of the Massachusetts convention on January 9, 1788, opposition seriously threatened ratification. The presiding officer, John Hancock, avoided defeat by suggesting that a resolution accompany ratification, recommending to Congress the adoption of certain amendments to the Constitution. Hancock's plan succeeded and provided a model for other state conventions. The New Hampshire, New York, North and South Carolina, Rhode Island, and Virginia conventions all ratified the Constitution with proposals for amendments.

In the Virginia and New York conventions the controversy over omission of a declaration of rights and, in particular, protection for speech and press became paramount. In the Virginia convention Patrick Henry, then governor, led the opposition, arguing:

> If we must adopt a constitution ceding away such vast powers, express and implied, and so frought with danger to the liberties of the people, it ought at least to be guarded by a bill of rights; that in all free governments, and in the estimation of all men attached to liberty, there were certain rights unalienable—imprescriptible—and of so sacred a character, that they could not be guarded with too much caution; among these were the liberty of speech and of the press—what security had we, that even these sacred privileges would not be invaded? Congress might think it necessary, in order to carry into effect the given powers, to silence the clamors and censures of the people; and if they meditated views of lawless ambition, they certainly will so think; what then would become of the liberty of speech and of the press?[50]

From the ensuing debate two committees were formed: the first to prepare and report the necessary amendments; the second to prepare a draft of the ratification resolution. Within a few days the committee drafting the proposed amendments set forth a resolution recommending adoption of a

Declaration or Bill of Rights including: "That the people have a right to freedom of speech, and of writing and publishing their sentiments; that the freedom of the press is one of the greatest bulwarks of liberty, and ought not to be violated."[51] The convention approved the ratification resolution and proposed Bill of Rights, enjoining the state representatives in Congress to obtain ratification of the amendments. The New York convention was initially similarly inclined to require adoption of a bill of rights as a condition for ratification, but eventually passed a ratifying resolution "in confidence that the proposed amendments would receive the early and mature consideration of Congress."

The bitter debates within and without the state conventions over the necessity of a declaration of rights provide a basis for comprehending the prevailing understanding of freedom of speech and press. The debates centered around those who embraced or with slight modification endorsed the Blackstonian or common law understanding of freedom of speech and press and more libertarian thinkers such as James Madison and Thomas Jefferson. That the predominant understanding was neo-Blackstonian is evident from Alexander Hamilton's leadership in the New York convention and eloquent defense under the pseudonym of Publius of both the Constitution and the omission of a bill of rights, and from devotees of the Constitution like James Wilson at the Pennsylvania convention as well as from the antifederalists, such as Richard Henry Lee, in opposition to the Virginia convention.[52]

Adoption of a bill of rights, Alexander Hamilton argued in his celebrated essay Number 84 of *The Federalist Papers*, would be "not only unnecessary . . . but would even be dangerous." An enumeration of rights was unnecessary because "the Constitution is itself, in every rational sense, and to every useful purpose, A BILL OF RIGHTS." More generally, parchment guarantees would prove dangerous, he thought, because they would prohibit the exercise of governmental power when authority for that power had not been previously granted by the Constitution. "Why, for instance, should it be said that the liberty of the press shall not be restrained, when no power is given by which restrictions may be imposed?" Continuing, he posed the persistently vexatious definitional questions: "What signifies a declaration that 'the liberty of the press shall be inviolably preserved?' What is the liberty of the press? Who can give it any definition which would not leave the utmost latitude for evasion?" Hamilton concluded "it to be impracticable" to define freedom of the press "and from this [he inferred] that its security, whatever fine declarations may be inserted in any constitution respecting it, must altogether depend on public opinion, and on the general spirit of the people and of the government." Hamilton nonetheless made clear his acceptance of the Blackstonian definition of freedom of the press, remarking in a footnote that "it is notorious that the press no where enjoys greater liberty than in [England]."[53]

Libertarians like James Madison and Thomas Jefferson contributed powerful arguments for securing the adoption of a bill of rights, but they did not successfully challenge the widely accepted Blackstonian understanding of freedom of speech and press. Madison, like Hamilton, worried about the potential problems arising from a declaration of rights. In a letter to Jefferson, he explained:

> My own opinion has always been in favor of a bill of rights; provided it be so framed as not to imply powers not meant to be included in the enumeration. . . . At the same time I have never thought the omission a material defect, nor been anxious to supply it even by subsequent amendment, for any other reason than that it is anxiously desired by others. I have favored it because I suppose it might be of use, and if properly executed could not be a disservice. I have not viewed it in an important light . . . [b]ecause there is a great reason to fear that a positive declaration of some of the most essential rights could not be obtained in the requisite latitude.[54]

In response, Jefferson wrote:

> Your thoughts on the subject of the Declaration of rights in the letter of Oct. 17 [1788] I have weighed with great satisfaction. Some of them had not occurred to me before, but they were acknowledged [sic] just in the moment they were presented to my mind. In the arguments in favor of a declaration of rights, you omit one which has great weight to me, the legal check which it puts into the hands of the judiciary. This is a body, which if rendered independent, and kept strictly to their own department merits great confidence for their learning and integrity."

The Madison-Jefferson correspondence reflects their concern that "[a] positive declaration of some essential rights could not be obtained in the requisite latitude," but also their conviction (and response to Hamilton's arguments) that "Half a loaf is better than no bread. If we cannot secure all our rights, let's secure what we can.[55] Both Madison and Jefferson viewed a bill of rights as providing through the judiciary a crucial legal check on the exercise of coercive governmental power, and the Ninth Amendment, specifically, as providing the courts with a rule of construction for ensuring the requisite latitude of individuals' civil liberties and civil rights.

Madison and Jefferson did not share the generally accepted Blackstonian approach to freedom of speech and press. Madison's view of free speech and press was far too libertarian for his contemporaries. Jefferson's position was more congenial to the common law approach and yet prophetic of constitutional developments. Jefferson lamented "the putrid state into which our newspapers have passed, and the malignity, the vulgarity, and mendacious spirit of those who write them. . . . These ordures are rapidly depraving the public taste. . . . It is however an evil for which there is no remedy, our liberty depends on the freedom of the press, and that cannot be limited without being lost."[56] Yet, Jefferson, unlike Madison, embraced both Zengerian principles and the common law of libel. That is, unlike religious freedom, which he deemed an "unceded" or natural right, freedom of the press was primarily a means for checking abusive government power. No freedom, of course, is unconditional, and even religious freedom could permissibly be restricted when religious principles "break out into overt act against peace and good order." In his *Bill for Establishing Religious Freedom* for the state of Virginia, he maintained that "the acts of the body," unlike "the operations of the mind, are subject to the coercion of the laws."[57] Although this broad libertarian principle could apply to both religious and political matters in terms of distinguishing between speech per se and conduct, with the latter "subject to the coercion of the laws," Jefferson did not go that far in his thinking about the scope of protection for political, in contrast to religious, publications. In 1783 when drafting a proposal for a new constitution for Virginia, Jefferson provided that "PRINTING PRESSES shall be subject to no other restraint than liableness to legal prosecution for false facts printed and published."[58] Even in response to the Sedition Act of 1798, Jefferson, unlike Madison, did not question the propriety of punishing the licentiousness of the press. Instead, he objected to the national government's exercise of that power. Jefferson made clear in the *Kentucky Resolutions* and in his letters that the states may properly punish seditious, false, and licentious publications.[59] Jefferson was not as libertarian as Madison, but more tolerant of the abuses of speech and press than his neo-Blackstonian contemporaries. Jefferson accepted in general the common law doctrines governing freedom of speech and press, and advocated the role of the states in constraining the licentiousness of the press.

The traditional common law principles were indeed widely accepted by the participants in the state ratifying conventions. James Wilson, for example, when defending the Constitution at the Pennsylvania convention argued: "What is meant by the liberty of the press is that there should be no antecedent restraint upon it; but every author is responsible when he attacks the security or welfare of the government, or the safety, character and propriety of the individual."[60] Likewise, in 1788 Chief Justice Thomas McKean, who had previously signed the Declaration of Independence and served as president of the Continental Congress, ruled in *Respublica* v. *Oswald* that freedom of the press meant precisely what it did at English and colonial common law.[61] So too, in the next year—the year the First Amendment was drafted—Massachusetts Chief Justice William Cushing and John Adams worried about whether common law principles could be modified to adopt the Zengerian principle that truth serves as a defense in libel actions.[62]

THE FIRST AMENDMENT AND COMMON LAW PRINCIPLES

Because a representative democracy requires some freedom of information concerning governmental affairs, and some limitations on public disclosure of such information, the First Amendment plays an important role in constitutional law and the political processes of the polity. As Justice Felix Frankfurter once observed: "Without a free press there can be no free society. Freedom of the press, however, is not an end in itself but a means to the end of a free society."[63] More generally Justice Frankfurter understood that the First Amendment was only a part of a complex constitutional scheme and political system. Far from guaranteeing an affirmative right to know, the fundamental question in adopting the First Amendment was whether the amendment simply gave constitutional effect to traditional common law principles or embodied more libertarian precepts, thereby granting broader protection for free speech and press. When examined, the argument that "explicit recognition by the courts that the constitutional right to know embraces the right of the public to obtain information from the government"[64] runs counter to the historical background of the First Amendment and the constitutional law that it spawned.

In 1789, when the first Congress entertained amendments to the Constitution, James Madison endeavored to give constitutional effect to his libertarian precepts and concomitant rejection of common law principles. He urged adoption of the following provision: "The people shall not be deprived or abridged of their right to speak, to write, or to publish their sentiments; and the freedom of the press, as one of the great bulwarks of liberty, shall be inviolable." Madison argued, as he did later when the Sedition Act of 1798 was passed, that "freedom of the press and rights of conscience, those choicest privileges of the people, are unguarded in the British constitution." In England, Parliament was considered to possess unlimited power to guard the people against the sovereign's unlawful acts. By contrast, in the United States the people are sovereign and their rights to free speech and press must therefore be guaranteed against both the executive and the legislature. For these reasons Madison not only rejected the application of Blackstonian-common law principles to the freedom of speech and press but also proposed as a constitutional amendment that "[n]o State shall violate the equal rights of conscience, or the freedom of the press."[65]

In rebuking the principal tenets of the Blackstonian-common law understanding Madison advanced perhaps the broadest possible view of freedom of speech and press. Considering a vigorous press, even with its potential for abuse, essential to free government, he rejected the imposition of sanctions for any licentiousness accompanying the exercise of freedom speech and press:

> Among those principles deemed sacred in America, among those sacred rights considered as forming the bulwark of liberty, which the Government contemplates with awful reverence and would approach only with the most cautious circumspection, there is no one of which the importance is more deeply impressed on the public mind than the liberty of the press. That this *liberty* is often carried to excess; that it has sometimes degenerated into *licentiousness*, is seen and lamented, *but the remedy has* not yet been discovered. Perhaps it is an evil inseparable from the good with which it is allied; perhaps it is a shoot which cannot be stripped from the stalk without wounding vitally the plant from which it is torn. However desirable those measures might be which might correct without enslaving the press, they have never yet been devised in America.[66]

As Madison acknowledged, his understanding of an unconditional freedom of speech and press was simply not representative of the founding period or even of subsequent interpretations of those freedoms.[67] Since colonial experiences with censorship by the Crown and legislative assemblies fostered agreement that the rights of free speech and press, if not Madison's "rights of conscience," should be protected, there was little debate in the first Congress on adopting a provision for the freedom of speech and press. Those who feared the abuse of these freedoms expected the states to continue common law restrictions on libel and other licentious publications.

The primary concern during the congressional debates over what became the First Amendment was whether by guaranteeing the freedoms of speech, press, and assembly representatives would be constitutionally required to give legislative effect to the expressions of public opinion. Madison settled that issue by maintaining that the guarantees no more granted the people a right to control congressional debates than they imposed upon representatives an obligation to act on their constituents' opinions:

> The right of freedom of speech is secured; the liberty of the press is expressly declared to be beyond the reach of this Government; the people may therefore publicly address their representatives, may privately advise them, or declare their sentiments by petition to the whole body; in all these ways they may communicate their will. If gentlemen mean to go further, and to say that the people have a right to instruct their representatives in such a sense as that the delegates are obliged to conform to those instructions, the declaration is not true.[68]

Although Madison's resolution of the controversy was accepted, his proposal for expressly prohibiting the states from limiting the freedom of speech and press was rejected in the final draft. Ratified on December 15, 1791, the First Amendment provides: "Congress shall make no law respecting an establishment of religion, or prohibiting the exercise thereof; or abridging the freedom of speech, or of the press; or the right of the people peaceably to assemble." The amendment was so worded precisely because it was adopted by representatives who understood the amendment to give constitutional effect to Blackstone's all-too-definitive view of the freedom of speech and press. The amendment was thought to protect only against prior restraint by the national government; it did not provide absolute immunity for what speakers or publishers might utter or print. Thus the First Amendment was in Hamiltonian terms superfluous, whereas from Madison's vantage point it did not sufficiently safeguard individuals' freedom, and from Jefferson's perspective the amendment reaffirmed both the limits of the national government's power and the reserved powers of the states.

Less than a decade later, the initial constitutional and political crisis over the First Amendment arose when Congress passed the Alien and Sedition Acts of 1798. The Sedition Act, in particular, imposed criminal sanctions on individuals who made "any false, scandalous writing against the government of the United States."[69] The act was designed by the Federalists in Congress to politically censure and turn public opinion against the Jeffersonsian Republicans, if not to ensure a single party system. In terms of legal theory, the act responded to the Jeffersonians' position that libel and licentiousness could only be tried in state courts. The Federalists' enactment of the Sedition Act legitimated their political preference for using federal courts, staffed largely with Federalist judges, instead of state courts in which the judges tended to be Republicans. More significant, the act incorporated earlier libertarian demands for demonstration of criminal intent and for the Zengerian principle of truth as a defense in libel actions as well as for jury determination of whether publications constituted, as a matter of law and of fact, seditious libel. Nonetheless, the ensuing controversy produced further confirmation of the predominant Blackstonian approach to speech and press.

The congressional reports on the repeal of the Sedition Act on February 25, 1799, amply illustrate the acceptance of Blackstonian principles. The majority report defended the constitutionality of the act on four grounds. First, punishment of seditious libel did not constitute an abridgement of freedom of speech and press, since those freedoms never included "a license for every man to publish what he pleases without being liable to punishment." Second, although little more than a restatement of the first point: The laws of the states and national government, as well as those of England, never extended "to the publication of false, scandalous, and malicious writings against the Government." Third, the Sedition Act was not unconstitutional because it was "merely declaratory of the common law, and useful for rendering that law more generally known, and more easily understood." Fourth, and most interesting, the committee, like Jefferson, drew a crucial distinction between the religious and the speech and press freedoms protected by the First Amendment. The amendment provides that "*Congress shall make no law respecting* an establishment of religion, *or prohibiting* the free exercise thereof," implying that the national government is absolutely barred from legislating on religious matters. By contrast, the amendment literally forbids Congress from only passing legislation "*abridging* the freedom of speech, or of the press." From that language, the committee surmised that Congress was not precluded from passing legislation *respecting* speech and press; and, in any case, the Sedition Act did not abridge any freedom recognized by the prevailing common law understanding that undergirded the First Amendment's guarantee for speech and press.[70]

In the House, representatives such as Albert Gallatin, Edward Livingston, John Nicholas, and Nathaniel Macon argued against the Sedition Act because "[t]he States have complete power on the subject."[71] Likewise, Thomas Jefferson insisted that under the First Amendment the states alone possess the power to initiate libel actions. The minority report on the repeal of the Sedition Act further emphasized that the act was designed to proscribe precisely that kind of speech and press that is essential to free government, namely, political commentary and criticism:

> It must be agreed that the nature of our Government makes a diffusion of knowledge of public affairs necessary and proper, and that the people have no mode of obtaining it but through the press. The necessity for their having this information results from its being their duty to elect all the parts of the Government, and, in this way, to sit in judgment over the conduct of those who have been heretofore employed. The most important and necessary information for the people to receive is, of the misconduct of the Government; because their good deeds, although they will produce affection and gratitude to public officers, will only confirm the existing confidence, and will, therefore, make no change in the conduct of the people. The question, then, whether the Government ought to have control over the persons who alone can give information throughout a country, is nothing more than this, whether men interested in suppressing information necessary for the people to have, ought to be entrusted with the power, or whether they ought to have a power which their personal interest leads to the abuse of?[72]

In urging the unconstitutionality of the Sedition Act, the minority report, like Madison and other influential libertarians such as George Hay, Tunis Wortman, John Thomson, and the prominent College of William and Mary law professor, St. George Tucker, drew attention to the import of political criticism and to the necessity for popular and accessible information about the conduct of government officials and public affairs.[73] In so doing these libertarians rejected the Blackstonian approach to the First Amendment.

Madison poignantly asserted: "[i]t would seem a mockery to say that no laws shall be passed for punishing them in case they should be made."[74] The very idea of seditious libel was repugnant and, as Wortman observed, could "never be reconciled to the genius and constitution of a Representative Government."[75]

The libertarians were not entirely persuasive because they were neither in agreement nor consistent in their views on freedom of speech and press. The Jeffersonian Republicans waxed and waned in their belief that the only permissible restrictions on speech and press could originate from state legislation. Continued federal prosecutions for seditious libel after the Sedition Act expired underscores the inconsistencies in the Jeffersonian Republican position and the intractability of the common law understanding of freedom of speech and press.

Moreover, members of the Supreme Court accepted the constitutionality of the Sedition Act and the common law of seditious libel. Justices William Patterson and Samuel Chase presided over some prosecutions, Justice William Cushing defended the act before a Virginia grand jury on September 23, 1798, as did Justice James Iredell a year later, and, finally, correspondence between Justice Oliver Ellsworth and Timothy Pickering indicate that Ellsworth also approved of the Sedition Act.[76]

There were no prosecutions under the Sedition Act after 1801, when the act expired and Thomas Jefferson became president, but seditious libel remained a crime at common law. In 1804, while quarrelling with Chief Justice John Marshall over the role of the Supreme Court, President Jefferson wrote Mrs. John Adams explaining his pardoning of those convicted under the Sedition Act, insisting that the "law [was] a nullity as absolute and as palpable as if Congress had ordered us to fall down and worship a golden image; and that it was as much my duty to arrest its execution at every stage as it would have been to rescue from the fiery furnace those who should have been cast into it for refusing to worship the image."[77] Eloquent in describing his rage against Federalists' prosecutions under the act, Jefferson was no less vengeful in recommending prosecutions of Federalist editors! A year earlier he wrote to Governor McKean of Pennsylvania:

> The federalists have failed in destroying the freedom of the press by their gag-law, seem to have attacked it in the opposite form, that is by pushing it's licentiousness & it's lying to such a degree of prostitution as to deprive it of all credit. And the fact is that so abandoned are the tory presses in this particular that even the least informed of the people have learnt that nothing in a newspaper is to be believed. This is a dangerous state of things, and the press ought to be restored to its credibility if possible. The restraints provided by the laws of the states are sufficient for this if applied. And I have therefore long thought that a few

prosecutions of the most prominent offenders would have a wholesome
effect in restoring the integrity of the presses. Not a general prosecution,
for that would look like persecution: but a selected one . . . If the same
thing be done in some other of the states it will place the whole band
more on their guard.[78]

Enclosing a copy of what he deemed seditious articles, Jefferson again
showed that he was not above political intrigue and that the First Amendment did not alter the common law of freedom of speech and press. Rather,
it only prohibited Congress from legislating on such matters: "While we
deny that Congress have a right to control the freedom of the press, we have
ever asserted the right of the states, and their exclusive right to do so."[79]

That Jeffersonian Republicans, like the Federalists, clung to the
Blackstonian understanding of freedom of speech and press was exemplified
by their prosecutions for seditious libel after the expiration of the Sedition
Act. In *People* v. *Croswell* (1803), for instance, Republicans prosecuted a
New York Federalist editor for seditious libel against President Jefferson![80]
Three years later the Republicans were still using federal courts to prosecute
individuals for seditious libel against the president. Not until 1812, in
another action for libel against the president, did the Supreme Court finally
rule, in *United States* v. *Hudson and Goodwin*, that there was no federal
common law of crimes, including the crime of seditious libel.[81] State judges
like Massachusetts Chief Justice Parker nevertheless stood on firm common
law principles when declaring: "The liberty of the Press, not its licentiousness; this is the construction which a just regard to the other parts of that
instrument [the Constitution], and to the wisdom of those who founded it,
requires. . . . The liberty of the Press was to be unrestrained, but he who
used it was to be reasonable in case of its abuse; like the right to keep
firearms, which does not protect him who uses them for annoyance or
destruction."[82]

In 1833 the most widely read and knowledgeable commentator on the
Constitution within a generation of the founding period, and also a member
of the Supreme Court, Joseph Story, observed that "[t]here is a good deal of
loose reasoning on the subject of the liberty of the press, as if it inviolability
were constitutionally such." The import of his observations consists not only
in comprehending the meaning of free speech and press after the founding
period but also in addressing claims that the press enjoys special privileges so
it can inform the public and vindicate the public's right to know. That the
press should enjoy special privileges, Story remarked, "is too extravagant to
be held by any sound constitutional lawyer." Story, like those who drafted
and ratified the First Amendment, endorsed Blackstone's interpretation of
freedom of speech and press: The First Amendment guarantees individuals
the right to express their views in speech or print without prior restraint.

More than 30 years after the Sedition Act, Story remained uncertain of whether the First Amendment prohibited Congress from "punishing the licentiousness of the press," but he did not doubt that the states could prosecute individuals for libelous and "other mischievous publications."[83]

By the late nineteenth century another authority on the Constitution, Thomas Cooley, recognized that the press has assumed an increasingly important role in society as a result of technological innovations. Cooley agreed with Madison that "[r]epression of full and free discussion is dangerous in any government resting upon the will of the people." Unlike Story he also appreciated as constitutionally significant the difference between defamation of private individuals on the one hand, and of public officials on the other. Prosecutions for libel of private individuals, but not public officials and political actors, were constitutionally permissible. Like Story and the authors of the First Amendment, however, he continued to view the First Amendment in terms of common law principles and practices. The First Amendment, he thought, guarantees "a right to freely utter and publish whatever the citizen may please, and to be protected against any responsibility for so doing, except so far as such publications, from their blasphemy, obscenity, or scandalous character, may be a public offense, or as by their falsehood and malice they may injuriously affect the standing, reputation, or pecuniary interests of individuals."[84]

Cooley also rejected the claim that the press enjoys special privileges: "When the authorities are examined, it appears that they have generally held the proprietors of public journals to the same rigid responsibility with all other persons who publish what is injurious. If what they give as news proves untrue as well as damaging to individuals, malice in the publication is presumed." While appreciating that the "public demand and expect accounts of every important meeting, . . . and of all events which have a bearing upon trade and business, or upon political affairs," he expressly denied that the press enjoys special privileges under the First Amendment or at common law to obtain and publish confidential information concerning government proceedings whether they be ex parte proceedings, preliminary examinations, trials, or legislative proceedings.[85]

From the founding period and throughout the nineteenth century the First Amendment was comprehended in terms of developing common law principles and practices. The Supreme Court repeatedly confirmed that freedom of speech and press was limited by common law proscriptions of licentious publications and by political and constitutional determinations that the states, but not the national government, may legislate on these freedoms. In 1833, in one of Chief Justice John Marshall's last major decisions, the Court ruled in *Barron* v. *Baltimore* that the Bill of Rights applied solely to the federal government, and partially justified its holding on the First Amendment's proscribing that only Congress shall make no law abridging freedom of speech and press.[86] Consequently, state prosecutions for licentious publications were constitutionally permissible. In 1894, in *Mattox* v. *United States*, the Court further stated: "We are bound to interpret the Constitution in light of the law as it existed at the time it was adopted . . . as securing to every individual such [rights] as he already possessed as a British Subject—such as his ancestors had inherited and defended since the days of Magna Charta."[87] Three years later, in *Robertson* v. *Baldwin*, the Supreme Court again asserted that "[t]he law is perfectly well settled that the first ten amendments to the Constitution, commonly known as the Bill of Rights, were not intended to lay down any novel principles of government, but simply to embody certain guarantees and immunities which we had inherited from our English ancestors."[88]

Not until the mid-twentieth century, when the Supreme Court held that the basic guarantees of the First Amendment extended to the states under the Fourteenth Amendment's due process clause, did federal courts recognize jurisdiction over challenges to state legislation infringing on the freedom of speech and press.[89] Yet when the Court initially turned to the task of interpreting the First Amendment and its applicability to the states it did so on the basis of common law principles. In 1907, for instance, Justice Oliver Wendell Holmes observed: "In the first place, the main purpose of such constitutional provisions is to 'prevent all such *previous restraints* upon publications as had been practiced by other governments,' and they do not prevent the subsequent punishment of such as may be deemed contrary to the public welfare. . . . The preliminary freedom extends as well to the false as to the true; the subsequent punishment may extend as well to the true as to the false."[90] Only in the 1930s did members of the Court begin to question reliance on common law principles when construing the First Amendment. In the landmark case of *Near* v. *Minnesota*, Chief Justice Charles Evans Hughes, while affirming common law principles, indicated that "[t]he conception of the liberty of the press in this country had broadened with the exigencies of the colonial period and with the efforts to secure freedom from oppressive administration."[91] Finally, in 1936, in *Grosjean* v. *American Press Co.*, Justice George Sutherland declared:

> It is impossible to concede that by the words "freedom of the press" the framers of the amendment intended to adopt merely the narrow view then reflected by the law of England that such freedom consisted only in immunity from previous censorship; for this abuse then permanently disappeared from British practice. . . . Undoubtedly, the range of a constitutional provision phrased in terms of the common law sometimes may be fixed by recourse to the applicable rules of law. But the doctrine which justifies such recourse, like other canons of construction, must yield to more compelling reasons whenever they exist.[92]

Still, two decades later commentators and judges, including Justice Frankfurter, confidently maintained that *Roberston* v. *Baldwin* expressed the "authentic and genuine view" of the First Amendment.[93]

CONSTITUTIONAL HISTORY AND THE RIGHT TO KNOW

During the founding period the First Amendment comprehended common law doctrines for freedom of speech and press. Public access to government information and the political ideal of the public's right to know was concomitantly and indirectly ensured by the amendment's proscription of prior governmental restrictions on individuals' communications. The crucial role that the First Amendment assumes in the polity arises precisely because the electorate must be able to inform its representatives concerning issues of public moment and be informed by critical appraisals of official activity and the operations of government. Still although the First Amendment prohibits prior censorship of "information and communication among the people which is indispensible to the just exercise of their electoral rights,"[94] the broad freedom of political commentary and criticism that is enjoyed was not the achievement of architectonic design but of the long arduous struggle for free speech and press that emerged prior to and continued throughout the bicentennary of the founding of the republic.

There exists no historical basis for the proposition that the First Amendment was designed to guarantee to individuals and to the press an affirmative constitutional right to demand access to government facilities or materials. In view of the bitter struggle over individuals' freedom from prior censorship and subsequent punishment for licentious speech and press, arguments for an affirmative right to demand access to government facilities are misleading and counterhistorical. In sum, the argument that the public's right to know attains constitutional legitimacy in terms of the historical background of the First Amendment is a pretense with no basis in the debates over the adoption, ratification, and interpretation of the First Amendment.

To conclude that historical arguments for the constitutional legitimacy of an enforceable right to know are ill founded because the First Amendment reflected common law practices, which recognized no such affirmative right of the people, presents no less vexing issues about the scope of judicial creativity in constitutional interpretation. In *Grosjean*, although underestimating the controlling influence of the common law on judicial construction of the First Amendment, Justice Sutherland keenly perceived that common law principles would prove inadequate for constitutional interpretation in the forthcoming decades and in accommodating the increasingly difficult issues raised by litigation over press freedom and the public's right to know.

Justice Sutherland apprehended, as Madison understood, that the First Amendment is integral to the political enterprise of sustaining a system of free government. Madison, like Justice Black in *Griswold*, appreciated that the Constitution is subverted as much by judicial self-restraint that renders constitutional provisions contingent on developments in public policy as by judicial activism that turns the Constitution into a mandate for constitutional common law via judicial articulation of extraconstitutional rights. The Constitution and the First Amendment requires that the Supreme Court articulate constitutional principles based on parchment guarantees by reflecting on the perennially perplexing dilemma of balancing freedom and restraint.

NOTES

1. David Mitchell Ivester, "The Constitutional Right to Know," 4 *Hastings Constitutional Law Quarterly* 109, 119 (1977).

2. Letter from James Madison to W. T. Barry (August 4, 1822), reprinted in *The Writings of James Madison*, ed. Gaillard Hunt (New York: Putnam's Sons, 1906-1910), vol. 9, 103. The testimonial is cited in support of a constitutional right to know by, for example, Thomas I. Emerson, "Colonial Intentions and Current Realities of the First Amendment," 125 *University of Pennsylvania Law Review* 737, 754-55 (1977); *Branzburg* v. *Hayes*, 408 U.S. 665, 723 (1972) (Douglas, J., dis. op.); *Environmental Protection Agency* v. *Mink*, 410 U.S. 73, 110 (1973) (Douglas, J., dis. op.); and the U.S. Senate interpreted Madison to provide a "theory of an informed electorate" in U.S., Congress, Senate, *Senate Report on the Freefom of Information Act*, S. Rep. 813, 89th Cong., 1st Sess. 3 (1965).

3. See, for example, Ivester, "The Constitutional Right to Know"; Edward Bloustein, "The First Amendment and Privacy: The Supreme Court and the Philosopher," 28 *Rutgers Law Review* 41 (1974); and William Brennan, "The Supreme Court and the Meiklejohn Interpretation of the First Amendment," 79 *Harvard Law Review* 1 (1965).

4. Thomas Hennings, Jr., "The People's Right to Know," 45 *American Bar Association Journal* 667, 668 (1959).

5. James Madison, *The Complete Madison*, ed. Saul Padover (New York: Harper & Row, 1953) 341.

6. Ivester, "The Constitutional Right to Know," at 119.

7. *De Scandalis Magnatum*, 3 Edward I, c. 34 (1274); 2 Richard II, Stat. 1, c. 5 (1378); 1 Elizabeth, c. 6 (1559). See, generally, Fredrick Seaton Siebert, *Freedom of the Press in England 1476-1776* (Urbana: University of Illinois, 1965); and Sir Thomas Erskine May, *Treatise on the Law, Privilege, Proccedings, and Usage of Parliament*, 16th ed. (London: Butterworth, 1957).

8. *De Libellis Famosis*, 3 Coke's Reports 254, 255 (1605).

9. *Trial of William Prynn*, 3 Howell's State Trials 561 (1632).

10. See, generally, Clyde A. Duniway, *The Development of Freedom of the Press in Massachusetts* (New York: Longmans, Green, 1906); *Albert* v. *Dicey, Introduction to the Study of the Law of the Constitution*, 10th ed. (London: Macmillan, 1959); and Edward G. Hudon, *Freedom of Speech and Press in America* (Washington, D.C.: Public Affairs Press, 1963).

11. The Stamp and Advertising Act, 10 Anne, c. 19 (1711).

12. Sir William Blackstone, *Commentaries on the Laws of England* (Oxford: Clarendon Press, 1766), vol. 4, 151-52.

13. *Trial of H. S. Woodfall*, 20 Howell's State Trials 895, 903 (1770).

14. *Trial of Dean of St. Asaph*, 21 Howell's State Trials 847, 1040 (1783-1784).

15. Fox Libel Act, 32 George III, c. 60 (1791).

16. *Trial of Thomas Paine*, 22 Howell's State Trials 357 (1792).

17. Thomas Erskine May, *The Constitutional History of England* (New York: Longmans, Green, 6th ed., 1878), 2.

18. Lord Campbell's Act, 6 & 7 Vict., c. 96 (1843).

19. See Thomas B. MacCaulay, *The History of England* (London: Dent, 1906), vol. 4, 248.

20. John P. Roche, *Shadow and Substance* (New York: Macmillan, 1964) 11. See also Leonard Levy, *The Legacy of Suppression* (Cambridge, Mass.: Belknap, 1960).

21. Duniway, *The Development of Freedom of the Press in Massachusetts* at 16. See also Kenneth E. Michael, "Freedom of the Press Under Our Constitution," 53 *West Virginia Law Quarterly* 29 (1926-1927).

22. 2 Hennings Statutes at Large (Virginia), 1619-1792 (1819-1823) 517, quoted by Michael, "Freedom of the Press Under Our Constitution," at 36; and Thomas Cooley, *A Treatise on The Constitutional Limitations*, 8th ed. (Boston: Little, Brown, 1927), vol. 2, 822.

23. Quincy's Massachusetts Reports, 1761-1772, at 266.

24. John Milton, *Areopagitica*; and see William C. Clyde, *The Struggle for the Freedom of the Press from Caxton to Cromwell* (London: Oxford, 1934) 79-80 and 171-73.

25. John Locke, "A Letter Concerning Toleration," in *The Works of John Locke*, 11th ed. (London: W. Otridge, 1812), vol. 4, 45-46.

26. See Benjamin Franklin, *The Writings of Benjamin Franklin*, ed. Albert H. Smyth (New York: Macmillan, 1905-1907), vol. 2, 172-79; *Cato's Letters: Or, Essays on Liberty, Civil and Religious*, reprinted in *The English Libertarian Heritage: From the Writings of John Trenchard and Thomas Green*, ed. David L. Jacobson (Indianapolis: Bobbs-Merrill, 1965); and *Freedom of the Press from Zenger to Jefferson*, ed. Leonard Levy (New York: Bobbs-Merrill, 1966) 10-24.

27. Cato, "Reflections on Libelling," reprinted in Levy, *Freedom of the Press from Zenger to Jefferson* at 12.

28. *The Trial of John Peter Zenger*, 17 Howell's State Trials 675, 682 (1735). See, generally, Livingston Rutherford, *John Peter Zenger, His Press, His Trial, and a Bibliography of Zenger Imprints* (New York: Dodd, Mead & Co., 1904).

29. There were two subsequent trials before royal judges. See Julius Goebel, Jr., and T. Raymond Naughton, *Law Enforcement in Colonial New York: A Study in Criminal Procedure (1664-1776)* (New York: Commonwealth Fund, 1944) 99n.

30. James Alexander, *Pennsylvania Gazette* (Philadelphia, November 17 to December 18, 1737) and Andrew Bradford, The *American Weekly Mercury* (Philadelphia, April 25, 1734), both reprinted in Levy, *Freedom of the Press from Zenger to Jefferson* at 62-63, 41-42.

31. William Livingston, *The Independent Reflector or Weekly Essays on Sundry, Important, Subjects*, ed. Milton Klein (Cambridge, Mass.: Belknap, 1963).

32. William Bollan, *The Freedom of Speech and Writings Upon Public Affairs, Considered, with a Historical View* (London: S. Baker, 1766) 3-4.

33. See, Mary Patterson Clarke, *Parliamentary Privilege in American Colonies* (New Haven: Yale University Press, 1943).

34. Francis Thorpe, *The Federal and State Constitutions, Colonial Charters, and Other Organic Laws* (Washington, D.C.: 1909), vol. 3, 1872 (Massachusetts Constitution of 1780); and vol. 5, 3083-90 (Pennsylvania Constitution of 1776).

35. *Journals of the Continental Congress 1774-1789*, ed. W. Ford, et al. (Washington, D.C.: Government Printing Office 1904-1937), vol. 1, 108, quoted in *Near* v. *Minnesota*, 283 U.S. 697, 717 (1931).

36. See, for example, *Respublica* v. *Oswald*, 1 Dallas (Penn.) Reports 319 (1788).

37. *Journals of the Continental Congress*, vol. 19, 214.

38. Letter from Thomas Jefferson to Edward Carrington (January 16, 1787), reprinted

in *The Papers of Thomas Jefferson*, ed. Julian Boyd (Princeton: Princeton University Press, 1955), vol. 11, 49.

39. See Robert E. Kling, Jr., *The Government Printing Office* (New York: Praeger, 1970) 8–10.

40. Letter from Thomas Jefferson to Edward Carrington. Ibid.

41. Irving Brant, "The Constitution and the Right to Know," in *Mass Media and the Law*, ed. David C. Clark and Earl Hutchison (New York: Wiley Interscience, 1970) 76. See also Jonathan Elliot, ed., *The Debates in the Several State Conventions on the Adoption of the Federal Constitution* (New York: Burt Franklin Reprint, 1974) [Hereinafter referred to as *Elliot's Debates*], vol. 5, 558 (statements by Messrs. King and Wilson, suggesting that the Journals of the Convention be either destroyed or deposited in government custody).

42. *Elliot's Debates*, vol. 5, 408.

43. *Elliot's Debates*, vol. 3, 315, 396–98.

44. *Elliot's Debates*, vol. 3, 170.

45. *Elliot's Debates*, vol. 3, 409, 460.

46. See, for example, *Elliot's Debates*, vol. 2, 52 (Massachusetts delegates); vol. 3, 169, 201–2, 233, 315, 396–98, 404, 409, 459–60 (Virginia delegates); vol. 4, 72–73 (North Carolina delegates), 264 (South Carolina delegates); and *Annals of Congress 1789–1791* (Washington, D.C.: Gales and Seaton, eds. & compilers, 1834), vol. 1, 16.

47. On July 10, 1979, the House of Representatives rejected 79 to 321 an amendment to an intelligence authorization bill that would direct the president to disclose foreign intelligence appropriations totals for fiscal 1980. The proposed amendment was the first since a similar amendment was defeated in 1974. See *Access Reports* (July 24, 1979) at 8–9; and Comment, "The CIA Secret Funding and the Constitution," 84 *Yale Law Journal* 608 (1975).

48. *United States* v. *Richardson*, 418 U.S. 166 203 (Douglas, J. dis. op.). On another occasion, however, Justice Douglas did acknowledge that "there may by situations and occasions in which the right to know must yield to other competing and overriding interests." *Gravel* v. *United States*, 408 U.S. 606, 643 n.10 (1972) (Douglas, J., dis. op.).

49. James Monroe, "Seventh Annual Message of the President," in *A Compilation of the Messages and Papers of the Presidents*, (Washington, D.C.: Government Printing Office, 1897).

50. William Wirt, *Sketches of the Life and Character of Patrick Henry* 2d ed. (Philadelphia: William Brown, 1818) 204.

51. *Elliot's Debates*, vol. 3, 659.

52. See Alexander Hamilton, *The Federalist Papers*, No. 84, ed. Clinton Rossiter (New York: Mentor Books, 1961), 510–20; James Wilson in *Pennsylvania and the Federal Constitution*, eds. John B. McMaster and Fredrick D. Stone (Philadelphia: Historical Society of Pennsylvania, 1888) 308–9; and Richard Henry Lee, *An Additional Number of Letters from the Federal Farmer to the Republican* (Chicago: Quadrangle, 1962) 151–53.

53. Hamilton, *The Federalist Papers*, No. 84, at 513–14.

54. Letter from James Madison to Thomas Jefferson (October 17, 1788), *The Papers of Thomas Jefferson*, vol. 14, at 16 & 18.

55. Letter from Thomas Jefferson to James Madison (March 15, 1789), Ibid., at 659.

56. Letter from Thomas Jefferson to Dr. J. Currie (1786), in *The Writings of Thomas Jefferson*, eds. Andrew Lipscomb and Albert E. Bergh (Washington, D.C., 1904–1905), vol. 15, 214.

57. See, for example, "A Bill for Establishing Religious Freedom" (1779) in *The Writings of Thomas Jefferson*, ed. Paul Ford (New York: Putnam's Sons, 1892–1899), vol. 2, 237–39; and Letter from Thomas Jefferson to Noah Webster (1790), *The Writings of Thomas Jefferson*, eds. Lipscomb and Bergh, vol. 8, 112–13.

58. Thomas Jefferson, "Draught of a Fundamental Constitution for the Commonwealth of Virginia" (1783), in *The Papers of Thomas Jefferson*, vol. 6, 304. See also Thomas Jefferson,

"Second Inaugural Address, March 4, 1804," in *The Writings of Thomas Jefferson*, ed. Ford, vol. 8, 346–47.

59. See Thomas Jefferson, Kentucky Resolutions of 1798 and 1799, in *Elliot's Debates*, vol. 4, 540–44.

60. James Wilson, *Pennsylvania and the Constitution*, at 308.

61. *Respublica* v. *Oswald*, 1 Dallas (Penn.) Reports 319 (1788).

62. See letter from William Cushing to John Adams (February 18, 1789) and letter from John Adams to William Cushing (March 17, 1789), reprinted in *Freedom of Press from Zenger to Jefferson*, at 147–53.

63. *Pennekamp* v. *Florida*, 328 U.S. 331, 354 (1946) (Frankfurter, J., con. op.).

64. Thomas Emerson, "Legal Foundations of the Right to Know," 1976 *Washington University Law Quarterly* 1, 14.

65. *Annals of Congress*, vol. 1, 453. See also James Madison's "Report of the Virginia Resolutions," in *Elliot's Debates*, vol. 4, 569–70.

66. James Madison, *The Writings of James Madison*, vol. 6, 336.

67. See, for example, letter from James Madison to Edward Everrett (August 28, 1830), in *The Writings of James Madison*, vol. 9, 383.

68. *Annals of Congress*, vol. 1, 766. See statements by Messrs. Hartley, Page, Clymer, Sherman, Jackson, Gerry, Madison, Smith, Stone, and Livermore, at 761–74.

69. See An Act concerning Aliens (June 25, 1798), Ch. 74, 1 Stat. 570–572; An Act respecting Enemies (July 6, 1798), Ch. 74, 1 Stat. 577–578; An Act in addition to the act, entitled "An act for the punishment of certain crimes against the United States," (The Sedition Act) (July 14, 1798), Ch. 14, 1 Stat. 596–597. On the Alien and Sedition Acts, see, generally, James M. Smith, *Freedom's Fetters: The Alien and Sedition Laws and American Civil Liberties* (Ithaca: Cornell University, 1956).

70. *Majority Report on Repeal of the Sedition Act*, *Annals of Congress*, 5th Cong., 3d Sess. 2987–90 (February, 25, 1799).

71. See statements by Messrs. Gallatin, Livingston, Nicholas, and Macon in *Annals of Congress*, 5th Cong., 2d Sess. (1798) at, respectively, 2160–66, 2153–54, 2138–43, and 2106 and 2152.

72. *Minority Report on Repeal of the Sedition Act*, *Annals of Congress*, 5th Cong., 3d Sess 3003–14 (February 25, 1799), pp. 3003–3014.

73. See, "Hortensius" (George Hay), *An Essay on the Liberty of the Press, Respectfully Inscribed to the Republican Printers Throughout the United States* (Richmond: Samuel Pleasants, Jr., 1803); Tunis Wortman, *A Treatise Concerning Political Enquiry, and the Liberty of the Press* (New York: Forman, 1800) (reprinted, New York: Da Capo Press, 1970); John Thomson, *An Enquiry, Concerning the Liberty, and Licentiousness of the Press, and the Uncontroulable Nature of the Human Mind* (New York: Johnson and Styker, 1801); and St. George Tucker, *Blackstone's Commentaries: with Notes of Reference, to the Constitution and Laws, of the Federal Government of the United States; and the Commonwealth of Virginia* (Philadelphia: William Y. Birch and Abraham Small, 1803).

74. *Madison's Report on the Virginia Resolutions*, in *Elliot's Debates*, vol. 4, 569.

75. Wortman, *A Treatise Concerning Political Enquiry, and the Liberty of the Press*, at 68.

76. See Charles Warren, *The Supreme Court in United States History* (Boston: Little, Brown, 1922), vol. 2, 166 n2.

77. Letter from Thomas Jefferson to Abigal Adams (September 11, 1804), in *The Writings of Thomas Jefferson*, ed. Ford, vol. 8, 310.

78. Letter from Thomas Jefferson to Thomas McKean (February 19, 1803), in *The Writings of Thomas Jefferson*, ed. Ford, vol. 8, 218–19.

79. Letter from Thomas Jefferson to Abigal Adams, in *The Writings of Thomas Jefferson*, ed. Ford, vol. 8, 310.

80. *People* v. *Croswell*, 3 Johnson's (N.Y.) Cases 336 (1804).

81. *United States* v. *Hudson and Goodwin*, 1 Cranch 32 (1812).

82. *Commonwealth* v. *Blanding*, 3 Pick. 304, 313 (Mass., 1825).

83. Story, *Commentaries on the Constitution of the United States*, at 735.

84. Thomas Cooley, *A Treatise on The Constitutional Limitations*, vol. 2, 886.

85. Ibid., at 931–40.

86. *Barron* v. *Baltimore*, 7 Peters 243, 32 U.S. 243 (1833). But see also *Van Ness* v. *Pacard*, 2 Peters 137 (1829).

87. *Mattox* v. *United States*, 156 U.S. 237 (1894).

88. *Robertson* v. *Baldwin*, 165 U.S. 275, 281 (1897). See also *Prudential Insurance Company* v. *Cheek*, 259 U.S. 530 (1922).

89. The Supreme Court found First Amendment guarantees "implicit in the concept of ordered liberty" and under the Fourteenth Amendment selectively applied those guarantees against the states in the following cases: *Fiske* v. *Kansas*, 274 U.S. 380 (1927), *Gitlow* v. *New York*, 268 U.S. 652 (1925) (dictum), and *Gilbert* v. *Minnesota*, 254 U.S. 325 (1920) (dictum) (freedom of speech); *Near* v. *Minnesota*, 283 U.S. 697 (1931) (freedom of the press); *Hamilton* v. *Regents of University of California*, 293 U.S. 245 (1934) (dictum) (freedom of religion); *DeJonge* v. *Oregon*, 299 U.S. 353 (1937) (freedom of assembly); *Cantwell* v. *Connecticut*, 310 U.S. 296 (1940) (freedom of religious exercise); *Everson* v. *Board of Education*, 330 U.S. 1 (1947) (separation of church and state; freedom from the establishment of religion).

90. *Patterson* v. *Colorado*, 205 U.S. 454, 462 (1907) (citations omitted).

91. *Near* v. *Minnesota*, 283 U.S. 697, 716, 717 (1931).

92. *Grosjean* v. *American Press*, Co., 297 U.S. 233, 248, 249 (1936).

93. See, for example, *Dennis* v. *United States*, 341 U.S. 494, 524 (Frankfurter, J., con. op.).

94. *Madison's Report on the Virginia Resolutions*, in *Elliot's Debates*, vol. 4, 574.

CHAPTER 3

SPEECH, PRESS, AND THE SUPREME COURT

A free press stands as one of the great interpreters between the government and the people. To allow it to be fettered is to fetter ourselves.

Justice George Sutherland, *Grosjean* v. *American Press* (1935)

The purpose of the Constitution was not to erect the press into a privileged institution but to protect all persons in their right to print what they will as well as to utter it.

Justice Felix Frankfurter, *Pennekamp* v. *Florida* (1945)

In the twentieth century the Supreme Court gradually articulated constitutional principles for First Amendment protection, and in so doing endorsed the public's right to know as an important abstract political right but not a concrete constitutional guarantee. Recognizing that "speech concerning public affairs . . . is the essence of self-government,"[1] the Court acknowledged the necessity for popular information about governmental affairs; indeed, the "profound national commitment to the principle that debate on public issues should be uninhibited, robust, and wideopen."[2] Consistent with the understanding that the First Amendment "rests on the assumption that the widest possible dissemination of information from diverse and antagonistic sources is essential to the welfare of the public,"[3] the Court interpreted the freedom of speech and press to serve "the paramount public interest in a free flow of information to the people."[4] Thus "[a]ny system of prior restraint of expression . . . [bears] a heavy presumption against its constitutional validity."[5] Perhaps more important, since the 1930s the Supreme Court extended the scope of First Amendment protection to various modes of disseminating information; that is, pamphlets, leaflets, signs, magazines, advertisements, books, motion pictures, radio, and television.[6]

In the late 1960s and throughout the 1970s, members of the press endeavored to further enlarge the scope of the First Amendment by contending that the amendment embodies both an enforceable right to know and special privileges for the press to obtain information that it deems necessary for an informed public.[7] Prior to the 1960s, First Amendment litigation principally involved challenges to restrictions on the dissemination of information. Individuals could claim constitutional guarantees for only the freedom from restraints on their communications, but not for a right to obtain access to governmental information. First Amendment litigation over an enforceable public's right to know and a preferred status for the press therefore engenders an extraordinary degree of controversy over First Amendment principles.

Some constitutional scholars boldly proclaim that the Supreme Court fashioned a "new" press guarantee and that the right to know is "an emerging constitutional right." Thomas Emerson, for example, asserts: "The Supreme Court has recognized a constitutional guarantee of the right to know."[8] That assessment, however, is neither correct nor accurate. Although a plurality of the Court endorsed the legitimacy of a right to know, a majority has not formally denominated such a constitutional guarantee. A majority of the Court, likewise, has not declared that the press has a constitutionally preferred status upon the First Amendment. In the major cases where claims to a First Amendment right to know were raised, approval of a limited but constitutionally enforceable right to know was given by five justices writing or concurring in dissenting opinions: Justice Douglas, six times;[9] Justice Brennan, three times;[10] Justice Powell, twice;[11] Justice Marshall, twice;[12] and Justice Stevens, once.[13] Moreover, although a majority of the Court failed to agree that the First Amendment guarantees either an enforceable right to know or press privileges, the intimation of such guarantees prompted Chief Justice Burger and Justice Rehnquist to specifically repudiate the constitutional legitimacy of the public's right to know.[14]

The narrow and controversial rulings in *Branzburg* v. *Hayes*,[15] holding that news reporters do not have a privilege of confidentiality before grand jury investigations, and in *Zurcher* v. *Stanford Daily*,[16] ruling that newspaper offices are not exempt from third-party searches conducted under a valid warrant, as well as several decisions rejecting claims to affirmative rights of access to government facilities and materials[17] exemplify the salience of First Amendment litigation and the divisions within the Court over the meaning of the First Amendment and the constitutional legitimacy of the public's right to know.

Justice Potter Stewart's remarks in 1974 at the Yale Law School Sesquicentennial Convocation underscored the import of First Amendment litigation in the 1970s. The First Amendment, he declared, "is, in essence, a *structural* provision of the Constitution" that specifically recognizes the autonomy or "institutional independence" of the press and thereby confers a preferred constitutional status on "the organized press" or "the daily newspapers and other established news media." The amendment's "primary purpose," Justice Stewart asserted, "was to create a fourth institution outside the Government as an additional check on the three official branches." "The publishing business is, in short, the only organized private business that is given explicit constitutional protection."[18] Analogous to the First Amendment's establishment clause, which effects a complete separation of religion from the government, the preferred status of the press is ostensibly legitimated by the language of the amendment and by the policy determination that the press serves as a guardian of informed public opinion. Although claims for press privileges might imply that the First Amendment interests of the press are distinct from those of the public,[19] typically the claims purport that recognition of press privileges enhances the public's right to know since the press is unconditionally free in its pursuit and publication of information. In defending a First Amendment news reporter's privilege after *Branzburg* and in urging the enactment of a federal press shield law, for instance, Walter Cronkite implored: "Why can't the American people see that freedom of the press is not some privilege extended to a favored segment of the population but is purely and simply their own right to be told what their government and its servants are doing in their name?"[20]

If Justice Stewart's remarks registered the import of press litigation, he also registered the departure in the 1970s from the traditional understanding of the speech and press clauses as being constitutionally redundant. Throughout the nineteenth century and into the twentieth century the constitutional protection accorded the press was parallel to that accorded the individual. The speech and press clauses were comprehended to ensure the interests both of individual self-expression and of an informed public and electorate. Justice Stewart's views, therefore, oppose much of constitutional history and the prevailing assumption that "[w]hat [the First Amendment] should protect is not the *institution*, but the *role* of the press: To afford a vehicle of information and opinion, to inform and educate the public, to offer criticism, to provide a forum for discussion and debate, and to act as a surrogate to obtain for readers news and information that individual citizens could not or would not gather on their own."[21]

Justice Stewart's interpretation of the First Amendment, however, did not embrace all of the claims made by members of the press. Specifically, he rejected press claims for denomination of an enforceable public's right to know. As Chapter 4 shows, Justice Stewart steadfastly voted with the majority of the Court in holding that "[t]he First and Fourteenth Amendments do not guarantee the public a right of access to information generated or controlled by government, nor do they guarantee the press any basic right of access superior to that of the public generally."[22] Yet he dissented along with Justices Brennan, Marshall, and Douglas in *Branzburg*, arguing that a news reporter's testimonial privilege derives from the First Amendment. Similarly, dissenting with Justices Marshall and Stevens in *Zurcher* v. *Stanford Daily*, he observed:

> Perhaps as a matter of abstract policy a newspaper office should receive no more protection from unannounced police searches than, say, the office of a doctor or the office of a bank. But we are here to uphold a Constitution. And our Constitution does not explicitly protect the practice of medicine or the business of banking from all abridgment by the government. It does explicitly protect the freedom of the press.[23]

Justice Stewart is not inconsistent. He maintains that the preferred status of the press ensures that it may publish what information it obtains with security from governmental intrusions into its editorial processes. However, neither the First Amendment nor the preferred status of the press grants affirmative rights of access.

For Justice Stewart, denomination of the public's right to know as a First Amendment penumbral guarantee constitutes unacceptable judicial activism, whereas a strict construction of the amendment and recognition that the press serves as the guardian of the public's right to know justifies the preferred status of the press within our constitutional system. Concurring in the Court's holding in *Landmark Communications, Inc.* v. *Virginia* that any person is constitutionally protected in divulging the name of a judge under disciplinary investigation despite a criminal statute prohibiting such disclosures, Justice Stewart further explained his theory of press exceptionalism:

> If the constitutional provision of a free press means anything, it means that government cannot take it upon itself to decide what a newspaper may and may not publish. Though government may deny access to information and punish its theft, government may not prohibit or punish the publication of that information once it falls into the hands of the press.[24]

Precisely because Justice Stewart's particular understanding of the First Amendment holds that the press has a preferred status and that the amendment does not grant an enforceable right to know, his opinions are the focus of controversy for members of and commentators on the Supreme Court. Shortly after Justice Stewart's speech at Yale, Chief Justice Burger responded in *First National Bank* v. *Bellotti* by pointing out that the press clause was simply "complementary to and a natural extension of Speech Clause liberty." The Chief Justice further drew attention to the fact that "[t]he Court has not yet squarely resolved whether the Press Clause confers upon the 'institutional press' any freedom from governmental restraint not enjoyed by all others."[25]

The preferred constitutional status of the press endorsed by Justice

Stewart created a good deal of controversy off the bench as well. A few journalists such as Pulitzer Prize winner and *New York Times* contributor Anthony Lewis lamented that "[t]he Press does itself no good when it claims special privileges under the Constitution" and that the strategy of the press to use constitutional adjudication to secure "different and better treatment under the Constitution" is a "fundamental mistake."[26] The vast majority of news reporters, however, decried the general trend of the Court's rulings, specifically the *Branzburg* v. *Hayes* decision. Their condemnation of the Court's rulings reinforced pressures on legislative arenas for enactment of statutory protection for the press. Before *Branzburg* only eighteen states had press shield laws, but immediately following the decision no less than eight other states enacted similar statutes (see Appendix C for a compilation of state press shield laws). In 1972 Congress also responded to *Branzburg* with the introduction of more than 55 bills to establish a federal shield law. Although none of the bills introduced that year or subsequently found its way into law, the spate of legislative activity reflects the intense political salience of claims to press exceptionalism and the public's right to know.[27]

In reflecting on Justice Stewart's structuralist theory of the First Amendment, there is no gainsaying that the Supreme Court duly acclaimed the role of the press as a "mighty catalyst in awakening public interest in government affairs, exposing corruption among public officers and employees."[28] In the 1830s the always perceptive political observer Alexis de Tocqueville likened the press to an "eye . . . constantly open to detect the secret springs of political designs and to summon the leaders of all parties in turn to the bar of public opinion."[29] More than a century later, and yet a decade before the press became a *cause celebre* in the political tragedy of Watergate, the Supreme Court reiterated that the press functions as a "powerful antidote to any abuses of power by government officials"[30] and guards "against the miscarriage of justice by subjecting the police, prosecutors, and judicial processes to extensive public scrutiny and criticism."[31] Even when denying claims to a reporter's testimonial privilege in *Branzburg* the Court hastened to emphasize that "news gathering is not without its First Amendment protections" and that "without some protection for seeking out the news, freedom of the press could be eviscerated."

Justice Stewart's structuralist theory and litigation over the public's right to know and press privileges requires examination of the First Amendment not only in terms of constitutional history but with regard to the politics of First Amendment adjudication. "In seeking out the news the press acts as an agent of the public at large,"[32] but does that necessitate that the press merits or that the First Amendment contemplates a constitutionally preferred status for the press? Is press exceptionalism and a structuralist interpretation defensible in terms of developing constitutional law, judicial approaches to the First Amendment, and considerations of public policy?

Traditionally the central meaning of the First Amendment has been that "[t]hose guarantees [for free speech and press] are not for the benefit of the press so much as for the benefit of all of us."[33] The long struggle for free speech and press established that "freedom of speech, freedom of press, freedom of religion are available to all, not merely to those who can pay their own way."[34] The amendment protects the "lonely pamphleter" and the "citizen-critic" as much as the "institutional press" precisely because the speech and press clauses are coequal and coterminous and thus a constitutional redundancy.[35] In 1776, for instance, the editors of the *Virginia Gazette* wrote "[T]he liberty of the press is inviolably connected with the liberty of the subject . . . The *use* of speech is a *natural right*, which must have been reserved when men gave up their natural rights for the benefit of society. PRINTING is a more extensive improved kind of right."[36] Much later, when summarizing the historical basis for freedom of speech and press and the essential role of the First Amendment in securing popular information, the Supreme Court observed:

> The freedom of speech and of the press guaranteed by the Constitution embraces at least the liberty to discuss publicly and truthfully all matters of public concern without previous restraint or fear of subsequent punishment. The exigencies of the colonial period and the efforts to secure freedom from oppressive administration developed a broadened conception of these liberties as adequate to supply the public need for information and education with respect to the significant issues of the times. . . . Freedom of discussion, if it would fulfill its historical function in this nation, must embrace all issues about which information is needed or appropriate to enable the members of society to cope with the exigencies of their period.[37]

There is a crucial difference between pointing out that the press was considered an important institution in a free society and claiming that the authors of the First Amendment intended to confer special constitutional immunities on the institutional press. Members of the press mistakenly allege that press privileges are constitutionally implied, that "the framers of the Constitution knew how crucial a role it would play in shaping government, and . . . [k]nowing all this, they chose to emphasize the special significance to them of liberty of the press, and to accord that liberty a central role in the litany of freedoms."[38] The problematic character of demonstrating conclusively that the founders specifically intended a preferred status for the press under the First Amendment, of course, diminishes arguments drawn from history. Nevertheless, assuming, as Zechariah Chafee does, that "the framers had no clear idea as to what they meant,"[39] the debates over the amendment and the prevailing common law of freedom of speech and press yield no justification for press exceptionalism. In the absence of such evidence constitutional history therefore indicates that the freedom of speech and the freedom of the press were used interchangeably and that the First Amendment is indeed constitutionally redundant.

The speech and press clauses are a constitutional redundancy, but, as such, neither superfluously nor paradoxically redundant. The freedoms are coequal and coterminous and require a functional analysis because they simultaneously bear on the self-determination of each individual and on the self-governance of all citizens composing the body politic. The propriety of a functional analysis and the constitutional redundancy of the First Amendment is further demonstrated by the political and judicial history of the amendment. The amendment, as judicially enforced, guarantees that the press may publish without recrimination what information it acquires even in circumstances where there are countervailing interests in national security and personal privacy.[40] Broad press freedom emerged not from acceptance of a structural interpretation of the First Amendment. Instead, a functional analysis of the speech and press clauses revealed the import of safeguarding "the paramount public interest in a free flow of information to the people."[41] Because freedom of speech and freedom of press are two interrelated means of disseminating information essential to an informed public, those freedoms acquired coequal and coterminous constitutional protection to foreclose individual favoritism and press exceptionalism.

Inasmuch as a functional analysis of the First Amendment demands that governmental regulations be neutrally applied to both speech and press, that analysis also informs judicial determinations of the constitutionality of any restrictions on the content of communications. Just as any legal right is not absolute or unconditional, constitutional politics has established that a First Amendment "right is not an absolute one, and the State in the exercise of its police power may punish the abuse of this freedom."[42] Consistent with common law practice and the understanding of the amendment during the founding period, the Court maintains that some categories of speech and press receive no First Amendment protection. In *Chaplinsky* v. *New Hampshire* the Court eloquently set forth its functional analysis of the First Amendment, proclaiming that the amendment does not constitutionally protect those categories of speech or print that by definition have no relationship to an informed public and self-governing polity:

> There are certain well-defined and narrowly limited classes of speech, the prevention and punishment of which have never been thought to raise any Constitutional problem. These include the lewd and obsence, the profane, the libelous, and the insulting or 'fighting words.' . . . It has been well observed that such utterances are no essential part of any exposition of ideas, and are of slight social value as a step to truth that any benefit that may be derived from them is clearly outweighed by the social interest in order and morality.[43]

In addition, the Supreme Court has repeatedly sustained the validity of regulations concerning reasonable time, place, and manner regulations applied in an even-handed fashion to public places or forms, and thereby recognized that, although the dissemination of information may serve vital public interests, an individual "has no right to force his message upon an audience incapable of declining to receive it."[44]

The unenviable judicial task of articulating constitutional principles for the protection of speech and press engendered bitter controversy among members of the Court. Indeed, the constitutional law of free speech and press was forged by conflicting judicial approaches ranging from endorsements of Blackstonian principles, through various techniques of balancing individual and societal interests, to Justice Hugo Black's "absolutist-literalist" interpretation, and to what Harry Kalven called "the two-level theory" of the First Amendment.[45] These competing judicial approaches are the external deposits, as Martin Shapiro emphasizes, "of the deeper struggle between [judicial] activism and modest [self-restraint] tendencies on the Court."[46] That is, judicial approaches to the First Amendment manifest differences in judicial temperament and policy orientations toward either a position of deference to legislative restrictions on speech and press or an activist posture that challenges and invalidates limitations on First Amendment freedoms. Figure 3.1 illustrates the connection between different judicial approaches to the amendment and judicial orientations toward either self-restraint or activism. Still, as the following discussion shows, these competing judicial approaches to the First Amendment diverge as much as the result of orientations toward self-restraint or activism as of the consequence of basic jurisprudential differences in articulating constitutional principles for reconciling First Amendment freedoms with other governmental interests. More important, these judicial approaches, whether rooted in a jurisprudence of self-restraint or activism, are fundamentally guided by functionalist analysis of the First Amendment.

Examination of judicial approaches to and the evolution of constitutional protection accorded speech and press serves to explicate the central place of a functional analysis in the Court's interpretation of the First Amendment, to show how upon that analysis the public's right to know as an abstract right emerged with judicial expansion of the scope of the amendment, and, finally, to provide the background for exploring (in Chapter 4) litigation over First Amendment affirmative rights for the press and the public.

BLACKSTONE'S LIBERTY AND LICENTIOUSNESS

Sir William Blackstone's definition of the common law of speech and press served as the touchstone for understanding those freedoms for more than a century. According to Blackstone, the liberty of speech and press meant the absence of prior restraints but also the permissibility of subsequent punishment for speech or print that was deemed "improper, mischievous or illegal." Blackstone distinguished between liberty and licentious-

FIGURE 3.1

Judicial Approaches to the First Amendment

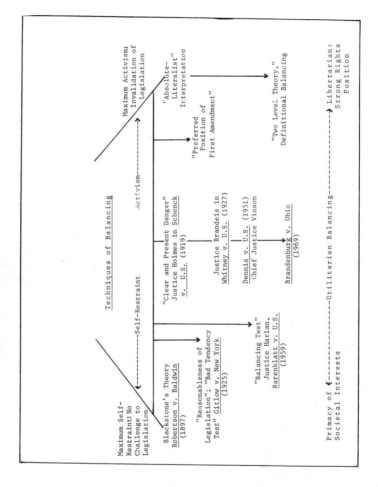

Maximum Activism:
Invalidation of
Legislation

"Absolute-
Literalist"
Interpretation

"Preferred
Position of
First Amendment"

"Two Level Theory,"
Definitional Balancing

Libertarian:
Strong Rights
Position

Techniques of Balancing

Activism

Self-Restraint

"Clear and Present Danger"
Justice Holmes in Schenck
v. U.S. (1919)

Justice Brandeis in
Whitney v. U.S. (1927)

Dennis v. U.S. (1951)
Chief Justice Vinson

Brandenburg v. Ohio
(1969)

Blackstone's Theory
Robertson v. Baldwin
(1897)

"Reasonableness of
Legislation"; "Bad Tendency
Test" Gitlow v. New York
(1925)

"Balancing Test"
Justice Harlan,
Barenblatt v. U.S.
(1959)

Maximum Self-
Restraint: No
Challenge to
Legislation

Primacy of
Societal Interests

Utilitarian Balancing

ness, or protected and unprotected communications, yet failed to articulate the criteria for determining what and when speech and printing constitutes an abuse of liberty. Rather, he assumed that legislatures, public opinion, and common law judges would determine the nature of licentiousness. Implicit in the Blackstonian-common law conception, nonetheless, was a functionalist view of freedom of speech and press: Claims to free speech and press were to be adjudicated in terms of the content of the communication and its relationship to other societal interests.

The Blackstonian jurisprudence of liberty versus licentiousness undergirded governmental policies and practices toward speech and press throughout the nineteenth and into the twentieth centuries. In the early nineteenth century the Supreme Court's interpretation of the First Amendment as applying only against the national government deprived federal courts of jurisdiction over challenges to state legislation restricting speech and press. After the public outcry against the Sedition Act and the subsequent ruling that there was no federal common law of seditious libel, the national government in the first half of the nineteenth century left the punishment of licentious publications largely to the states and public opinion. Historically, public opinion reflected in state legislation and by administrative regulations proved particularly powerful in checking the dissemination of unpopular, licentious materials. The shifting tides of public opinion, in the absence of constitutional restraints, determined what materials the public had (or should have) no interest in obtaining, but also thereby frequently deprived the right of minorities to express unpopular views.

Beginning in the 1830s and throughout the Civil War the dissemination of information about slavery was punished in the North and the South by enthusiasts both of abolition and of the institution of slavery. In the North, crusading vigilante committees fomented mob action that led to the tarring and feathering, clubbing, whipping, and shooting of abolitionists. William Lloyd Garrison, for instance, was stripped half naked and paraded through the streets of Boston, Massachusetts. In Illinois, Elijah Lovejoy died at the hands of a mob while resisting the destruction of his printing press. In the South, legislation punished abolitionist sentiments as not merely licentious but as also "incendiary," "inflammatory," and "provoking servile insurrection." State legislation was reinforced by administrators' censorship of the mails. Indeed, the precedent for administrative censorship of the mails emerged in 1835 from the refusal by a Charleston, South Carolina, postmaster to deliver abolitionist mail in the South. The postmaster general, along with President Andrew Jackson and John C. Calhoun, endeavored to secure congressional enactment of a statute authorizing such administrative actions. Although Congress, on the urging of Daniel Webster and Henry Clay that such legislation abridged freedom of the press, ultimately passed a law to the contrary, state statutes punishing dissemination of abolitionist materials were enforced by postmasters and effectively nullified federal law.

By the Civil War, attorneys general and postmasters general largely accepted the principle of state nullification, broadly interpreting their powers to fit their own political preferences and notions of licentiousness.[47] Moreover, major newspapers in the North and South during the war challenged President Abraham Lincoln's conduct of the war no less than the purposes of the war. And President Lincoln finally but reluctantly ordered the New York *World* and New York *Journal of Commerce* closed and the editors arrested. Post office censorship was firmly established and vigilantes frequently determined newspapers' editorial policies.[48]

If abolitionist sentiments were *contra bonos mores* in the early nineteenth century, lewd and obscene materials were the object of condemnation in the latter part of the century. Postmasters general had previously suppressed mailings of such materials, but in 1865 Congress expressly authorized punishment of purveyors of obscenity. Less than a decade later Congress expanded the law with the Comstock Act of 1873, named after Anthony Comstock, a tireless crusader against impure and lustful publications.[49] Federal courts upheld congressional delegation of the power to suppress obscene materials, applying the extremely restrictive English common law test for determining obscenity, the so-called *Hicklin* rule, "whether the tendency of the matter charged as obscenity is to deprave and corrupt those whose minds are open to such immoral influences and into whose hands a publication of this sort might fall."[50]

After 1879 and into the twentieth century federal and state courts relied on the *Hicklin* rule in upholding legislative and administrative bans against publishing, importing, mailing, and purchasing not only pornographic materials but also literature by Balzac, Flaubert, James Joyce, and D. H. Lawrence as well as Theodore Dreiser's *An American Tragedy*! The *Hicklin* rule exemplifies the narrow and rigid functionalist view in the nineteenth century of the line between liberty and licentiousness, between the public's proper and improper interests in information. The rule balanced individual and societal interests by focusing on the tendency of the material as a whole, rather than the effect of isolated passages, and the influence of the material on the weakest members of society (for example, children and the mentally disturbed). Even no less a devotee of judicial self-restraint than Justice Felix Frankfurter was moved to comment that "the incidence of this standard is to reduce the adult population of [the country] to reading only what is fit for children."[51] Yet not until the mid-twentieth century did the Supreme Court finally repudiate the rule and endeavor to articulate a less restrictive constitutional standard for reconciling individuals' claims to free speech and press with societal interests in both obtaining information and punishing, if not eliminating, licentious publications.

Along with a mounting number of obscenity prosecutions, actions for criminal libel increased in the last quarter of the nineteenth century, with more than 100 prosecutions between 1890 and 1900.[52] At the turn of the century, public opinion became aroused by doctrines of socialism, anarchism, syndicalism, and the specter of violent revolution raised by radical political groups, especially communists. The assassination of President William McKinley epitomized for the public the dangers to the public order of such doctrines. Consequently, after a century there was a resumption of legislation against that kind of licentiousness feared more than any: seditious libel. Political commentaries and criticism of the government once again were not condoned. Unsuccessfully, the "old Rough-Rider" President Theodore Roosevelt sought criminal punishment of Joseph Pulitzer's New York *World* and the Indianapolis *News* for editorials charging corruption in acquisition of the Panama Canal.[53] The president did manage to persuade Congress to pass the Immigration Act of 1903, barring entry into the country of any individual advocating the overthrow of government. Inevitably, minority rights and individuals' claims to the liberty of speech and press gave way under the weight of demands for majority rule, and majoritarian sensibilities determined what the public has a right to know. By the end of World War I no less than 32 states enacted laws against criminal syndicalism or sedition; more than 1,900 individuals were prosecuted for seditious libel and more than 100 newspapers, pamphlets, and other periodicals were subjected to judicial and administrative recrimination.[54]

The Espionage Act of 1917 was the primary source of federal restrictions in the early twentieth century. Under the act, prosecutions were conducted against dissident or subversive individuals and groups; indeed, the major newspapers during World War I, unlike during the Civil War, cooperated with the government and often engaged in self-censorship.[55] The provisions of the Espionage Act rested on the traditional dichotomy of liberty versus licentiousness and a functionalist view of the difference between legitimate communications and licentious *cum* seditious ideas and information. The act imposed criminal liability on any individual who, when the country was at war, would "make or convey false reports or false statements with the intent to interfere with the operations or success of the military or naval forces of the United States or to promote the success of its enemies" or to "willfully cause or attempt to cause insubordination, disloyalty, mutiny, or refusal of duty, in the military or naval forces of the United States" or to "willfully obstruct the recruiting or enlistment service of the United States, to the injury of the service of the United States."[56]

When First Amendment challenges to state and federal sedition laws reached the Supreme Court on appeal, the convictions were upheld. These cases, however, forced the Court to directly confront two long-avoided tasks: first, whether the First Amendment applied equally against the states and the national government; second, articulation of constitutional standards for freedom of speech and press. In the nineteenth century the Court had held that the Bill of Rights applied to only the national government and, in cases such as *Robertson* v. *Baldwin*, that those guarantees merely gave constitutional effect to common law principles. Accordingly, the Court was reluctant in the twentieth century to rule otherwise and was compelled to observe that "the Constitution of the United States imposes upon the states no obligation to confer upon those within its jurisdiction . . . the right to free speech."[57]

The wartime convictions presaged vexing issues with broad political consequences for the judiciary, civil liberties/civil rights and federalism. The due process clause of the Fourteenth Amendment eventually provided the vehicle for the Court's "nationalization" or application of the Bill of Rights to the states. Enacted during the Reconstruction era to protect Blacks, the Fourteenth Amendment in part provides that "No state shall deny any person . . . of life, liberty or property without the due process of law." In the late nineteenth century a majority of the Court, in a notorious exercise of judicial activism, construed the due process clause of the Fourteenth Amendment to protect a judicially created "liberty of contract," and thereupon reviewed and invalidated state and federal regulation of business practices.[58] In constructing a "liberty of contract" the Court gave substance to the due process clause.

Substantive due process analysis, as it turned out, initially provided a way of dealing with restrictions on speech. Two cases are particularly illustrative. In 1923, *Meyer* v. *Nebraska* presented a challenge to a state law, promulgated during the World War I hysteria, forbidding the teaching of the German language in private schools.[59] The Court resolved the issue not as a civil liberties matter but as an impermissible attack on the economic livelihood of German-language teachers under the due process clause of the Fourteenth Amendment. Two years later the Court struck down a Ku Klux Klan-backed amendment to the Oregon state constitution that prohibited parents from sending their children to parochial schools, again with the reasoning that the law destroyed the proprietary rights of the schools.[60]

Not until the late 1920s did the Court extend the First Amendment to the states under the Fourteenth Amendment. And only after wide-ranging condemnation of the Court's assumption of the power of a "super-legislature" in invalidating "New Deal" legislation and President Franklin Roosevelt's "Court-Packing Plan" in 1937 did a majority of the Court, led by Chief Justice Charles Evans Hughes, abandon supervision of economic regulation and the enterprise of substantive due process. Indeed, although as early as 1920, in *Gilbert* v. *Minnesota*, the Court mentioned in *dicta* the possible application of the First Amendment guarantee for freedom of speech and press, two decades passed before all of the provisions of the amendment were extended to the states.[61]

Gilbert v. *Minnesota* illustrates the legacy of the Blackstonian-common law approach to freedom of speech and press. Gilbert was convicted under a wartime state sedition law for false and malicious speech concerning the motives and objectives of the nation upon entry into World

War I. Gilbert argued that the state infringed his guaranteed right of free speech—a right that he claimed was a natural and inherent political right. Justice Joseph McKenna conceded *arguendo* the permissibility of his claim, but pointed out that no right is absolute and unconditional: The right does not "give immunity for every possible use of language." In any event, Gilbert's speech was seditious and for which the state properly sought prosecution. The majority of the Court upheld his conviction, observing that "[i]t would be a travesty on the constitutional principle he invokes to assign him its protection."

"REASONABLENESS OF LEGISLATION" AND THE "BAD TENDENCY" TEST

Seditious communications historically were punishable because they cast government into disrepute and thereby tended to encourage violence and disruption of the public order. Yet in both the nineteenth and twentieth centuries legislation often aimed at unpopular ideas. Inexorably, the Court was drawn into the political contests over free speech and press and was forced to determine the nature and scope of those freedoms under the First Amendment. As it was, the rush of convictions under the Espionage Act after World War I necessitated that the Court develop an approach to the First Amendment, to articulate a constitutional standard for defining the scope of protected speech and press.

Schenck v. *United States* was the first of the cases under the Espionage Act to reach the Supreme Court. As secretary of the Socialist party, Schenck was responsible for printing and distributing leaflets that advocated opposition and resistance to the draft during World War I. A unanimous Court upheld the Act and his conviction. In the opinion for the Court, Justice Oliver Wendell Holmes initially intimated that the standard for determining the scope of protected speech and press was whether the communications posed a "clear and present danger." In his classic formulation he observed:

> The character of every act depends upon the circumstances in which it is done. . . . The most stringent protection of free speech would not protect a man falsely shouting fire in a theatre and causing a panic . . . The question in every case is whether the words are used in circumstances and are of such a nature as to create a clear and present danger that they bring about the substantive evils that Congress has a right to prevent. It is a question of proximity and degree.[62]

The "clear and present danger" test suggested by Justice Holmes was a potentially broad libertarian standard by which courts would in each case juxtapose the circumstances of speech or print with the words themselves. Traditionally judges simply deferred to legislative determinations of the nature and possible affects of licentious and seditious words.

Although implicitly challenging the traditional approach, Justice Holmes retreated, basing his opinion on the old common law standard: "If the act (speaking, or circulating a paper), its tendency and intent with which it is done are the same, we perceive no ground for saying that success alone warrants making the act a crime." Within a week, in two more unanimous Court opinions, he again upheld convictions under the Espionage Act upon the standard of whether the words have, or may reasonably be thought to have, a "bad tendency." In sustaining the guilty verdict of Eugene Debs, Justice Holmes explained: "Disapproval of war is, of course, not a crime, nor is the advocacy of peace a crime under this law, unless the words or utterances by which the expression or advocacy is conveyed shall have been willfully intended by the person making them to commit the acts forbidden by this law, and, further, not even then unless the natural and reasonable probable tendency and effect of such words and language as he may use will have the effect and consequences forbidden by the law."[63]

In four subsequent Espionage Act cases decided by the Court, Justice Holmes, along with Justice Louis Brandeis, embraced the "clear and present danger" approach, but only in dissenting opinions.[64] In the 1920s the majority of the Court continued to maintain that individuals have no legitimate claims to, nor does the public have interests in, speech and print that carries the possibility of pernicious effects on society. The Court thus applied the "bad tendency" test—"whether the statements contained in the [communication] had a natural tendency to produce the forbidden consequences"[65]—to both federal and state prohibitions on speech and press.

Gitlow v. *New York* illustrates the Court's treatment in the 1920s of litigation over state legislation imposing on the freedom of speech and press. Benjamin Gitlow was convicted for writing a socialist pamphlet, declaring the inevitability of a proletarian revolution, under a peacetime statute prohibiting the advocacy of criminal anarchy—"the doctrine that organized government should be overthrown by force or violence, or by the assassination of the executive head or of any of the executive officials of government, or by any unlawful means." While upholding Gitlow's conviction, the majority presumed what it had previously denied; namely, that the First Amendment was applicable to the states under the Fourteenth Amendment. Justice Edward Sanford merely noted that "[w]e may and do assume that freedom of speech and of the press . . . are among the fundamental rights and liberties protected . . . from impairment by the states." Turning to the constitutionality of the state statute, Justice Sanford reiterated that no First Amendment right is absolute and that states may punish "utterances inimical to the public welfare, tending to corrupt public morals, incite to crime, or disturb the public peace." Courts, moreover, should exercise judicial self-restraint when reviewing state legislation: Judges should presume the "reasonableness of the legislation." Judges may permissibly invalidate only legislation that appears arbitrary or unreasonable; that is, if courts find that a reasonable man would reach the same determination as the legislature in proscribing certain kinds of speech and press, then the legislation must be upheld. Justice Sanford thus rationalized on traditional common law principles the legislative power to determine the boundaries between liberty and licentiousness. So, also, he drew on common law doctrines in articulating the Court's standard for reviewing the line drawn between protected and unprotected speech: Were Gitlow's statements worthy of censure? Justice Stanford, no less eloquent than Justice Holmes, declared:

> Such utterances, by their very nature, involve danger to the public peace and to the security of the State. They threaten breaches of the peace and ultimate revolution. And the immediate danger is none the less real and substantial, because the effect of a given utterance cannot be accurately foreseen. The State cannot reasonably be required to measure the danger from every such utterance in the nice balance of a jeweler's scale. A single revolutionary spark may kindle a fire that, smouldering for a time, may burst into a sweeping and destructive confragration.[66]

In retrospect, judicial deference to the "reasonableness of legislation" and adoption of the "bad tendency" test in drawing the line between the use and abuse of First Amendment freedoms partly reflected the proclivities of the Court in the 1920s to give greater weight to proprietary rights than to civil liberties/civil rights. The Court's approach also appeared defensible in terms of constitutional history. For more than a century, First Amendment guarantees had been interpreted to give constitutional effect to common law principles and the "organic institutions transplanted from English soil."[67] Broader, more libertarian standards such as the "clear and present danger" test bode unprecedented judicial activism and "not only to turn one's back on history but also to indulge in an idle play on words, unworthy of constitutional adjudication."[68]

Constitutional adjudication, nevertheless, requires more than mere rehearsal of common law principles. The Court's responsibility is to articulate constitutional standards based on a critical review of legislation in terms of the primary rights embodied in the Bill of Rights. The "reasonableness of legislation" and "bad tendency" approach was little more than a judicial rationalization of legislative determinations of the perniciousness of certain kinds of communications. Moreover, as Justices Holmes and Brandeis perceived, the approach was so ambiguous and overinclusive as to provide no basis for establishing the constitutional boundaries between protected and unprotected communications and ensuring that an individual's right to express unpopular views would not be thwarted by shifting majoritarian sensibilities.

THE RISE OF THE "CLEAR AND PRESENT DANGER" APPROACH

In *Schenck* and two other unanimous opinions for the Court, Justice Holmes intimated the more libertarian standard of "clear and present danger," but then rested on the "bad tendency" approach. In the same year (1919), however, he dissented, along with Justice Brandeis, in *Abrams* v. *United States* and endeavored to persuade the Court of the propriety of the "clear and present danger" approach.[69] Justice Holmes's dissent in *Abrams* was followed by four other biting dissents and one concurring opinion, establishing the foundations for the evolution of this most famous of judicial approaches to the First Amendment.[70]

In only one of the six cases—three, including *Abrams*, arising under the Espionage Act and three others challenging state criminal anarchy and syndicalism statutes—did Justices Holmes and Brandeis not stand together. In *Gilbert* v. *Minnesota* the two justices differed over the validity of the criminal anarchy statute, thereby registering their differing judicial philosophies. In dissent, Justice Brandeis objected to the law's absolute restriction on certain kinds of speech and press, rather than the prohibition of speech and press constituting a "clear and present danger." He also contended that the state in enacting the law before the federal Espionage Act had no legitimate interest in forbidding criticisms of the national government's conduct of the war, and in any event had gone beyond even those prohibitions imposed by the federal Espionage Act. Justice Brandeis was a social reformer, yet more critical of legislative experimentation than was Justice Holmes. In his view, social legislation should not only not infringe on the rights of minorities but have demonstrable utility and efficacy for the public good.[71] By contrast, Justice Holmes's concurring opinion in *Gilbert*, disagreeing only with the majority's reasoning, evidenced the skepticism that informed his understanding of the "clear and present danger" standard. For Justice Holmes, truth emerges only from the competition in the marketplace of ideas, and the people's representatives may experiment with socioeconomic legislation so long as that experimentation does not completely annihilate the legal rights of minorities. The "Boston Brahmin's" skepticism thus accounts for his writing the unanimous opinions for the Court in *Schenck*, *Frowerk* v. *United States*, and *Debs* v. *United States*.[72] Justice Holmes was as much irritated by his brethren on the bench and their particular economic theories and certitude of the perniciousness of doctrines of socialism and communism as he found dissident political expression foolish, boorish, and unlikely to have any practical political consequence. In letters to Sir Edward John Pollock he complained about the difficulties of writing opinions for the Court since "[t]he boys generally cut one of the genitals out of mine, in the form of some expression that they think too free." After his opinion in *Debs* he wrote: "Those whose cases have come before us have seemed to me poor fools whom I should have been inclined to pass over if I could. The greatest bores in the world are the come-outers who are cocksure of a dozen nostrums. The dogmatism of a little education is hopeless."[73]

Abrams involved the conviction of five individuals under the Espionage Act for their printing and distributing leaflets condemning the government war effort and intervention in Russia, and calling for a general strike of workers in protest. The leaflet was but a rhetorical tirade against the government. *Abrams*, however, provided the occasion for Justice Holmes to refine the "clear and present danger" standard.[74] In his masterful dissenting opinion he rejected the majority's presumption that the First Amendment simply gave effect to common law principles, and ridiculed the notion that individuals are guilty of criminal intent merely because they express ideas that would be punishable if borne out in action. In rejecting the "bad tendency" test, Justice Holmes eloquently argued: "Only the emergency that makes it immediately dangerous to leave the correction of evil counsels to time warrants making any exception to the sweeping command, 'Congress shall make no law . . . abridging the freedom of speech.'"[75]

In the two subsequent Espionage Act cases he joined Justice Brandeis's dissents, which again urged that the "clear and present danger" the standard was required to ensure freedom of speech and press "both from suppression by tyrannous, well meaning majorities and from abuse by irresponsible minorities."[76] Together they set forth their position in dissenting opinions when the Court sanctioned convictions under state criminal anarchy and syndicalism acts. In *Gitlow*, with another illustrious dissent, Justice Holmes reiterated the propriety of the "clear and present danger" test: "If in the long run the beliefs expressed in a proletarian dictatorship are destined to be accepted by the dominant forces of the community, the only meaning of free speech is that they should be given their chance to have their way."[77] Two years later, in *Whitney* v *California*, which involved the conviction of a communist under a state syndicalism act, Justice Brandeis endeavored to further explicate the broad protection that the standard accorded speech and press. Even in the face of legislation the First Amendment forbids restrictions short of demonstrating an *imminent* clear and present danger, "[o]nly an emergency can justify repression."[78]

TOWARD A "PREFERRED POSITION"

In the two decades following *Abrams* the "clear and present danger" approach was almost totally eclipsed. In only one instance during the 1920s did a majority discuss, and then set aside, the standard.[79] In the 1930s the standard was again occasioned—and rejected—only once by a majority, and defended in a sole dissenting opinion.[80] Not until the 1940s did the "clear and present danger" standard enjoy a renaissance.

In the initial decades of the twentieth century the Court was bitterly divided over judicial approaches to the First Amendment. Ironically, under the leadership of Chief Justice Charles Evans Hughes in the 1930s the Court substantially undermined reliance on the "reasonableness of legislation" *cum* "bad tendency" approach while declining to endorse the "clear and present danger" standard. In terms of constitutional development the chief justice charted a course midway between both approaches and did so on a case-by-case basis just as he shifted the Court's position from reviewing economic legislation to the as yet largely uncharted area of civil liberties/civil rights. The political context in which the Court found itself in the 1930s was also substantially different from that of previous decades. The World War I hysteria subsided and the paranoia that would grow during World War II and the Cold War remained in the distant, imperceptible future.

Before appointment to the Supreme Court, Hughes prophetically expressed his view of both the crucial role that the Supreme Court should assume in safeguarding free speech and press and the futility of rigidly applying fixed standards: "The division in the Court [during the 1920s] illustrates the vast importance of its function, as, after all, the protection both of the rights of the individuals and those of society rests not so often on formulas, as to which there may be agreement, but on a correct appreciation of social conditions and a true appraisal of the actual effect of conduct."[81] During his tenure on the bench (1930–41) the Court continued the nationalization of First Amendment guarantees and expanded the scope of those guarantees as well. The Court nevertheless remained as sharply divided on the First Amendment as were the attorneys for the government and defendants. In 1937, for instance, the Court reviewed the conviction and 18- to 20-year prison sentence of Angelo Herndon, a member of the Communist party of Atlanta, for possessing a pamphlet advocating the "Self-Determination of the Black Belt." The Georgia attorney general urged the reasonableness of the statute and the application of the "bad tendency" test, whereas Herndon's counsel insisted on the "clear and present danger" standard. A majority—the Chief Justice and Justices Owen Roberts, Louis Brandeis, Harlan Stone, and Benjamin Cardozo—declined both invitations, overturning the conviction because the statute as applied amounted to "a dragnet which may enmesh anyone who agitates for a change of government if a jury can be persuaded that he ought to have foreseen his words would have some effect in the future conduct of others."[82]

Significantly, the Hughes Court enlarged the scope of the First Amendment by rejecting any tacit structural analysis of the amendment's provisions. In a series of cases the Court interpreted First Amendment freedoms to protect more than the "institutional press" or major newspapers and periodicals.[83] In several Jehovah's Witnesses' cases the Court affirmed that pamphlets and leaflets receive First Amendment protection,[84] as does peaceful picketing, because, in Justice Frank Murphy's words, the amendment guarantees "the liberty to discuss publicly and truthfully all matters of public concern without previous restraint or fear of subsequent punishment."[85] In addition, Chief Justice Hughes resurrected the old common law doctrine of no prior restraint and gave it constitutional status as a standard for reviewing restrictions on speech and press.

In the 1940s the "clear and present danger" approach enjoyed a renaissance buttressed by Chief Justice Hughes's precedents and resurrection of the doctrine of no prior restraint. Yet during that decade and the tenures of Harlan F. Stone and Fred M. Vinson as chief justices (respectively, 1941–46 and 1946–53), "clear and present danger" underwent a metamorphosis in form and application.

The initial Holmes-Brandeis formulation was aimed at evidentiary considerations or the application of statutory prohibitions to particular circumstances, and did not purport to establish a standard for reviewing the constitutionality of the legislation per se. Moreover, their formulation focused on the content, rather than the form (time, place and manner), of speech and press. Finally, the "clear and present danger" standard was employed in only national security cases.

By comparison, "clear and present danger" evolved in the 1940s into an approach for determining the constitutionality of both the application of statutes and their legitimacy per se; and served as a basis for reviewing restrictions on speech and press, regardless of whether those restraints were imposed on the content or the form of communications; and, furthermore, was applied to a variety of circumstances, not only national security cases. The approach thus was used to further expand the amendment's protection for peaceful picketing,[86] but not violence that might accompany such activities,[87] because "[a]bridgment of the liberty of such discussion [concerning labor disputes] can be justified only where the clear danger of substantive evil arises under circumstances affording no opportunity to test the merits of ideas by competition for acceptance in the market of public opinion."[88] Similarly, "clear and present danger" became the standard for deciding cases involving Jehovah's Witnesses' challenges to state statutes and municipal ordinances restricting or prohibiting handbill distribution and solicitation,[89] and to compulsory flag-salute laws[90] as well as cases arising from contempt of court convictions for publications concerning pending trials and individuals' speeches before public assemblies.[91]

The Jehovah's Witnesses cases exemplify the Court's juxtaposition of the policy of no prior restraint and the "clear and present danger" standard. In *Cantwell* v. *Connecticut*, the Court reversed the convictions of several Jehovah's Witnesses for soliciting money and accosting passersby on city streets and urging them to listen to phonograph records describing their religious materials and condemning the Roman Catholic church. As it happened, one day they stopped two Roman Catholics who became outraged by the recordings and promptly complained to the local police, precipitating the Jehovah's Witnesses' arrest and conviction. The Supreme Court dismissed the convictions for soliciting, striking down as prior restraint the statute that forbade any solicitation for religious, charitable, or philanthropic purposes without prior official approval. Since one of the group had also been convicted for breach of peace, the Court employed the "clear and present danger" standard as well. The Court noted that "[w]hen clear and present danger of riot, disorder, interference with traffic upon the public streets, or other immediate threat to public safety, peace or order, appears, the power of the State to prevent or punish is obvious," but found "in the absence of a statute narrowly drawn to define and punish specific conduct as constituting a clear and present danger to a substantial interest of the state," that the conduct did not constitute a clear or a present danger.[92]

Because the Jehovah's Witnesses cases frequently raised claims to both free speech and religious freedom under the First Amendment, they prompted the move by some members of the Court to an even broader libertarian approach based on the presumption of the "preferred position" of the First Amendment. By the mid-1940s the Court had repudiated its previous elevation of proprietary rights to a high standard of judicial review, indicating that henceforth civil liberties/civil rights were the preferred freedoms in our constitutional scheme. The Jehovah's Witnesses cases led Chief Justice Stone, along with Justices Hugo Black, William Douglas, Frank Murphy, and John Rutledge, to insist that the First Amendment itself has a "preferred position." In 1943, on the rehearing of a case involving a license tax on the activities of religious sects, the chief justice initially employed the phrase, observing that "[t]he First Amendment is not confined to safeguarding freedom of speech and freedom of religion against discriminatory attempts to wipe them out. On the contrary, the Constitution, by virtue of the First and Fourteenth Amendments, has put those freedoms in a *preferred position*."[93]

The "preferred position" approach evolved as the logical extension of the Court's growing preoccupation with civil liberties/civil rights and the principal tenets of the "clear and present danger" standard as reformulated in the 1940s. Throughout the decade, members of the Court no longer uncritically accepted legislative determinations of licentiousness. The "preferred position" approach manifested a reversal in judicial doctrine and posture: Legislation impinging on speech and press was viewed as presumptively invalid, instead of as a reasonable legislative enactment; and judicial activism, not self-restraint, was to be the fare. The "preferred position" approach, however, implied neither special privileges for the press nor a structuralist interpretation of the First Amendment. A functionalist analysis was explicitly employed, but the balance between freedom and restraint was tipped toward the former, with the judiciary, not the legislature, asserting the ultimate decision on the legitimacy of any imposition on First Amendment freedoms.

FROM "CLEAR AND PRESENT DANGER" TO AD HOC BALANCING

The assumption in the 1940s of activism on a reformulation of the "clear and present danger" standard and the articulation of the "preferred position" of the First Amendment was not without opposition from within the Court. Throughout his 23 years on the bench (1939-62), Justice Felix Frankfurter criticized his more activist colleagues for their "idle play on words" and "perversion" of the Holmesian-Brandeis formulation, and, attending to claims for a "preferred position," ridiculed his brothers for devising a "deceptive formula . . . [that] makes for mechanical jurisprudence."[94] As important as his criticisms and his own advocacy of judicial self-restraint was Justice Frankfurter's perception that "clear and present danger" was used as a technique for balancing on an ad hoc or case-by-case basis. That perception was undeniably reinforced by the incremental development and recasting of the standard as the Court unsuccessfully sought consensus on a single approach to the First Amendment.

The divisions within the Court were further exacerbated by the political currents of the 1940s and 1950s. Beginning in the early 1940s, political passions again swept the country, with dire warnings about fascism and communism. In 1940 Congress enacted the Alien Registration Act or "Smith Act," the first federal peacetime sedition act since the Alien and Sedition Acts of 1798. Less restrictive than the Sedition Act, which forbid political criticism of the government, the Smith Act made it a crime to advocate or to belong to an organization that advocated the forceful overthrow of the government.[95] Subsequently, Congress passed legislation requiring loyalty oaths and statements of non-Communist affiliation from public and private sector employees.[96] The paranoia over communists continued through the 1950s with the passage over President Harry Truman's veto of the Internal Security Act of 1950 (the McCarran Act), requiring all members of the Communist party to register with the U.S. attorney general; and the infamous hearings and investigations by Senator Joseph McCarthy's subcommittee and the Special House Committee on Un-American Activities as well as numerous state legislative committees' investigations of individuals' loyalty.[97] Bitterly divided over interpeting the First Amendment, the Court affirmed the constitutionality of both the Smith Act and the McCarran Act in, respectively, *Dennis* v. *United States* (1951) and *Communist Party* v. *Subversive Activities Control Board* (1961).[98]

Dennis remains the watershed case in which the Court waxed and waned over the construction and application of "clear and present danger," exemplifying the futility of further judicial reliance on the standard. The source of judicial disagreement over "clear and present danger" ironically derived from its expansive use during the 1940s and the unsuccessful transformation of the Holmesian evidentiary rule into a constitutional panacea.

Dennis was presaged by Chief Justice Vinson's opinion in *American Communications Association* v. *Douds* upholding the non-Communist affidavit requirement of the Labor-Management Relations Act. In their briefs to the Supreme Court the unions argued that only actual or potentially widespread political strikes constitute a "clear and present danger" and, in any case, mere belief in communism did not constitute such a danger to the country; to wit, it was extremely difficult "to conceive how the expression of belief, or the joining of a political party, without more, could ever constitute such a danger."[99] The chief justice thought otherwise: The threat of communism was substantial, considerably greater than when Holmes proposed his "clear and present" approach, and therefore justified congressional legislation. Equally important, he rejected "clear and present danger" as a touchstone or mechanical rule for First Amendment adjudication. Instead, "clear and present danger" was simply a technique for balancing interests, and in striking a balance between individual and societal interests the Court must remain cognizant of the doctrines and dangers that threaten a free society. The chief justice concluded:

> [E]ven harmful conduct cannot justify restrictions upon speech unless substantial interests of society are at stake. But in suggesting that the substantive evil must be serious and substantial, it was never the intention of this Court to lay down an absolutist test measured in terms of danger to the Nation. When the effect of a statute or ordinance upon the exercise of First Amendment freedoms is relatively small and the public interest to be protected is substantial, it is obvious that a rigid test requiring a showing of imminent danger to the security of the Nation is an absurdity.[100]

"Clear and present danger" in Chief Justice Vinson's hands became a balancing technique and a justification for convictions, rather than for setting individuals free![101]

Eugene Dennis and ten other leaders of the U.S. Communist party were indicted under the Smith Act for willfully and knowingly conspiring to teach and advocate the forceful and violent overthrow and destruction of the government. After a nine-month trial Dennis and the others were found guilty, whereupon they appealed their convictions. At the Court of Appeals, Judge Learned Hand upheld their convictions with another of his celebrated and scholarly opinions. Noting the extensive freedom of political commentary and criticism enjoyed since World War I, he reviewed the evolution of "clear and present danger" from *Schenck* to *Douds*, concluding that the "clear and present danger" standard was no more than a balancing technique. Judge Hand did give "clear and present danger" greater precision by adding that courts must consider "whether the gravity of the 'evil,' discounted by its improbability, justifies such invasion of free speech as is necessary to avoid the danger." Accordingly, restrictions on speech and press are permissible only if they pose a clear and not merely present but imminent and probable danger. As reformulated, "clear and present danger" was sharper than Justice Holmes's initial formulation, yet it permitted changing political circumstances to determine the scope of constitutional guarantees. Turning to international events and the threat of communism, Judge Hand could not imagine "a more probable danger, unless one must wait till the actual eve of hostilities."[102]

Eight years later, when delivering the Oliver Wendell Holmes Lecture at Harvard University, Learned Hand expressed "doubt that the ["clear and present danger"] doctrine will persist and I cannot help thinking that for once Holmer nodded."[103] The doctrine proved unsalvageable, however, precisely because of Chief Justice Vinson's adoption of Hand's version of "clear and present danger." In *Dennis*, with Justice Tom Clark not participating, six justices voted to uphold the convictions, but they could not agree on an opinion for the Court, let alone attain a consensus on the formulation and application of "clear and present danger." Chief Justice Vinson, joined by Justices Stanley Reed, Harold Burton, and Sherman Minton, wrote the plurality opinion, applying "clear and present danger" as reformulated by Judge Hand. Concurring, Justice Frankfurter again rejected the Court's substitution of that approach for deference to the reasonableness of the legislation, and Justice Roberts, also concurring, found the convictions permissible but thought that "clear and present danger" was not applicable in the present case. In dissent, Justices Hugo Black and William Douglas reaffirmed their understanding of "clear and present danger" as a libertarian approach to the First Amendment.

The opinions in *Dennis* exemplify the frustrations of formulating and applying "clear and present danger." For Chief Justice Vinson and three other justices, "clear and present danger," as "succinct[ly] and inclusive[ly]" rephrased by Judge Hand, was simply a useful balancing technique that "takes into consideration those factors which we deem relevant, and relates their significance. More we cannot expect from words."[104] The promise of "clear and present danger," for Justice Frankfurter, remained nothing more than a pretense "to make of it an absolute dogma and definitive measuring rod for the power of Congress to deal with assaults against security through devices other than overt physical attempts." Once again he criticized judicial activism under the guise of the "clear and present danger" approach: "How best to reconcile competing interests is the business of legislatures, and the balance they strike is a judgment not to be displaced by ours, but to be respected unless outside the pale of fair judgment."[105]

By contrast, dissenting Justice Black presaged his "absolutist-literalist" interpretation of the First Amendment, rehearsing his position expressed in *Bridges* v. *California* that "At least as to speech in the realm of public matters, I believe that the 'clear and present danger' test does not 'mark the furthermost constitutional boundaries of protected expression' but does 'no more than recognize a minimum compulsion of the Bill of Rights.'" And, as typical of dissenting opinions, he appealed to the future, "that in calmer times, when present pressures, passions and fears subside, this or some later Court will restore the First Amendment liberties to the high preferred place where they belong in a free society."[106]

Justice Douglas confronted the fundamental issues raised by Justices Frankfurter and Black; namely, whether the exercise of judicial power is appropriate when, as Chief Justice John Marshall understood, legislation registering the "transitory will" of a majority overrides the ostensible rights of minorities, and what the permissible scope of judicial review is if the Constitution as judicially enforced provides Madison's legal check on political passions. Like Justice Black, he knew all too well that the Truman administration commenced *Dennis* after Republican accusations of being "soft on communism," and that the tides of political passions ebb and flow. Still, like Justice Frankfurter, he recognized that "[t]he freedom to speak is not absolute; the teaching of methods of terror and other seditious conduct should be beyond the pale along with obscenity and immorality." So too, he understood "clear and present danger" as a balancing technique that turned on the likelihood of immediate injury to society. Here, Justice Douglas found no "clear and present danger," because Dennis and the others were not indicted for conspiring to commit violent overthrow of the government but only conspiring to advocate and organize to teach Marxist-Leninist doctrines that may be found in books not forbidden by law!

Dennis registers the Court's uncertainty over the formulation and application of "clear and present danger." During the 1950s and 1960s the Court gradually repudiated "clear and present danger," asserting a functional analysis of constitutionally protected and unprotected communications by expressly balancing First Amendment freedoms with competing societal interests. Abandonment of "clear and present danger" proceeded in the same areas in which the approach had been so useful only a decade earlier: During the 1950s in adjudicating picketing[107] and Jehovah's Witnesses cases,[108] the Court never even mentioned "clear and present danger"! Likewise, in later subversive cases the Court refused to employ "clear and present danger" even as recast in *Dennis*.

When the Court's second opportunity to interpret the Smith Act arose with *Yates* v. *United States* there was anticipation that the result would be different from that of *Dennis*. Oleta Yates and 13 other second-string functionaries of the Communist party were prosecuted by the government shortly after the *Dennis* ruling. Each was found guilty, fined $10,000, and sentenced to a 5-year prison term. Subsequently, all appealed their convictions to the Supreme Court. When the Court granted *certiorari* in October 1955, calmer times prevailed and the Court's composition had changed. President Dwight Eisenhower appointed in 1953 the popular governor of California, Earl Warren, as chief justice, and Reed, Jackson, and Minton were replaced by Charles E. Whittaker, John M. Harlan, Jr., and William J.

Brennan. Thus, Chief Justice Vinson and his three principal supporters in *Dennis* were gone. The Warren Court, in a six-to-one decision, with newly appointed Justices Whittaker and Brennan not participating, nevertheless did not challenge the Smith Act. The majority, however, did reverse five of the convictions and ordered retrials for the others, setting forth certain conditions for applying the Smith Act that made future convictions exceedingly difficult. Only Justice Tom Clark voted to uphold all of the convictions in *Yates*. Justices Black and Douglas, in opinions that concurred and dissented in part, voted on the basis of their dissents in *Dennis* to acquit all 14 defendants.

Justice Harlan wrote the Court's opinion, as he was to do so in later subversive activities cases. Abandoning the "clear and present danger" standard, he insisted that the essence of *Dennis* lay in distinguishing advocacy of abstract doctrine from advocacy of action: "The essential distinction is that those to whom the advocacy is addressed must be urged to *do* something, now or in the future, rather than merely to *believe* in something." The First Amendment protects advocacy of abstract doctrine, but not advocacy of unlawful action. Consequently, individuals are not culpable for mere association in organizations that advocate unpopular doctrines, but are liable if evidence shows direct conspiracy to bring about or advocate violent, unlawful action. By explicitly balancing individual and societal interests, Justice Harlan partially vindicated the position advanced by Justices Black and Douglas in *Dennis*: Individuals cannot be convicted on the basis of "what Marx or Engels or someone else wrote or advocated as much as a hundred or more years ago"![109]

The Court's balancing of First Amendment freedoms against societal interests in self-preservation became more explicit in Justice Harlan's other opinions for the Court in the vexing cases arising out of congressional investigations of subversive activities. Along with *Yates* in 1957, the Court, without a majority opinion, voted in two cases that the due process clauses of the Fifth and Fourteenth Amendments provide limits to legislative inquiries. In both cases Chief Justice Earl Warren in *dictum* noted that "the First Amendment may be invoked against infringement of the protected freedoms by law or by lawmaking [for example, inquiries and investigations pursuant to legislation]."[110] In one of the cases a leader of the labor movement appeared before a subcommittee of the House Committee on Un-American Activities to testify about his activities in the Communist party. Although admitting to personal cooperation with the party, he refused to answer questions about the past activities of other individuals whom he thought were members of the Communist party, whereupon he was cited in contempt of Congress. Here, the chief justice found that an individual could not determine what questions were relevant and pertinent to the investigation, because the subcommittee's authorization for its inquiry was unconstitutionally broad. Although not clarifying the application of the First Amendment in the congressional context, he suggested that,

[t]he critical element is the existence of, and the weight to be ascribed to, the interest of the Congress in demanding disclosures from an unwilling witness. We cannot simply assume, however, that every congressional investigation is justified by a public need that overbalances any private rights affected. To do so would be to abdicate the responsibility placed by the Constitution upon the judiciary to ensure that the Congress does not unjustifiably encroach upon an individual's right of privacy nor abridge his liberty of speech, press, religion or assembly.[111]

In 1959, two years after writing for the Court in *Yates* and joining the chief justice in the two previous legislative investigation cases, Justice Harlan provided the voice for a bare majority in *Barenblatt* v. *United States*, another case growing out of the House Un-American Activities committee's investigation of communism. Barenblatt, a college professor, refused to answer questions concerning his alleged membership in the Communist party, but did so not by claiming the Fifth Amendment's privilege against self-incrimination. Rather, he claimed the First Amendment protection and broadly contested the inquiry into his political and religious beliefs and private affairs. Unlike the two earlier cases, Justice Harlan found that the subcommittee's authorization was not too broad or vague, and that here the questions were pertinent to the investigation of communist infiltration of education. Turning then to Barenblatt's First Amendment claim, Justice Harlan advanced a position of explicit balancing of First Amendment freedoms and the right of self-preservation, "the ultimate value of any society."[112] He concluded that "the balance between the individual and the government interests here at stake must be struck in favor of the latter, and that therefore the provisions of the First Amendment have not been offended."

Justice Harlan's articulation of an express "balancing" position replaced the "clear and present danger" approach to the First Amendment. In subsequent legislative inquiry cases, in 1961, the Court remained bitterly divided over balancing, with the votes consistently five to four, the chief justice and Justices Black, Douglas, and Brennan in dissent. In his sharp dissenting opinion in *Barenblatt*, Justice Black lambasted the notion "that laws directly abridging First Amendment freedoms can be justified by a congressional or judicial balancing process:"

To apply the Court's balancing test under such circumstances is to read the First Amendment to say "Congress shall pass no law abridging freedom of speech, press, assembly and petition, unless Congress and the Supreme Court reach the joint conclusion that on balance the interest of the Government is stifling these freedoms is greater than the interest of the people in having them exercised.[113]

Dennis thus embodies the final reformulation of "clear and present danger." The approach had evolved from the original Holmesian formulation into a broad technique for balancing and then gave way in the 1950s to the Court's express balancing of private and public interests. Justice Harlan's balancing approach, however, was accepted by only a bare majority in the legislative investigation cases because, though theoretically useful as a libertarian measure, as applied it only masked a position of judicial self-restraint. Indeed, after 1961 the Warren Court—with the addition of Justice Potter Stewart in 1958 and Justices Byron White and Arthur Goldberg in 1962—reversed further contempt convictions by requiring that a "compelling state interest" govern the authorization and the scope of legislative investigations and by enforcing procedural guarantees and rules on the pertinency of the inquiry. Although upholding a First Amendment "right of associational privacy" within the context of congressional inquiries,[114] the Court typically avoided deciding cases on the basis of the First Amendment.[115]

The Warren Court endeavored to avoid First Amendment issues because intepretation of the amendment so profoundly divided the justices. When the Court entertained First Amendment claims in subversive activities cases the justices split five to four. The point of disagreement was over balancing, with Justice Stewart as the swing vote. A bare majority upheld in *Scales* v. *United States* the Smith Act's prohibition on membership in subversive organizations, and, in *Communist Party of the United States* v. *Subversive Activities Control Board* (SCAB), the registration requirements for all members of subversive organizations, as established by the Internal Security Act of 1950.[116] In *Scales*, Justice Harlan upheld the membership clause by distinguishing between mere, or passive, members—the "foolish, deluded, or perhaps merely optimistic"—and those knowing, active members with the requisite specific intent "to bring about the overthrow of the government as speedily as circumstances would permit." Over the four dissenters' objections that the decision legitimated "guilt by association," the majority thought that there existed adequate evidence that Scales was an "active" member and engaged in illegal advocacy.

In the second case involving the SCAB, Justice Harlan's ally concerning judicial self-restraint and principles of separation of powers and federalism, Justice Frankfurter, performed the delicate task of writing the opinion for another bare majority. He admitted that the registration requirements impinged on the First Amendment freedom of association, "[b]ut where the problems of accommodating the exigencies of self-preservation and the values of liberty are as complex and intricate as they are in the situation [here,] . . . the legislative judgment as to how [the threat of communism] may best be met consistently with the safeguarding of personal freedom is not to be set aside merely because the judgment of judges would, in the first instance, have chosen other methods."[117]

In both cases the chief justice and Justices Black, Douglas, and Brennan dissented. One week later, in another contempt case for refusing to answer questions before a subcommittee of the House Committee on Un-American Activities, Justice Stewart swung over to the dissenters to form a majority for reversing the conviction. Still, this majority also refused rule on the First Amendment claims![118]

Following *Scales*, prosecutions under the Smith Act were largely abandoned, and by the mid-1960s—with the appointment of Abe Fortus and Thurgood Marshall as associate justices—the Warren Court struck down, albeit again not on First Amendment grounds, portions of the McCarran Act. Because of congressional refusal to appropriate funds, the SCAB was finally abandoned in 1973 over the objections of President Richard Nixon, who as a congressman in 1950 had been one of its sponsors. A year later the House Committee on Un-American Activities was abolished and its duties transferred to the House Judiciary Committee.

In the last term of Chief Justice Earl Warren the Court rendered a remarkable *per curiam* (unsigned) opinion in *Brandenburg* v. *Ohio* (1969) that laid to rest the long line of cases approving convictions for membership in subversive organizations and for advocacy of unpopular political doctrines. Charles Brandenburg, the leader of a Ku Klux Klan group, was convicted under a Ohio criminal syndicalism statute for an address to a small rally of hooded men, some of whom were carrying firearms, in which he declared that if the president, Congress, and the Court continued "to suppress the white, Caucasian race, it's possible that there might have to be revengenance taken." The Court held that *Whitney* had been thoroughly discredited and overruled *sub silentio* by later cases that "fashioned the principle that the constitutional guarantees of free speech and free press do not permit a State to forbid or proscribe advocacy of the use of force or of law violation except where such advocacy is directed to *inciting or producing imminent lawless action* and is likely to incite or produce such action."[119] In brief concurring opinions, Justices Black and Douglas gave their final requiem for "clear and present danger," observing that there is "no place in the regime of the First Amendment for any 'clear and present danger' test, whether strict and tight as some would make it, or free-wheeling as the Court in *Dennis* rephrased it."

AN "ABSOLUTIST-LITERALIST" APPROACH AND DEFINITIONAL BALANCING

After 50 years the "clear and present danger" approach to the First Amendment was laid to rest. In only one case in the 1960s did "clear and present danger" surface,[120] and during the 1970s the phrase achieved only rhetorical use.[121] A majority of the Warren Court also repudiated the ad hoc balancing approach advanced by Justice Harlan. Two years before *Brandenburg*, in a six to two decision in *United States* v. *Robel*, with Justices Harlan and White in dissent and newly appointed Justice Marshall not participating, Chief Justice Warren proclaimed unconstitutional the provision of the McCarran Act that forbade any member of the Communist party to be employed in any defense facility. The chief justice, along with Justices Black, Douglas, Stewart, Fortus, and Brennan, issued the following disclaimer of ad hoc balancing:

> Faced with a clear conflict between a federal statute enacted in the interests of national security and an individual's exercise of his First Amendment rights, we have confined our analysis to whether Congress has adopted a constitutional means in achieving its concededly legitimate legislative goal. In making this determination we have found it necessary to measure the validity of the means adopted by Congress against both the goal it has sought to achieve and the specific prohibitions of the First Amendment. But we have in no way "balanced" those respective interests. We have ruled only that the Constitution requires that the conflict between congressional power and individual rights be accommodated by legislation drawn more narrowly to avoid the conflict. [122]

The practice of ad hoc balancing, whether on a "clear and present danger" formula or Justice Harlan's express "balancing" position, suffered three generic defects. Ad hoc balancing, in the first place, is ambiguous and unpredictable. The vicissitudes of "clear and present danger" formulations made this painfully obvious to members of the Court. [123] In the second place, ad hoc balancing in theory and practice fails to establish a constitutional standard for adjudicating claims in a principled fashion and for sharply defining the scope of First Amendment freedoms. In this respect there exists little jurisprudential difference between the "bad tendency" approach and the Holmesian version, or even the 1940s formulation of "clear and present danger," and Justice Harlan's explicit balancing of interests. With all the approaches, and especially through 50 years of twisting "clear and present danger," the Court made utilitarian calculations of permissible and punishable communications on an ad hoc basis. Finally, in practice, ad hoc balancing tended to legitimate restrictions on speech and press because First Amendment claims were construed as private claims to be juxtaposed with public interests (for example, in self-preservation and punishing licentiousness). By contrast, Justices Holmes and Brandeis and later justices advocating a "preferred position," and a majority of the Warren Court comprehended the First Amendment as guaranteeing not merely a personal right but safeguarding the public's interests in freedom of information. Yet not until the late 1960s did the Warren Court move toward a more sophisticated functional analysis of protected and unprotected communications: Fundamentally, interests—both of the individual and the public—in freedom of information must be reconciled with those competing interests registered in governmental restrictions on speech and press.

Over his more than 30 years on the high bench, Justice Black unsuccessfully sought to persuade a majority of his brethren of the merits of his alternative to "balancing"; namely, an "absolute-literalist" interpretation. In 1968, reflecting on his theory of constitutional interpretation during his presentation at the Columbia University School of Law James S. Carpenter Lecture Series, he summarized his unequivocal approach to the First Amendment:

> My view is, without deviation, without exception, without any ifs, buts, or whereases, that freedom of speech means that government shall not do anything to people, or, in the words of the Magna Carta, move against people, either for the views they have or the views they express or the words they speak or write. Some people would have you believe that this is a very radical position, and maybe it is. But all I am doing is following what to me is the clear wording of the First Amendment that "Congress shall make no law . . . abridging the freedom of speech [,] or of the press."[124]

Throughout his judicial career Justice Black was repelled by balancing and utilitarian calculations of the social benefits and costs of restraining or permitting unpopular communications. More, he thought his absolutist-literalist interpretation was justified by constitutional history and firm canons of judicial construction as well as by considerations of public policy. For him, the history of the founding period justified a Madisonian construction of the First Amendment, and no degree of judicial creativity was required to show that "'Congress shall make no law' means Congress shall make no law." Because of his Madisonian view of the amendment he unblushingly denied Justice Frankfurter's deference to federalism and supported the application of the Bill of Rights to the states. Thus, Justice Black's interpretation on the one hand rejected balancing for a literal interpretation of the Constitution, and on the other hand sacrificed jurisprudential consistency by endorsing the nationalization of the First Amendment. As such, his approach was without qualification neither "absolute" nor strictly "literal," and reflected as much the influence of Madison as his own undoubted faith that as a matter of public policy "the best way to protect and preserve the country is to keep speech and press free."

Conspicuous in Justice Black's absolutist-literalist interpretation is a functional analysis that places inestimable value on free speech and press. Like Madison, Justice Black, and also Justice Douglas, rebuked the Court for approving laws proscribing obscenity and libel no less than laws punishing the advocacy of unpopular political doctrines: Neither legislatures nor courts should determine the public's interests in obtaining information or restrict the free flow of communications. However, he also embraced Jefferson's distinction between speech and overt action, or speech versus conduct; and thereupon drew the line at extending unconditional First Amendment protection to conduct, as presented in picketing and demonstration cases. Reasonable and nondiscriminatory regulations governing the time, place, and manner of communications plus conduct were constitutionally permissible, he said, for "while the First Amendment guarantees freedom to write and speak, it does not guarantee that the people can, wholly regardless of the rights of others, go where they please and when they please to argue for their views."

The Warren Court's abandonment of ad hoc balancing is perhaps a measure of Justice Black's contribution to the constitutional politics of the First Amendment. The majority of Justice Black's colleagues and a good number of the Court's commentators nevertheless could not embrace in naked form his absolutist-literalist position. During the Warren Court era, criticism of ad hoc balancing precipitated a judicial approach to the amendment that, as it were, balanced interests in freedom and restraint in a principled, rather than an ad hoc, manner. A majority agreed that ad hoc balancing was ambiguous, unprincipled, and unpredictable in application and deprecated the public's interests in the availability of even unpopular information. Not without justification, Justice Black had denounced ad hoc balancing both as an abdication of the judicial responsibility to articulate constitutional principles and for rendering constitutional rights contingent on a parade of possible horrors. Similarly, Laurent Frantz thoughtfully argued:

> If the arguments employed to justify balancing are carried to their logical conclusion, then the Constitution does not contain—and is not even capable of containing—anything whatever which is unconditionally obligatory? . . . Anything which the Constitution says *cannot* be done *can* be done, if Congress thinks and the Court agrees (or is unwilling to set aside the congressional judgment) that the interests thereby served outweighed those which were sacrificed. Thus the whole idea of a government of limited powers, and of a written constitution as a device for attaining that end, is at least potentially at stake.[125]

Although echoing Justice Black's dissent in *Barenblatt*, Frantz, like a majority of the Warren Court, could not endorse an absolutist-literalist approach to the First Amendment. Instead of maintaining "that courts should *never* balance," he argued that "they should not, especially in free speech cases, employ balancing as a substitute for an effort to find a rule or principle that can guide decision."[126]

In repudiating ad hoc balancing, court watchers and a majority of the Warren Court advanced an approach of principled or definitional balancing by which categories of speech were defined as protected or unprotected per se. Actually, in 1942, Justice Murphy, for a unanimous Court in *Chaplinsky* v. *New Hampshire*, intimated such a definitional balancing approach or "two-level theory" of the First Amendment.[127] Here the Court upheld a conviction under a statute forbidding the use of offensive or derisive language in public. Chaplinsky, at the time of his arrest for creating a public disturbance, called the arresting officer "a Goddamned racketeer" and "a damned Fascist." In contemplating these fighting words Justice Murphy ruled that the First Amendment provides no protection for such language because "such utterances are no essential part of any exposition of ideas." Certain categories of speech such as insulting or fighting words and the obscene or libelous have minimal if any social value, and therefore are not worthy of constitutional protection. In the same year the Court also ruled, in *Valentine* v. *Christensen*, that commercial speech was "less protected" than other forms of permissible speech.[128] Consequently, the purview of the First Amendment falls short of protecting fighting words, obscenity, libel, and commercial speech. Justice Murphy thus implied a two-level theory of the First Amendment: The amendment safeguards communications that have social value, but not those categories of speech that constitute "no essential part of any exposition of ideas" and are "clearly outweighed by the social interest in order and morality." In drawing a line between categories of constitutionally protected and unprotected speech he explicitly employed a functional analysis of the kinds of communications of interest to the public and worthy of constitutional protection.

Definitional balancing remains no less problematic than ad hoc balancing, since the Court must define with some precision the categories of protected and unprotected speech; that is, fighting words, obscenity, libel, and commercial speech. Because of the Court's preoccupation with subversive political speech throughout the early part of the twentieth century and because of deference to legislative and common law proscriptions, occasions for further defining these categories of unprotected speech were avoided until the era of the Warren Court.

Although for a century federal and state laws forbade and punished obscene publications, not until June 24th, 1957, in the companion cases of *Roth* v. *United States* and *Alberts* v. *California*, did the Court squarely rule on the constitutionality of federal and state obscenity laws. With the old antagonists Justices Black, Douglas, and Harlan in dissent, the majority's watershed opinion was written by Justice Brennan, who had arrived on the bench only nine months earlier. Drawing on *Chaplinsky*, Justice Brennan ruled that obscenity is not within an area of constitutionally protected speech. The First Amendment, he observed, "was fashioned to assure unfettered interchange of ideas for the bringing about of political and social changes desired by the people . . . [b]ut implicit in the history of the First Amendment is the rejection of obscenity as utterly without redeeming social importance." Turning then to what constitutes obscenity, he rejected the common law *Hicklin* rule as too restrictive, holding instead that the test for obscenity is "whether to the average person, applying contemporary community standards, the dominant theme of the material taken as a whole appeals to the prurient interests."[129]

Justice Brennan's *Roth* opinion exemplifies the Warren Court's functional analysis and definitional balancing of the public's interests in protected and unprotected speech. Constitutional protection extends to only those forms of communication that possess some social redeeming value, regardless of whether the First Amendment is claimed by individuals or the institutional press. The *Roth* definition of obscenity, unlike the old *Hicklin* rule, also illustrates the Court's greater sensitivity to the broad and vital interests of the public in freedom of information: Obscenity is to be measured in terms of the morality of the average person, not the most susceptible person, and the dominant theme, rather than isolated passages.

The precision of the *Roth* definition was nevertheless illusory. Who is an "average person," what are "contemporary community standards," how and where are those standards to be determined, and, finally, what is "prurient interest"? In dissent, Justices Black and Douglas further objected that, even with *Dennis* subversive political speech was punishable only because it bore some relation to illegal action, whereas with *Roth* obscenity was punishable simply because it presumably stimulates impure thoughts. Justice Harlan was no less criticial of definitional balancing and not surprisingly emphasized the necessity for an ad hoc balancing approach: "The Court seems to assume that 'obscenity' is a peculiar *genus* of 'speech and press,' which is as distinct, recognizable, and classifiable as poison ivy is among other plants. . . . But surely the problem cannot be solved in such a generalized fashion. Every communication has an individuality and 'value' of its own."

The *Roth* prurient interest definition of obscenity was indeed problematical and opened the floodgates for obscenity litigation in the 1960s–70s. During the remaining years of the Warren Court, with Justices Black and Douglas often rather vehemently attacking both ad hoc and definitional balancing, a majority sought to refine and sharpen the *Roth* definition. Gradually the Court required that obscene materials, even films and motion pictures, not be prosecuted for thematic obscenity but only when demonstrably appealing to prurient interests in a patently offensive way or shown to be utterly without redeeming social importance. By the mid-1960s a majority agreed that allegedly obscene material could be successfully prosecuted if and only if the material met each of three criteria: that the material was not merely thematically objectionable as *contra bonos mores*, but appealed to prurient interests in a patently offensive way, and was devoid of redeeming social value. [130] Again writing for the majority, Justice Brennan (who for almost a decade became, so to speak, the Court's custodian of obscenity law) overturned a lower court's judgment that *Fanny Hill* was obscene, ruling that material must fail all three criteria and that the community standards on which turns the social value of materials must be determined according to national community standards.

Thus, by 1969 and the ascendance of Warren E. Burger as chief justice, a majority of the Court had firmly established obscenity as outside the purview of the First Amendment while sharply limiting the number of successful prosecutions for obscenity. Much to the ire of the new chief justice, the "liberalizing" or narrow construction of obscenity encouraged the proliferation of sex-related magazines and businesses. Yet the Warren Court also ruled that obscene materials may constitutionally be restricted or prohibited in public, but not private, places because of their commercial exploitation of erotica and possible adverse "effects" on minors.[131] The Warren Court, for instance, upheld the convictions of Ralph Ginzburg for pandering by advertising the sale of his magazine *Eros* from such places as Middlesex, New Jersey, and Intercourse, Pennsylvania, and of Sam Ginsberg for selling two "girlie" magazines to a 16-year-old boy.[132]

More important, while refining the criteria for determining obscenity, a majority of the Warren Court agreed to disagree on the vexing problem of precisely defining the nature of obscenity. In *Roth*, Justice Brennan not entirely perspicaciously pointed out that "sex and obscenity are not synonymous. On the other hand, obscene material is material which deals with sex in a manner appealing to prurient interests." Unable to agree on further refinement of the *Roth* prurient interest formulation, the Warren Court did agree that essentially only hard-core pornography was excluded from First Amendment protection. Justice Black, of course, found the *Roth* test "uncertain, if not more uncertain than is the unknown substance of the Milky Way."[133] Justice Harlan concluded that obscenity is "that prurient material that is patently offensive or whose indecency is self-demonstrating," only to confirm Justice Stewart's "I know it when I see it"[134] approach to the matter. The latter's view reportedly prompted Chief Justice Warren's quip from the bench: "Don't you mean, my brother, you know it when you feel it?" Whether apocryphal or not, there exists a modicum of wisdom in that sardonic comment, for *Webster's* definition of "prurient" is "to itch or long for a thing, be lecherous, having lustful ideas or desires, lustful, lewd, itching." In sum, the vexatious definitional problem ultimately eluded a definitive judicial solution because of the open texture of language and the diversity and multiplicity of human experience and pleasures: "One man's vulgarity is another man's lyric."[135]

By 1970 definitional balancing was also firmly, if no less problematically, established with regard to libel. As in *Roth*, Justice Brennan wrote the Warren Court's watershed decision in *New York Times Co.* v. *Sullivan*. This remarkable case commenced in 1960 after the New York *Times* published a full-page paid advertisement/article entitled, "Heed Their Rising Voices." The advertisement/article criticized the treatment of blacks by police during peaceful protests in Montgomery, Alabama, and appealed for funds to support the student movement, the right-to-vote movement, and the legal defense of Martin Luther King, Jr., against a perjury indictment pending in Montgomery. Although no city official or member of the police was identified by name (and of the 650,000 circulation of that edition of the *Times* only 35 copies were distributed in Montgomery County), L. B. Sullivan, one of three elected city commissioners, contended that the criticism of the police constituted libel of him in his official capacity as commissioner of public affairs. After instituting a civil libel action against both the clergy sponsoring the ad and the New York *Times*, a jury awarded Sullivan $500,000 in damages and the state supreme court of Alabama affirmed the award. The New York Times Company appealed to the U.S. Supreme Court.

In handing down the Court's ruling, Justice Brennan initially rejected the contention that the ad constituted commerical speech not protected by the First Amendment, insisting that the ad was not commercial per se because it communicated information about a movement "whose existence and objectives are matters of highest public interest and concern." Then, reaffirming *Roth*'s definitional balancing and functional analysis of First Amendment freedoms, he reiterated that the amendment "was fashioned to assure unfettered interchange of ideas for the bringing about of political and social changes desired by the people." Unlike prosecutions for obscenity, civil libel actions by governmental officials against citizens must be considered "against the background of a profound national commitment to the people that debate on public issues should be uninhibited, robust and wide-open, and that it may well include vehement, caustic, and sometimes unpleasantly sharp attacks on government and public officials." Accordingly, he found occasion to rule that the Sedition Act of 1798 was inconsistent with the First Amendment "because of the restraint it imposed upon criticism of government and public officials." For a unanimous Court, Justice Brennan declared that the central meaning of the amendment is "to secure 'the widest possible dissemination of information from diverse and antagonistic sources'." [136]

Broad freedom of political commentary and criticism, for Justice Brennan and his brethren, was justified both by the historical abuses in suppressing dissenting political opinions following the founding of the republic and continuing into the twentieth century, and on the Court's premise that the First Amendment fundamentally guarantees freedom of information essential to an informed citizenry. The extensive protection for freedom of political commentary recognized by *Sullivan* nevertheless was not unlimited. Justice Brennan fashioned the constitutional rule that public officials are precluded from recovering damages for libel unless they prove "that the statement was made with 'actual malice'—that, with knowledge that it was false or with reckless disregard of whether it was false or not." The actual malice rule thus drew "the line between speech unconditionally guaranteed and speech which may legitimately be regulated." Here, even though the advertisement/article contained several factual errors, in applying the Court's new rule Justice Brennan found no evidence that Sullivan had suffered actual malice and reversed the Alabama Supreme Court's judgment.

Concurring in *Sullivan*, Justices Black, Douglas, and Goldberg foresaw the attendant definitional problems that eventually would arise with the Court's ruling. Justice Black, again arguing that the First Amendment does not merely "delimit" but completely prohibits libel actions, suggested that actual malice was "an elusive, abstract concept, hard to prove and hard to disprove." Likewise, Justice Goldberg complained that the Court should have simply proclaimed an unconditional freedom to criticize official conduct. Equally important, he worried about the gray areas that would arise in applying the Court's dichotomy between public officials and private individuals. Public officials may recover damages on showing actual malice, whereas private individuals do not have to meet that difficult burden of proof; but when and how to distinguish between the two remained unclear.

Application of the actual malice rule to those "gray areas" was uncertain. In 1966 the Court applied the rule for public officials to a former county recreation supervisor who claimed to have been libeled.[137] A year later the Court was badly split over application of the rule to public figures. In two cases, *Associated Press* v. *Walker* and *Curtis Publishing Company* v. *Butts*, both involving public figures—ostensibly in the gray area between public officials and private individuals—the Court was divided five to four, with the chief justice as the swing vote.[138] In the first case, Edwin A. Walker, a well-known, retired right-wing general, sought libel damages for a news report that he personally "took command" of a violent crowd protesting the enrollment of James Meredith, a black, at the University of Mississippi. Walker claimed to have been libeled as a private individual and won a jury award of $500,000 in compensatory damages (damages for actual financial loss) and $300,000 in punitive damages (compensation for mental suffering). However, the trial judge found no malice in the publication and struck the latter award. An appellate court affirmed. The Supreme Court unanimously reversed, but disagreed on the standard to be applied. Justices Brennan, Douglas, Black, and White, along with the chief justice, thought that the actual malice rule should apply to both public officials and public figures. By contrast, Justices Clark, Stewart, and Fortus joined Justice Harlan's allowing of public figures to recover damages not on the difficult actual malice rule but, rather, on a showing of "highly unreasonable conduct constituting an extreme departure from the standards of investigation and reporting ordinarily adhered to by responsible publishers." In *Butts*, Justice Harlan and his three supporters from *Walker* were joined by the Chief Justice in upholding Wally Butts's libel award of $460,000. An article appeared in *The Saturday Evening Post*, alleging that Butts, a football coach at the University of Georgia, conspired to rig a game between his team and the University of Alabama. Although Butts, like Walker, was found to be a public figure, here the publication was not "hot news" and Justice Harlan applied his standard of highly unreasonable conduct in the investigation and reporting of the story. Although the Chief Justice concurred, he agreed with the four dissenters that the actual malice rule should apply to both public officials and public figures.

DEFINITIONAL BALANCING AND THE PUBLIC'S INTERESTS

In the 1970s the Supreme Court faced the unsettled and vexing problems attending the adoption and elaboration of a definitional balancing approach to the First Amendment. Although further refinement and application of First Amendment rules for balancing remained problematic, two factors were clear.

First, during the previous decade the Warren Court had successfully developed a broad libertarian approach to the First Amendment, based on a functional analysis and definitional balancing. Before 1970 "the Court's residual theory—its sole generalized formulation—[was] ad hoc balancing,"[139] but ad hoc balancing was repudiated by 1970 and simultaneously a majority of the Court advanced a definitional balancing approach, or two-level theory, of the First Amendment upon recognition of the vital interests of an informed public in securing freedom of information.

Second, the Court's further refinement and application of definitional balancing would proceed incrementally as the consequence of accommodating the views brought to the Supreme Court by Chief Justice Warren Burger and the addition of no less than four new associate justices. By 1975 the great stalwarts of the previous decade's Court—Earl Warren, Hugo Black, John Harlan, Jr., and William Douglas,—were replaced. Within a span of four years President Richard Nixon had the opportunity to secure the appointment of Warren E. Burger as chief justice (1969), Harry A. Blackmun (1970), and Lewis F. Powell, Jr., and William Rehnquist as associate justices (1971). After President Nixon's resignation during the Watergate scandals his appointed successor, Gerald Ford, filled Justice Douglas's chair on the high bench with the appointment of John Paul Stevens in 1975. Such dramatic changes in the Court's composition bode changes in constitutional politics, yet, perhaps unpredictably, the Burger Court continued to enlarge the scope of the First Amendment by refining categories of unprotected speech and by acknowledging the public's right to know as an abstract background right of the Constitution.

While the major changes during the 1970s in the Court's functional analysis and definitional balancing of First Amendment freedoms occurred in the areas of obscenity and commercial speech, there were significant rulings as well when the Court grappled with the vexing definitional problems arising over fighting words and libel actions. Not abandoning the category of fighting words, the Burger Court so narrowly applied the category as to virtually eliminate it. "Fighting words," as John Hart Ely puts it, are "no longer to be understood as a euphemism for either controversial or dirty talk but requires instead an unambiguous invitation to a brawl." [140] The Court, for example, reversed the conviction of a black man who rather unambiguously invited a brawl by calling a white police officer a son of a bitch and threatened to kill him. [141]

More difficult problems arose when applying libel standards and distinguishing among public officials, public figures, and private individuals. Initially the Burger Court extended the public figure category to a candidate for public office characterized in a newspaper article as a "former small-time bootlegger";[142] a real estate developer who had applied for zoning variances;[143] and a bookstore owner branded in a radio broadcast as a "smut peddler," but who was eventually acquitted of obscenity charges;[144] as well as a letter carrier listed as a "scab" in a union publication. [145] By 1974 the Court's safeguarding of the public's interests in the free flow of information appeared to substantially erode any protection for private individuals in defamation suits. Indeed, a decade after authoring the *New York Times* rule Justice Brennan was convinced that the First Amendment's guarantee of free and robust public debate required application of the rule "to all discussion and communication involving matters of public or general concern, without regard to whether the persons involved are famous or anonymous." [146]

A private individual was finally defined in *Gertz* v. *Robert Welch, Inc.* by a bare majority, with Justice Blackmun supplying the necessary fifth vote solely because a "definitive ruling [was] paramount" despite the "illogic" of the Court's ruling. Elmer Gertz was a private attorney who represented a couple in a civil action against a policeman who had shot and killed their son. The John Birch Society magazine *American Opinion* drew attention to the trial by inaccurately portraying Gertz as part of a nationwide communist conspiracy to discredit law enforcement agencies and by describing him as a "Leninist" and a "Communist-fronter." Gertz sought damages for defamation of character.

In a plurality opinion Justice Powell endeavored to sharply define both the category of private individuals and the applicable libel standards. Reviewing prior libel rulings he reiterated that the modern Supreme Court had established that "[u]nder the First Amendment there is no such thing as a false idea," just as the amendment's guarantee for religious freedom means that, politically, there exists no religious truth—all religious truths are matters of private opinion, not public concern. [147] The Court recognized that in a pluralistic and heterogeneous society, though communication of competing beliefs may at times misrepresent facts, "the public's interest in 'uninhibited, robust, and wide-open' debate on public issues" necessitates toleration of inevitable misrepresentations and falsehoods: "[t]he First Amendment requires that we protect some falsehood in order to protect speech that matters." In rehearsing the rationale for the actual malice rule of avoiding press self-censorship and thwarting the flow of information to the public, he defended the rule while refining its application.

Justice Powell initially noted that a more "utilitarian approach" to libel litigation might proceed via ad hoc balancing, but again rejected that approach as unpredictable, uncertain, and requiring unmanageable supervision of lower courts. He further justified the Court's actual malice rule on the ground that public officials and public figures have access to channels of communication to combat false accusations. By comparison, private individuals typically do not enjoy such opportunities for self-help, and therefore are more vulnerable amd more deserving of awards for defamation. Justice Powell thus reaffirmed that the actual malice rule applies to only public officials and public figures, and held that states may permit private individuals to recover commensatory damages on simply showing that a publisher was negligent in failing to exercise normal care in reporting. Because of the public's interests in freedom of information and the potential for press self-censorship, however, he further ruled that private individuals must demonstrate actual malice for any award of punitive damages Finally, in finding that Gertz was a private individual and not a public figure, Justice Powell endeavored to clarify the category of public figures, pointing out that such individuals are so designated as a consequence of either their achieving pervasive notoriety or their voluntary entry into some particular public controversy.

Gertz refined and sharpened the Court's definitional balancing approach to libel. Subsequent cases demonstrated that a majority of the Burger Court would take seriously the category of private individuals, and, no less important, that the rules ennunciated in *Gertz* were the result of its functional analysis of the First Amendment as a guarantee for freedom of information essential to informed public opinion. Two years after *Gertz*, in *Time, Inc.* v. *Firestone*, the Court ruled that Mary Alice Firestone, married to the scion of the Firestone industrial family, was a private individual, notwithstanding that she had called her own press conferences during her divorce proceedings. In her libel action over a newspaper's account of the divorce in which she was erroneously described as an "adultress," the Court held that she was entitled to the lesser standard of negligence in the normal care of news reporting in her quest for libel damages.[148]

In several other cases the Burger Court reinforced protection for the public's interests in freedom of information by holding that newspapers may lawfully publish whatever truthful information they obtain about matters of public significance even when individuals claim an invasion of their privacy. As a general rule the Court holds:

> If there are privacy interests to be protected in judicial proceedings, the States must respond by means which avoid public documentation of

other exposure of private information. Their political institutions must weigh the interests in privacy with the interests of the public to know and of the press to publish. Once true information is disclosed in public court documents open to public inspection, the press cannot be sanctioned for publishing it.[149]

In 1979 a unanimous Court went even further, upholding the right of a newspaper to publish the name of a juvenile arrested, although a state law prohibited such publications and the newspaper obtained the juvenile's name by monitoring the police radio frequency at the time of arrest.[150]

In 1979 the Burger Court, however, also ruled, in *Herbert* v. *Lando*, that members of the press have no privilege from testifying in libel cases and answering questions about editorial prepublication decisions. In the six and one-half to two and one-half decision (with Justice Brennan in part dissenting and in part concurring) Justice White, for the majority, held that unless such questions about journalists' "state-of-mind" in preparing articles are permissible it would be virtually impossible for public officials and public figures to prove actual malice. Justice Brennan conceded the necessity of such examinations of the editorial process, but only on a prima facie showing that the libel constituted a falsehood. Dissenting Justices Stewart and Marshall regretted the formulation of the actual malice rule and contended that the majority's ruling infringed upon the preferred status of the press and encouraged greater self-censorship, potentially diminishing the free flow of information to the public.

If the Burger Court's refinements in the law of libel were made on a retail scale, the revisions in the area of obscenity law were on a wholesale scale. Indicating the dramatic redefinition of the law of obscenity was the Burger Court's five to four rulings in no less than 11 cases decided on June 21, 1973. With the "intractable obscenity problem," the chief justice had his way, supported by Justices White, Blackmun, Powell, and Rehnquist. Almost 15 years after writing *Roth*, Justice Brennan was in dissent with Justices Douglas, Marshall, and Stewart. Justice Brennan rather dramatically abandoned his definitional approach to obscenity and embraced an absolutist-literalist interpretation along with Justices Douglas and Marshall. Remarkably, between 1957 and 1979 the Court rendered 38 decisions on obscenity, and Justice Brennan's turn-about is striking: During the Warren Court era (1957–69) Justice Brennan wrote no less than seven majority opinions and only one concurring and one dissenting opinion.[152] During the 1970s he wrote only two for the majority and a single concurrence, but personally issued 11 dissents and joined the numerous other dissenting opinions of Justices Douglas and Marshall.[153]

Handed down in 1973, *Miller* v. *California* remains the Burger Court's landmark obscenity decision. Here, the chief justice, writing for a bare majority, set out more concrete rules for obscenity prosecutions.[154] While maintaining the prurient interest test, the chief justice refined patently offensive as a test for "whether the work depicts or describes, in a patently offensive way sexual conduct specifically defined by state law;" thus, inviting states to precisely define obscenity in legislation. He went on to reject as too broad the utterly without redeeming social value test and devised his own more precise test, "whether the work, taken as a whole, lacks serious literary, artistic, political or scientific value." Finally, and perhaps most important, he reinterpreted contemporary community standards as local, not national, standards. As a result of *Miller*, obscenity is indeed a variable concept, and properly so according to the chief justice, for in a pluralistic, heterogeneous country public interests and standards markedly vary from state to state.

The other five to four decisions coming down with *Miller* buttressed the Burger Court's renewed deference to federalism. The majority, for example, upheld state regulation of "adult movie" houses against claims that the films were shown to only consenting adults, and affirmed regulations such as exclusionary zoning and restrictions on the public display and distribution of obscene materials.[155] The most vexing problems arose because the chief justice sanctioned obscenity prosecutions based on varying local community standards. At the federal level this encouraged prosecutors to "forum shop"; that is, to initiate their prosecutions in a district court located in a geographical area with strict community standards. The Court, for instance, refused to hear a case arising from an obscenity prosecution in Louisiana for materials produced in California and mailed to New York but that passed en route through Louisiana.[156] At the state level, material deemed obscene in one state may not be in another, therefore the Court must frequently render a final decision on the matter notwithstanding that local community standards are the touchstone for obscenity determinations. Thus the Court held that a movie, *Carnal Knowledge*, was not obscene although lower courts found it to be.[157]

The tenor of the Burger Court rulings gave greater flexibility to states and cities in maintaining and improving "the quality of life" of local communities with regulations on sex-related publications. The majority did not abandon a functionalist view of the First Amendment, but, rather, devised stricter rules to allow more community control over the dissemination of obscenity. As Justice Stevens observed: "[T]here is surely less vital interest in the uninhibited exhibition of material that is on the borderline between pornography and artistic expression than in the free dissemination of ideas of social and political significance."[158] In terms of constitutional politics the Burger Court reaffirmed that the states and legislatures are the proper arenas and decision-making bodies to register the public's sentiments about the dissemination of pornographic material.

By contrast, Justices Brennan, Marshall, and Douglas object that the majority of the Burger Court diluted the First Amendment's safeguard for freedom of information. Entirely recanting his earlier *Roth* position, Justice

Brennan found permissible only those restrictions the sale of obscene materials to minors.[159] In the dissenters' view the First Amendment's safeguard of the public's right to know necessitates unconditional protection for freedom of speech and press. Dissenting from the majority's 1973 rulings on obscenity, Justice Douglas, for example, argued that "imbedded in the First Amendment is the philosophy that the people have the right to know. Sex is more important to some than to others but it is of some importance to all."[160] Recourse to the right to know to support individuals' First Amendment claims against obscenity prosecutions nevertheless was misguided. The moral and constitutional issues raised by prosecutions for obscenity do not concern the public's interests in receiving information about sex education, but, rather, the permissibility of the legal enforcement of public morality. Moreover, notably without invoking the public's right to know, the ardent opponent of ad hoc and definitional balancing, Justice Black, argued that individuals have "an absolute, unconditional constitutional right to publish" under the First Amendment.

Apart from retrenchment in obscenity litigation during the 1970s, the Burger Court was sensitive to freedom of information and the political ideal of the public's right to know. The treatment of commercial speech litigation especially illustrates the Burger Court's functional analysis of the amendment's safeguard for popular information and an informed public. Until *Bigelow* v. *Virginia*, commercial speech appeared to constitute a category, along with obscenity and libel, of unprotected speech and press. Bigelow, an editor of a weekly newspaper, was convicted under a Virginia statute prohibiting anyone from "by publication, lecture, advertisement, or by sale or circulation of any publication . . . encourag[ing] or prompt[ing] the procuring of abortion or miscarriage." Bigelow had published an advertisement for an abortion clinic in New York state. With Justices Rehnquist and White dissenting, the Court held that the statute was an infringement of the First Amendment and limited the commercial speech doctrine enunciated in *Valentine* v. *Christensen* to the extent that the "commercial aspects" and "publisher's motives of financial gain" of advertisements do not "negate all First Amendment guarantees." Justice Blackmun, for the majority, found that "the advertisement conveyed information of potential interest and value to a diverse audience—not only to readers possibly in need of the services offered, but also to those with a general curiosity about, or genuine interest in, the subject matter or the law of another State and its development, and to readers seeking reform in Virginia."[161]

The following year, with only Justice Rehnquist dissenting, the Court extended its finding that public interests in commercial speech justify First Amendment protection. In *Virginia State Board of Pharmacy* v. *Virginia Citizens Consumer Council*, the Court upheld the advertising of prescription drug sales on the ground that the First Amendment is "primarily an instrument to enlighten public decision making in a democracy." Justice

Blackmun, again writing the majority's opinion, emphasized that "So long as we preserve a predominantly free enterprise economy, the allocation of our resources in large measure will be made through numerous private economic decisions. It is a matter of public interest that those decisions in the aggregate, be intelligent and well informed. To this end, the free flow of commercial information is indispensible." [162]

In dissent, Justice Rehnquist maintained his opposition. Justice Blackmun's public interest rationale was rejected with the quip: "I cannot distinguish between the public's right to know the price of drugs and its right to know the price of title searches or physical examinations or other professional services for which standardized fees are charged." And in a parody of Justice Douglas's argument against the law of obscenity, Justice Rehnquist condemned what he understood to be the Court's implicit acceptance of an enforceable right to know: "It is undoubtedly arguable that many people in the country regard the choice of shampoos as just as important as who may be elected to local, state, or national political office, but that does not automatically bring information about competing shampoos within the protection of the First Amendment." [163]

Despite Justice Rehnquist's misgivings about his colleagues' treatment commercial speech, the rulings demonstrate the majority's concern with broadly interpreting the First Amendment to safeguard the public's interests in popular information while declining to denominate a directly enforceable right to know. Though broadly construing the amendment to guarantee the public's interests in vital information, the Burger Court permits the government to impose prohibitions against "false, deceptive, and misleading commercial speech" [164] to ensure the public's interests in acquiring vital and accurate information. The Burger Court's functional analysis and refinement in definitional balancing of different kinds of speech and press (for example, compare political communications and commercial speech with hard-core pornography) therefore continues to enlarge the scope of freedom of speech and press upon recognition of the First Amendment's indirect, derivative protection for the public's right to know.

DOCTRINAL EVOLUTION, CONSTITUTIONAL REDUNDANCY, AND THE DILEMMAS OF PRESS PRIVILEGES

The tumultuous struggle for freedom of speech and press at the level of constitutional adjudication bode doctrinal evolution and expansion of the scope of the First Amendment. Although the constitutional law of free speech and press was forged by competing approaches to the First Amendment and diverging postures toward judicial self-restraint and activism, the Supreme Court historically embraced a functional analysis of First Amendment freedoms. A functionalist analysis was implicit at the turn of the century with the Court's deference to legislative determinations of the boundaries between liberty and licentiousness, and undergirded both modest and activist formulations of "clear and present danger" no less than the ad hoc balancing approach advanced most successfully during the 1950s. Doctrinal evolution and changes in the Court's composition promoted articulation of a definitional balancing approach towards constitutionally protected and unprotected communications. Thus, since the 1930s the Supreme Court increasingly acknowledged the public's interests in freedom of information or, as it were, the public's right to know as a political ideal and abstract right in the background of the First Amendment.

In comprehending the public's interests in freedom of information the Supreme Court applied its functional analysis and definitional balancing of First Amendment freedoms to both individuals and the institutional press.[165] When construing First Amendment claims the Court rejected demands for the preferred constitutional status of the press as a guardian of the public's right to know. Interpreting press freedom as an extension of individuals' First Amendment rights, the Court maintained, in Justice Powell's words, that "the [institutional] press does not have a monopoly on either the First Amendment or the ability to enlighten."[166]

Even before the Hughes Court's impressive expansion of First Amendment protection, when the institutional press claimed special privileges the Supreme Court accepted the constitutional redundancy of the amendment. In 1913, with an attack on congressional regulation of second-class mailing privileges, the American Newspapers Publishers Association initially claimed special press privileges in its first venture to the Supreme Court. The Court rejected the association's claim that press exceptionalism was essential "to secure to the public the benefits to result from the wide dissemination of intelligence as to current events."[167] Throughout the early twentieth century the Court, whether commanded by Chief Justice Melville Fuller (1888–1910), Edward White (1910–21), or William Taft (1921–30), consistently rejected a structuralist interpretation of the First Amendment. Accordingly, the Court rebuffed the press when it demanded special immunity from contempt-of-court citations and from the law of libel, while affirming the press's freedom to publish with impunity whatever information that it lawfully obtains.[168] In retrospect, whereas judicial self-restraint manifested in the late nineteenth and early twentieth centuries gave way by the 1930s to more activist judicial approaches to the First Amendment, the Supreme Court's enduring posture toward the institutional press was established by these early decisions.

During the 1930s–1940s the Supreme Court enlarged the scope of the First Amendment and, in particular, press freedom, but it did so without approving press exceptionalism. Chief Justice Hughes raised the common law doctrine of no prior restraint to the status of a constitutional rule and

simultaneously expanded First Amendment guarantees by broadly construing the press freedom to cover both the institutional and noninstitutional
press: "The press in its historic connotation comprehends every sort of
publication which affords a vehicle of information and opinion." [169] In the
landmark case of *Grosjean* v. *American Press Company*, for example, the
Hughes Court struck down a Louisiana 2 percent tax on the gross receipts of
all newspapers with a circulation of more than 20,000 copies per week that
had been adopted to stifle criticism of Huey Long's administration. In
reviewing the history of press freedom and censorship, the Court declared:
"In the ultimate, an informed and enlightened public opinion was the thing
at stake. . . . The predominant purpose of [the First Amendment] here
invoked was to preserve an untrammeled press as a vital source of public
information." [170] Yet when the institutional press claimed exceptionalism
from business regulations such as the Sherman Antitrust Act and the Fair
Labor Standards Act the Stone Court ruled against the claim, observing:
"Freedom to publish means freedom for all and not for some. Freedom to
publish is guaranteed by the Constitution, but freedom to combine to keep
others from publishing is not." [171] So, too, in the 1940s, when overturning
contempt-of-court convictions, the Stone and Vinson Courts acknowledged
that press freedom was to be given "the broadest scope that could be
countenanced in an orderly society" not because of the press's preferred
status but because of the public's interests in so-called sensational trials and
routine judicial proceedings. [172]

In the 1950s and 1960s the Warren Court continued to incrementally
broaden freedom of speech and press upon recognizing the import of the
availability of information to the public. *Mills* v. *Alabama*, for instance,
struck down as a prior restraint a state statute forbidding newspapers to
publish election-day editorials that urged voters to cast their ballots in a
certain way. Here, the Court noted that "[s]uppression of the right of the
press to praise or to criticize governmental agents and to clamor and
contend for or against change . . . muzzles one of the very agencies the
Framers of our Constitution thoughtfully and deliberately selected to
improve our society and keep it free." [173] The Warren Court did not thereby
intimate a preferred constitutional status for the press; instead, it acknowledged the important role that the press plays in disseminating information to
the public and the electorate. Consequently, when the institutional press
sought special privileges as the guardian of the First Amendment and the
public's right to know, the Warren Court resoundingly rejected those claims.

Likewise, the Burger Court affirmed the policy of no prior restraint
and the right of the press to publish information lawfully obtained from
public records and proceedings, even against competing claims of personal
privacy. Both individuals and the institutional press remain subject to the
rules governing libel and obscenity, and the Burger Court has held that
neither may be forced to disseminate information. [174] In more controversial

rulings the Court rebuffed the institutional press when it asserted special immunity from neutral regulatory schemes,[175] from testifying before grand juries,[176] and from third-party searches conducted by the police with properly issued search warrantes,[177] as well as when it claimed constitutional privileges apart from the general public in efforts to acquire access to government institutions.[178] The Burger Court's posture toward the institutional press, nevertheless, neither substantially changed from that of previous courts nor altered constitutional doctrine.

In the 1970s, claims by members of the institutional press multiplied and embraced a greater number of special privileges. Consequently, although the Burger Court's treatment of claims to press privileges remained consistent with prior rulings, increased litigation over press freedom in the 1970s gave the appearance of a new judicial posture—a posture of antagonism—toward the institutional press. Nor did the Burger Court deprecate the crucial role of the press in informing the public. Justice White's observations in *Cox Broadcasting Corporation* v. *Cohn* are illustrative:

> [I]n a society in which each individual has but limited time and resources with which to observe at first hand the operations of his government, he relies necessarily upon the press to bring to him in convenient form the facts of those operations. Great responsibility is accordingly placed upon the news media to report fully and accurately the proceedings of government, and official records and documents open to the public are the basic data of governmental operations. Without the information provided by the press most of us and many of our representatives would be unable to vote intelligently or to register opinions on the administration of government generally.[179]

The Burger Court's rejection of press exceptionalism and equation of broad press freedom with the public's interests in information was more explicit in 1978 in *Nixon* v. *Warner Communications* when denying claims to the public's right to know asserted by broadcasters desiring to copy and sell to the public portions of Richard Nixon's White House tape recordings that were played at the Watergate trial of his former chief of staff, H. R. Haldeman. Relying on *Cox*, Justice Powell reaffirmed "the right of the press to publish accurately information contained in court records open to the public. Since the press serves as the information-gathering agent of the public, it [can] not be prevented from reporting what it [learns] and what the public was entitled to know." Here, members of the press and the public heard the recordings in the courtroom and trial transcripts were available, so there was "no question of a truncated flow of information to the public." The issue was whether the media had a constitutional right to acquire, copy, and sell the Nixon tapes. Justice Powell recapitulated that "[t]he First Amendment generally grants the press no right to information about a trial superior to that of the general public." Justice Powell thought that Congress, by enacting the Presidential Recordings Act and empowering the administrator of General Services to supervise release of the tapes, had adequately considered the public's right to know and that the "presence of [this] alternative means of public access tips the scales in favor of denying release" of the tapes to Warner Communications.[180] Only Justices Stevens and Marshall dissented, not because they subscribed to press exceptionalism but because the Nixon tapes were "of great historical interest" and therefore should be readily available to members of the public.

The rejection of press exceptionalism reflects important considerations of public policy as much as constitutional principle. That is, apart from constitutional history and principle, claims for the preferred constitutional status for the institutional press as a guardian of the public's right to know pose fundamental political dilemmas for the judiciary, the press, and the public. Constitutional rights are personal, not institutional. Consequently, both individuals and the press enjoy freedom from accountability and external control. But if the institutional press were constitutionally denominated as it is often called, the fourth branch of government, then like other government institutions the press would be subject to principles of accountability or have a fiduciary duty to exercise protected freedoms responsibly and subject to the control and to the interests of the public.[181] As vigorously as special press privileges are defended, members of the institutional press vehemently oppose external control and direct accountability for editorial decisions. This dilemma posed by press exceptionalism has been circumvented because the Supreme Court historically embraced a functional, rather than a structural, analysis of the First Amendment.

There remains another dilemma posed by a structuralist theory of the First Amendment and litigation over press exceptionalism; namely, how to define "the press" or "institutional press." On a structuralist theory the Court must define "the press." And that definitional problem proves no less problematic than definitional balancing of protected and unprotected speech. In *Branzburg* v. *Hayes*, when denying the claim to a First Amendment testimonial privilege for news reporters, Justice White, for the majority, perceptively notes that special press privileges "present practical and conceptual difficulties of a high order."[182] The Supreme Court faced the equally difficult task of defining "religion" under the First Amendment.[183] Still, in proclaiming the constitutionality of press exceptionalism, the Court invites litigation over the protection accorded the non-institutional press, and with an underinclusive definition potentially diminishes the availability of information to the public. There are also problems of overinclusion in denominating press privileges. Justice Stewart recognized these definitional problems when directing questions to counsel during oral arguments in *Branzburg*:

> *Question:* And I suppose your argument, based as it is upon the First

Amendment, could not logically be confined to newsmen, however defined. I suppose everyone of use has the—is protected in his right to free speech and the right to speak also includes the right to keep silent. And I suppose, logically carried to its conclusion, your argument would be that anybody would be protected if he just said, "I don't want to talk."

Answer: "Well, I wouldn't know—"

Question: "Why is it confined to newsmen? We all have the right of free speech, do we not?" [184]

The Court could fashion a constitutional press privilege by following the lines drawn by legislatures in drafting press shield laws: either by defining members of the institutional press according to their employer, work schedule, or publication record; or by simply affording immunity for all who write professionally. For example, President James Carter, when proposing legislation to limit police searches of newsrooms after the Court's ruling in *Zurcher* v. *Stanford Daily*,* suggested immunity for "free-lance writers, radio and television stations, magazines, academics and any other person possessing materials in connection with the dissemination to the public of a newspaper, book, broadcast or other form of communication." [185] With either approach, however, the Court threatens to deny constitutional protection for the citizen-critic; whereas any broader definition of "the press" proves so overinclusive as to render meaningless press exceptionalism and a structuralist interpretation of the First Amendment.

Finally, litigation designed to secure press exceptionalism raises the perennial political issue concerning the legitimate exercise of judicial review and the permissible scope of judicial creativity in constitutional interpretation. In *Branzburg*, Justice White, echoing Chief Justice John Marshall, reiterated that "[t]he task of judges, like other officials outside the legislative branch, is not to make law but to uphold it in accordance with their oaths." Admittedly, denial of press privileges occasionally diminishes opportunities for gathering and reporting information, but under the Constitution only Congress and state legislatures are empowered to legislate special privileges and immunities for the press. [186] In contrast to the majority in *Branzburg*, dissenting Justice Douglas thought that "[t]he press has a preferred position in our constitutional scheme, not to enable it to make money, not to set newsmen apart as a favored class, but to bring fulfillment to the public's right to know." Unlike the majority, Justice Douglas was willing to pursue judicial creativity in constructing special press privileges because of the press's institutional role in informing the public. Similarly, Justice Stewart argues that "[t]he reporter's constitutional right to a confidential relation-

---

*On October 15, 1980, President James Carter signed the Privacy Protection Act of 1980 into law. The law undercuts the Supreme Court's ruling in *Zurcher* v. *Stanford Daily* (1978) by prohibiting unannounced searches of newsrooms by federal, state and local law enforcement officers, except in certain narrowly defined circumstances.

ship with his sources stems from the broad societal interest in a full and free flow of information to the public."[187] The majority nevertheless adhered to the constitutional redundancy of the First Amendment, reaffirming that within our constitutional and political system the propriety of press exceptionalism remains an issue to be resolved by the people's elected representatives.

The Supreme Court, in historical and political perspective, incrementally evolved a broad interpretation of the First Amendment upon considering the public's interests in freedom of information too precious either to permit excessive restraints on each individual's freedom of speech and press or to depend solely on the institutional press. With a functional analysis and broad construction of enumerated First Amendment guarantees, the Court indirectly, derivatively ensured the political ideal of the public's right to know. In adopting an activist jurisprudence and enlarging the scope of freedom of speech and press, the Court declined further invitations to fashion a constitutionally perferred position for the institutional press as the guardian of the public's right to know and thereby "embark the judiciary on a long and difficult journey to . . . an uncertain destination."[188]

NOTES

1. *Garrison* v. *Louisiana*, 379 U.S. 64, 74–75 (1964). See also *United States* v. *Cruikshank*, 92 U.S. 542, 554 (1876).

2. *New York Times Co.* v. *Sullivan*, 376 U.S. 254, 270–71 (1964).

3. *Associated Press* v. *United States*, 326 U.S. 1, 20 (1945).

4. *Garrison* v. *Louisiana*, 379 U.S. 64, 77 (1964).

5. *New York Times* v. *United States*, 403 U.S. 713, 714 (1971) (per curiam).

6. See *Lovell* v. *City of Griffin*, 303 U.S. 444 (1938) (pamphlets); *Schneider* v. *New Jersey*, 308 U.S. 147 (1939) (leaflets); *Thornhill* v. *Alabama*, 310 U.S. 88 (1940) (signs); *Roth* v. *United States*, 354 U.S. 376, 488 (1957) (dicta) (book); *Joseph Burstyn, Inc.* v. *Wilson*, 343 U.S. 495, 502 (1952) (motion pictures); *New York Times Co.* v. *Sullivan*, 376 U.S. 254, 266 (1964) (noncommercial advertisements); *Virginia State Board of Pharmacy* v. *Virginia Citizens Consumer Council*, 425 U.S. 748 (1976) (commercial advertisements); *Greenbelt Cooperative Publishing Association* v. *Bresler*, 398 U.S. 6, 11 (1970) (newspapers); *Time, Inc.* v. *Hill*, 385 U.S. 374, 388–89 (1967) (magazines); *Red Lion Broadcasting Co.* v. *Federal Communications Commission*, 395 U.S. 367 (1969) (radio); and *Estes* v. *Texas*, 381 U.S. 532 (1965) (dicta) (television).

7. See, generally, Floyd Abrams, "The Press *Is* Different: Reflections on Justice Stewart and the Autonomous Press," 7 *Hofstra Law Review* 559 (1979); and Randall P. Bezanson, "The Free Press Guarantee," 63 *Virginia Law Review* 731 (1977).

8. Thomas I. Emerson, "Colonial Intentions and Current Realities of the First Amendment," 125 *University of Pennsylvania Law Review* 737, 755 (1977).

9. See *Hamling* v. *United States*, 418 U.S. 87, 141 (1974) (Douglas and Brennan, JJ., dis. op.); *Pell* v. *Procunier*, 417 U.S. 817, 841 (1974) (Douglas, J., dis. op.); *Miller* v. *California*, 413 U.S. 15, 44 (1973) (Douglas, J., dis. op.); *Columbia Broadcasting System, Inc.* v. *Democratic National Committee*, 412 U.S. 94, 165 (1973) (Douglas, J., dis. op.); *Branzburg* v. *Hayes*, 408 U.S. 665, 721 (1972) (Douglas, J., dis. op.); and *Zemel* v. *Rusk*, 381 U.S. 1, 24 (1965) (Douglas, J., dis. op.).

10. See *Hamling* v. *United States*, 418 U.S. 87, 141 (1974) (Douglas and Brennan, JJ., dis. op.); *Saxbe* v. *Washington Post Co.*, 417 U.S. 843, 850 (1974) (Powell and Brennan, JJ., dis. op.); *Pell* v. *Procunier*, 417 U.S. 843, 850 (1974) (Douglas and Brennan, JJ., dis. op.).

11. See *Gannett Co.* v. *DePasquale*, 99 S.Ct. 2898, 2915 (1979) (Powell, J., con. op.); and *Saxbe* v. *Washington Post*, 417 U.S. 843, 873 (1974) (Powell, J., dis. op.).

12. See *Saxbe* v. *Washington Post Co.*, 417 U.S. 843, 850 (Powell, J., dis. op., joined by Brennan and Marshall, JJ.); *Pell* v. *Procunier*, 417 U.S. 817, 836 (1974) (Douglas, J., dis. op., joined by Brennan and Marshall, JJ.); *Rosenbloom* v. *Metromedia*, 403 U.S. 29, 78 (1971) (Marshall, J., dis. op.).

13. See *Houchins* v. *KQED*, 438 U.S. 1, 19 (1978) (Stevens, J., dis. op.).

14. See *Buckley* v. *Valeo*, 424 U.S. 1, 235 (1976) (Burger, C.J., con. and dis. op.); *New York Times Co.* v. *United States*, 403 U.S. 711, 749 (1971) (Burger, C.J., dis. op.); and *State Board of Pharmacy* v. *Virginia Citizens Consumer Council*, 425 U.S. 748, 785 (1976) (Rehnquist, J., dis. op.).

15. *Branzburg* v. *Hayes*, 409 U.S. 653 (1972). *Branzburg* was accepted on certiorari and decided with two other cases, *In re Pappas* and *United States* v. *Caldwell*.

16. *Zurcher* v. *Stanford Daily*, 436 U.S. 547 (1978).

17. See, for example, *Saxbe* v. *Washington Post*, 417 U.S. 843 (1974); *Pell* v. *Procuiner*, 417 U.S. 817 (1974); *Houchins* v. *KQED*, 438 U.S. 1 (1978); *Gannett Co.* v. *DePasquale*, 99 S.Ct. 2898 (1979); and *Richmond Newspapers, Inc.* v. *Virginia*, 100 S.Ct. 2814 (1980).

18. Potter Stewart, "Or of the Press," 26 *Hastings Law Journal*, 631–63 (1975).

19. See, for example, Randall P. Bezanson, "The New Free Press Guarantee," 63 *Virginia Law Review* 731, 735 (1977).

20. Walter Cronkite, in the introduction to Charles W. Whalen, Jr., *Your Right to Know* (New York: Vintage, 1973) x.

21. Robert D. Sack, "Reflections on the Wrong Question: Special Constitutional Privilege for The Institutional Press," 7 *Hofstra Law Review* 629, 633 (1979).

22. *Houchins* v. *KQED*, 438 U.S. 1, 16 (1978) (Powell, J., con. op.).

23. *Zurcher* v. *Stanford Daily*, 436 U.S. 547, 576 (1978) (Stewart, J., dis. op.)

24. *Landmark Communications, Inc.* v. *Virginia*, 98 S.Ct. 1535, 1547 (1978) (Stewart, J., dis. op.).

25. *First National Bank of Boston* v. *Bellotti*, 435 U.S. 765, 800 & 802 (1978) (Burger, C.J., con. op.).

26. Anthony Lewis, "Amending the Court," New York *Times*, June 26, 1978, at A19, col. 5. See also Lewis, "The Court and the Press," New York *Times*, June 8, 1978, at A27, col. 1; "A Depressing Tale," New York *Times*, December, 4, 1978, at A21, col. 3; "A Preferred Position for Journalism?" 7 *Hofstra Law Review* 595 (1979).

27. See Whalen, *Your Right to Know*; Maurice Van Gerpen, *Privileged Communications and the Press* (Westport, Conn.: Greenwood Press, 1979); and Henry Cohen, *Journalists' Privilege To Withhold Information In Judicial and Legislative Proceedings*, Report No. 78-220A (Washington, D.C.: Congressional Research Service, 1978).

28. *Estes* v. *Texas*, 381 U.S. 532, 539 (1965).

29. Alexis de Tocqueville, *Democracy in America*, vol. 1, ed. Phillips Bradley (New York: Vintage Books, 1945) 195.

30. *Mills* v. *Alabama*, 384 U.S. 214, 219 (1966).

31. *Sheppard* v. *Maxwell*, 384 U.S. 333, 350 (1966).

32. *Branzburg* v. *Hayes*, 408 U.S. 665, 707, 738 (1972).

33. *Saxbe* v. *Washington Post Co.*, 417 U.S. 843, 863 (1974) (Powell, J., dis. op.). See also *First National Bank of Boston* v. *Bellotti*, 435 U.S. 765, 776–78 (1978).

34. *Murdock* v. *Pennsylvania*, 319 U.S. 105, 111 (1942).

35. *Lovell* v. *City of Griffin*, 303 U.S. 444 (1938); and *New York Times* v. *Sullivan*, 376 U.S. 254, 282 (1964).

36. *Virginia Gazette*, May 18, 1776, at 1, col. 2, quoted by Lewis, "A Preferred Position for Journalism?", at 600.

37. *Thornhill* v. *Alabama*, 310 U.S. 88, 102 (1940).

38. Brief for respondents in *Herbert* v. *Lando*, 99 S.Ct. 1635 (1979) at 51, quoting Arthur Schlesinger, *Prelude to Independence* (1958) 45–46. See also Floyd Abrams, "The Press *Is* Different: Reflections on Justice Stewart and The Autonomous Press," 7 *Hofstra Law Review* 559 (1979).

39. Zechariah Chafee, book review, 62 *Harvard Law Review* 891, 898 (1949). See also Leonard Levy, *The Legacy of Suppression* (Cambridge, Mass.: Belknap, 1960), 308–9.

40. See, for example, *New York Times* v. *United States*, 403 U.S. 713 (1971); *Cox Broadcasting Corporation* v. *Cohn*, 420 U.S. 469 (1975); and *Smith* v. *Daily Mail Publishing Company*, 99 S.Ct. 2667 (1979).

41. *Garrison* v. *Louisiana*, 379 U.S. 64, 77 (1964).

42. *Stromberg* v. *California*, 283 U.S. 359, 359 (1931); see also *Whitney* v. *California*, 274 U.S. 357, 371 (1927); *Murdock* v. *Pennsylvania*, 319 U.S. 105, 122 (1942) (Reed, J., dis. op.); *Thornhill* v. *Alabama*, 310 U.S. 88, 105 (1939); *Bridges* v. *California*, 314 U.S. 252, 283 (1941) (Frankfurter, J., dis. op.); and *Associated Press* v. *United States*, 326 U.S. 1, 20 (1945).

43. *Chaplinsky* v. *New Hampshire*, 315 U.S. 568, 571–72 (1942).

44. See, for example, *Pell* v. *Procunier*, 417 U.S. 817, 826 (1974); *Grayned* v. *City of Rockford*, 408 U.S. 104, 115 (1972); *Police Department* v. *Mosley*, 408 U.S. 92, 98 (1972); *Cox* v. *Louisiana*, 379 U.S. 536, 554–55 (1965); *Poulos* v. *New Hampshire*, 345 U.S. 395, 398 (1953); *Schneider* v. *New Jersey*, 308 U.S. 147, 160 (1939); *Lehman* v. *City of Shaker Heights*, 418 U.S. 298, 307 (1974) (Douglas, J., con. op.); *Federal Communications Commission* v. *Pacifica Foundation*, 438 U.S. 726 (1978); *Rowan* v. *Post Office Department*, 397 U.S. 728, 736 (1970); *Public Utilities Commission* v. *Pollack*, 343 U.S. 451, 469 (1952); and *Martin* v. *City of Struthers*, 319 U.S. 141, 146–48 (1943).

45. Harry Kalven, Jr., "The Metaphysics of the Law of Obscenity," in *Supreme Court Review*, ed. Philip Kurland (Chicago: University of Chicago Press, 1960) 1–45.

46. Martin Shapiro, "The Balancing of Interests in Free Speech Cases: In Defense of an Abused Doctrine," 2 *Law in Transition Quarterly* 1, 18 (1965).

47. See, generally, Harold L. Nelson, ed., *Freedom of the Press from Hamilton to the Warren Court* (New York: Bobbs-Merrill, 1967) 167–235; John Lofton, *The Press as Guardian of the First Amendment* (Columbia: University of South Carolina, 1980) 79–102; and Russell B. Nye, *Fettered Freedom* (Urbana: University of Illinois Press, 1972) 115–21. On state nullification see U.S., Congress, *Register of Debates in Congress*, 24th Cong., 1st Sess., June 8, 1836, at 1721–27; and *Yazoo City Post Office Case*, 8 Opinion of Attorney General (1857), at 489; and U.S., Congress, House, "Postmaster General's Authority over Mailable Matter," in *House Miscellaneous Documents, No. 16*, 37th Cong., 3d Sess., January 20, 1863, at 4–9.

48. Abraham Lincoln, *Complete Works of Abraham Lincoln*, ed. John G. Nicolay and John Hay (New York: Francis D. Tandy Company, 1894), vol. ten, 108; and Edwin Emery and Henry Ladd Smith, *The Press and America* (New York: Prentice-Hall, 1954), 284–301.

49. See Anthony Comstock, *Traps for the Young* 2d ed. (New York: Funk & Wagnalls, 1884); and James C. N. Paul and Murray L. Schwartz, *Federal Censorship: Obscenity in the Mail* (New York: Free Press, 1961) 17–24.

50. *Queen* v. *Hicklin*, L.R. 3 QB 360 (1868). See also *Ex parte Jackson*, 96 U.S. 728 (1878); *United States* v. *Bennett*, 24 Fed. Cases 1,093 (1879) (applying *Hicklin* rule).

51. *Butler* v. *Michigan*, 352 U.S. 380, 383–84 (1957).

52. See, Tabulations of West Publishing Company, *American Digest, Decential Digest*, and *General Digest* (St. Paul, Minn.: West Publishing Co., 1902).

53. Theodore Roosevelt, *Special Message of the President of the United States to Congress*, House Document No. 1213, 60th Cong., 2d Sess., December 15, 1903, at 3–5.

54. See Fredrick Seaton Siebert, *The Rights and Privileges of the Press* (New York: D. Appleton-Century, 1934), 271, n.10; and Zechariah Chafee, Jr., *Free Speech in the United States* (Cambridge: Harvard University Press, 1941), 100–102, 298–305.

55. See Lofton, *The Press as Guardian of the First Amendment* at 231–78.

56. The Espionage Act of June 15, 1917, 40 Stat. 217; see also Act of May 16, 1918, 40 Stat. 553.

57. *Prudential Insurance Company* v. *Cheek*, 259 U.S. 530 (1922).

58. See, for example, *Lochner* v. *New York*, 198 U.S. 530 (1922).

59. *Meyer* v. *Nebraska*, 262 U.S. 390 (1923).

60. *Pierce* v. *Society of Sisters*, 268 U.S. 510 (1925).

61. *Gilbert* v. *Minnesota*, 254 U.S. 325, 333 (1920).

62. *Schenck* v. *United States*, 249 U.S. 47, 52 (1919).

63. Transcript of Record, *Eugene V. Debs* v. *United States*, case no. 714, October Term 1918, Supreme Court of the United States, at 279. See *Debs* v. *United States*, 249 U.S. 211 (1919) and *Frowerk* v. *United States*, 249 U.S. 204 (1919).

64. See *Abrams* v. *United States*, 250 U.S. 616 (1919); *Schaefer* v. *United States*, 251 U.S. 466 (1920); *Pierce* v. *United States*, 252 U.S. 239 (1920); and *Milwaukee Publishing Company* v. *United States*, 255 U.S. 407 (1921).

65. *Pierce* v. *United States*, 252 U.S. 239, 244 (1920).

66. *Gitlow* v. *New York*, 268 U.S. 652, 667, 669 (1925).

67. *Gompers* v. *United States*, 233 U.S. 604, 610 (1914).

68. *Bridges* v. *California*, 314 U.S. 252, 295 (1941) (Frankfurter, J., dis. op.).

69. *Abrams* v. *United States*, 250 U.S. 616 (1919).

70. Justice Holmes dissented in *Schaefer* v. *United States*, 251 U.S. 466 (1920); *Pierce* v. *United States*, 252 U.S. 239 (1920); *Gilbert* v. *Minnesota*, 254 U.S. 235 (1920); *Gitlow* v. *New York*, 268 U.S. 652 (1925); and concurred in *Whitney* v. *California*, 274 U.S. 357 (1927).

71. See, generally, Alpheaus T. Mason, *Brandeis: A Free Man's Life* (New York: Viking Press, 1946).

72. *Schenck* v. *United States*, 249 U.S. 47 (1919); *Frowerk* v. *United States*, 249 U.S. 204 (1919); and *Debs* v. *United States*, 249 U.S. 211 (1919).

73. Letter from Oliver Wendell Holmes to Sir John Pollock (January 24, 1981) in *Pollock-Holmes Letters*, ed. Mark DeWolfe Howe (Cambridge: Harvard University Press, 1942), vol. 1, 258; Letter from Oliver Wendell Holmes to Sir John Pollock (April 25, 1919), ibid., at 32.

74. Letter from Oliver Wendell Holmes to Sir John Pollock (December 14, 1919), ibid., at 32.

75. *Abrams* v. *United States*, 250 U.S. 616, 630–31 (1919) (Holmes, J., dis. op.).

76. *Schaefer* v. *United States*, 251 U.S. 466, 482 (1920) (Brandeis, J., dis. op.).

77. *Gitlow* v. *New York*, 268 U.S. 652, 673 (1925) (Holmes, J., dis. op.).

78. *Whitney* v. *California*, 274 U.S. 357, 375 (1927) (Brandeis, J., dis. op.).

79. *Gitlow* v. *New York*, 268 U.S. 652 (1925).

80. See, *Herndon* v. *Lowry*, 301 U.S. 242 (1937); and *Herndon* v. *Georgia*, 295 U.S. 441 (1935).

81. Charles Evans Hughes, *The Supreme Court of the United States* (New York: Columbia University Press, 1928) 165–66.

82. *Herndon* v. *Lowry*, 301 U.S. 242, 264 (1937).

83. See *Lovell* v. *City of Griffin*, 303 U.S. 444 (1938); *Schneider* v. *New Jersey*, 308 U.S. 147 (1939); *Marsh* v. *Alabama*, 326 U.S. 296 (1940); *Cantwell* v. *Connecticut*, 310 U.S. 296 (1940); and *Cox* v. *New Hampshire*, 312 U.S. 569 (1941).

84. *Cantwell* v. *Connecticut*, 310 U.S. 296 (1940).

85. *Thornhill* v. *Alabama*, 310 U.S. 88, 102 (1940).

86. See, for example, *Thornhill* v. *Alabama*, 310 U.S. 88 (1940); *Carlson* v. *California*, 310 U.S. 106 (1940); *Bakery & Pastry & Helpers* ·v. *Wohl*, 315 U.S. 769 (1942); and *Cafeteria Employees Union* v. *Angelos*, 320 U.S. 293 (1943).

87. See *Hotel & Restaurant Employees Local* ·v. *Wisconsin Employment Relations Board*, 315 U.S. 437 (1942); *Giboney* v. *Empire Storage and Ice Company*, 336 U.S. 409 (1949); *Milk Wagon Drivers Union* v. *Meadowmoor*, 312 U.S. 287 (1941); *American Federation of*

Labor v. *Swing*, 312 U.S. 321 (1941); and *Carpenters & Joiners Union* v. *Ritter's Cafe*, 315 U.S. 722 (1942).

88. *Thornhill* v. *Alabama*, 310 U.S. 88, 105 (1940).

89. See, for example, *Cantwell* v. *Connecticut*, 310 U.S. 296 (1940); *Douglas* v. *City of Jeanette*, 319 U.S. 157 (1943); *Jones* v. *Opelika*, 319 U.S. 103 (1943); *Murdock* v. *Pennsylvania*, 319 U.S. 105 (1943); and *Follet* v. *Town of McCormick*, 321 U.S. 573 (1944).

90. Compare *Minersville School District* v. *Gobitus*, 310 U.S. 586 (1940) with *West Virginia Board of Education* v. *Barnette*, 319 U.S. 624 (1943).

91. See *Bridges* v. *California*, 314 U.S. 252 (1941); *Pennekamp* v. *Florida*, 328 U.S. 331 (1946); *Craig* v. *Harney*, 331 U.S. 367 (1947) (contempt-of-court citations for publications concerning pending trials); and *Thomas* v. *Collins*, 323 U.S. 516 (1945), and *Terminello* v. *Chicago*, 337 U.S. 1 (1949) (public speeches).

92. *Cantwell* v. *Connecticut*, 310 U.S. 296, 308, 311 (1940).

93. *Jones* v. *Opelika*, 316 U.S. 584, 608 (1942) (Stone, J., dis. op.), adopted on rehearing, 319 U.S. 103 (1943). See also *Murdock* v. *Pennsylvania*, 319 U.S. 105, 115 (1943); *Marsh* v. *Alabama*, 326 U.S. 50 (1946); *Follet* v. *Town of McCormick*, 321 U.S. 573 (1944); *Herndon* v. *Lowry*, 301 U.S. 243 (1937); *Thomas* v. *Collins*, 323 U.S. 516, 529–30 (1945).

94. See *Bridges* v. *California*, 314 U.S. 252, 295 (1941); *Craig* v. *Harney*, 331 U.S. 367, 391 (1947); and *Kovacs* v. *Cooper*, 336 U.S. 77, 96 (1949).

95. Alien Registration Act of 1940, 54 Stat. 670. On the act, see Chafee, *Free Speech in the United States* at 440–90.

96. See, for example, Labor-Management Relations Act of 1947, 61 Stat. 136, Sec. 9(h).

97. The McCarran Act of 1950, 64 Stat. 987. See also Zechariah Chafee, *The Blessings of Liberty* (Philadelphia: J. B. Lippincott, 1957) 114–57.

98. *Dennis* v. *United States*, 341 U.S. 494 (1951); *Communist Party* v. *Subversive Activities Control Board*, 367 U.S. 203 (1961).

99. See Brief for Appellants, *American Communications Associations* v. *Douds*, case no. 10, October term, 1949, Supreme Court of the United States, at 58; Brief for the Petitioners, *Steelworkers of America* v. *National Labor Relations Board*, case no. 13, October Term, 1949, at 34.

100. *American Communications Association* v. *Douds*, 339 U.S. 382, 397 (1940).

101. See, for example, *Niemotko* v. *Maryland*, 340 U.S. 268 (1951) and *Feiner* v. *New York*, 340 U.S. 315 (1951).

102. *United States* v. *Dennis*, 183 F.2d 201, 212–13 (1950).

103. Learned Hand, *The Bill of Rights* (Cambridge: Harvard University Press, 1958) 59.

104. *Dennis* v. *United States*, 341 U.S. 494, 508 (1951).

105. *Dennis* v. *United States*, 341 U.S. 494, 543–44 (1951) (Frankfurter, J., con. op.).

106. Ibid., at 580 (Black, J., dis. op.), quoting *Bridges* v. *California*, 314 U.S. 252 (1941).

107. See, for example, *International Brotherhood of Electrical Workers* v. *National Labor Relations Board*, 341 U.S. 694 (1951); *Local Union No. 10 United Association of Journeymen Plumbers and Steamfitters* v. *Graham*, 345 U.S. 192 (1953); and *International Brotherhood of Teamsters* v. *Vogt*, 354 U.S. 294 (1957).

108. See, for example, *Fowler* v. *Rhode Island*, 345 U.S. 67 (1953); *Poulos* v. *New Hampshire*, 345 U.S. 395 (1953); *Breard* v. *City of Alexandria*, 341 U.S. 622 (1951); and *Staub* v. *City of Boxley*, 355 U.S. 313 (1958). See also *Talley* v. *California*, 362 U.S. 60 (1960).

109. *Yates* v. *United States*, 354 U.S. 178, 339 (1957) (Black and Douglas, JJ., con. and dis. op.).

110. *Watkins* v. *United States*, 354 U.S. 178, 198 (1957) and *Sweez* v. *New Hampshire*, 354 U.S. 234 (1957).

111. *Watkins* v. *United States*, 354 U.S. 178, 198–99 (1957).

112. *Barenblatt* v. *United States*, 360 U.S. 109, 127–28 (1959). See also *Uphaus* v. *Wyman*, 360 U.S. 72 (1959).

113. Ibid., at 145, 151–52 (Black, J., dis. op.).

114. See *Gibson* v. *Florida Legislative Committee*, 372 U.S. 539 (1963); *DeGregory* v. *Attorney General of New Hampshire*, 383 U.S. 825 (1966). On the Court's development of a First Amendment right of association and associational privacy, see David M. O'Brien, *Privacy, Law, and Public Policy* (New York: Praeger, 1979), 155–61.

115. See *Deutch* v. *United States*, 367 U.S. 456 (1961); *Yellin* v. *United States*, 374 U.S. 109 (1963); *Russell* v. *United States*, 369 U.S. 749 1962); *Slagle* v. *Ohio*, 366 U.S. 259 (1961); and *Gojack* v. *United States*, 384 U.S. 702 (1966).

116. *Scales* v. *United States*, 367 U.S. 203 (1961) and *United States* v. *Subversive Activities Control Board*, 367 U.S. 1 (1961).

117. *United States* v. *Subversive Activities Control Board*, 367 U.S. 1, 96–97 (1961).

118. *Deutch* v. *United States*, 367 U.S. 456 (1961).

119. *Brandenburg* v. *Ohio*, 395 U.S. 444, 445 (1969) (per curiam).

120. *Wood* v. *Georgia*, 370 U.S. 375 (1962).

121. See, for example, *Detroit Edison Company* v. *National Labor Relations Board*, 440 U.S. 301 (1979); *Federal Communications Commission* v. *Pacifica Foundation*, 438 U.S. 726 (1978); *Landmark Communications, Inc.* v. *Virginia*, 435 U.S. 829 (1978); *Procunier* v. *Navarette*, 434 U.S. 555 (1978); *Smith* v. *United States*, 431 U.S. 291 (1977); *Nebraska Press Association* v. *Stuart*, 427 U.S. 539 (1976); *Greer* v. *Spock*, 424 U.S. 828 (1976); *Pell* v. *Procunier*, 417 U.S. 817 (1974); *California* v. *LaRue*, 409 U.S. 109 (1972); *Branzburg* v. *Hayes*, 408 U.S. 665 (1972); *Cole* v. *Richardson*, 405 U.S. 676 (1972); *Cohen* v. *California*, 403 U.S. 15 (1971); *Younger* v. *Harris*, 401 U.S. 37 (1971).

122. *United States* v. *Robel*, 389 U.S. 258, 268 n.20 (1967).

123. Thomas I. Emerson, *The System of Freedom of Expression* (New York: Vintage Books, 1970) 16. For further criticisms of ad hoc balancing, see Thomas I. Emerson, "Toward A General Theory of the First Amendment," 72 *Yale Law Journal* 854, 912–14 (1963); Laurent B. Frantz, "The First Amendment in the Balance," 71 *Yale Law Journal* 1424, 1441–45 (1962); Robert McKay, "The Preference for Freedom," 34 *New York University Law Review* 1182 (1959); Samuel Kirslov, "From Ginzburg to Ginsberg: The Unhurried Children's Hour in Obscenity Litigation," in *Supreme Court Review*, ed. Philip Kurland (Chicago: University of Chicago, 1968) 153; Harry Kalven, "Uninhibited, Robust, and Wide-Open—A Note on Free Speech and the Warren Court," 67 *Minnesota Law Review* 289 (1968); and Melville Nimmer, "The Right to Speak From *Times* to *Time*: First Amendment Theory Applied to Libel and Misapplied to Privacy," 56 *California Law Review* 935 (1968). Compare Wallace Mendelson, "On the Meaning of the First Amendment: Absolutes in the Balance," 50 *California Law Review* 821 (1962); Dean Alfange, Jr., "The Balancing of Interests in Free Speech Cases: In Defense of an Abused Doctrine," 2 *Law in Transition Quarterly* 35 (1965).

124. Hugo LaFayette Black, *A Constitutional Faith* (New York: Alfred Knopf, 1969) 45.

125. Frantz, "The First Amendment in the Balance," at 1434.

126. Laurent B. Frantz, "Is the First Amendment Law? A Reply To Professor Mendelson," 51 *California Law Review* 729, 731–32 (1963).

127. *Chaplinsky* v. *New Hampshire*, 315 U.S. 568 (1942).

128. *Valentine* v. *Christensen*, 361 U.S. 52 (1942).

129. *Roth* v. *United States*, 354 U.S. 476 (1957) and *Alberts* v. *California*, 354 U.S. 476 (1957). Earlier in the term the Court struck down a statute forbidding "obscene and immoral language"; see *Butler* v. *Michigan*, 352 U.S. 380 (1957).

130. *Book Named "John Cleland's Memoirs of a Woman of Pleasure"* v. *Attorney General of Massachusetts*, 383 U.S. 913 (1966). See also *Kingsley International Pictures Corporation* v. *Regents*, 360 U.S. 684 (1959); *Manual Enterprises, Inc.*, v. *Day*, 370 U.S. 478 (1962); and *Jacobellis* v. *Ohio*, 378 U.S. 184 (1964).

131. See *Stanley* v. *Georgia*, 394 U.S. 557 (1969), discussed in O'Brien, *Privacy, Law, and Public Policy* at 150–54.

132. See *Ginzburg* v. *United States*, 383 U.S. 463 (1966); *Miskin* v. *New York*, 383 U.S.

502 (1966); *Ginsberg* v. *New York*, 390 U.S. 629 (1968); and *Redrup* v. *New York*, 386 U.S. 767 (1967).

133. *Ginzburg* v. *United States*, 383 U.S. 463, 480 (1969) (Black, J., dis. op.).

134. *Book Named "John Cleland's Memoirs of a Woman of Pleasure"* v. *Attorney General of Massachusetts*, 383 U.S. 913 (1966) (Harlan, J., dis. op.) and *Jacobellis* v. *Ohio*, 378 U.S. 476, 197 (1964) (Stewart, J., con. op.).

135. *Cohen* v. *California*, 403 U.S. 15, 15 (1971).

136. *New York Times Co.* v. *Sullivan*, 376 U.S. 254, 269, 270 (1964), quoting *Roth* v. *United States*, 354 U.S. 476, 484 (1957); and ibid., at 266, quoting *Associated Press* v. *United States*, 326 U.S. 1, 20 (1945).

137. *Rosenblatt* v. *Baer*, 383 U.S. 75 (1966).

138. *Associated Press* v. *Walker*, 388 U.S. 130 (1967) and *Curtis Publishing Co.* v. *Butts*, 388 U.S. 130 (1967).

139. Emerson, *The System of Freedom of Expression* at 16.

140. John Hart Ely, "Flag Desecration," 88 *Harvard Law Review* 1482, 1493 (1975).

141. See *Gooding* v. *Wilson*, 405 U.S. 518 (1972); *Watts* v. *United States*, 394, 705 (1969); and *Eaton* v. *City of Tulsa*, 415 U.S. 697 (1974).

142. *Monitor Patriot Corporation* v. *Roy*, 401 U.S. 265 (1971).

143. *Greenbelt Cooperative Publishing Association* v. *Bresler*, 398 U.S. 6 (1970).

144. *Rosenbloom* v. *Metromedia*, 403 U.S. 29 (1971).

145. *Old Dominion Branch No. 496* v. *Austin*, 418 U.S. 264 (1974).

146. *Rosenbloom* v. *Metromedia*, 403 U.S. 29, 31–32 (1971).

147. *Gertz* v. *Robert Welch, Inc.*, 418 U.S. 323, 339 (1974). See also Walter Berns, *The First Amendment and the Future of American Democracy* (New York: Basic Books, 1976).

148. *Time, Inc.* v. *Firestone*, 424 U.S. 448 (1976). See also *Wolston* v. *Reader's Digest*, 99 S.Ct. 2701 (1979).

149. See *Cox Broadcasting Corp.* v. *Cohn*, 420 U.S. 469, 496 (1975); and *Time Inc.* v. *Hill*, 424 U.S. 374 (1974) and *Cantrell* v. *Forest City Publishing Company*, 419 U.S. 245 (1974), discussed in O'Brien, *Privacy, Law, and Public Policy* at 161–67.

150. *Smith* v. *Daily Mail Publishing Company*, 99 S.Ct. 2667 (1979).

151. *Herbert* v. *Lando*, 99 S.Ct. 1635 (1979).

152. See *Roth* v. *United States*, 354 U.S. 476 (1957); *Marcus* v. *Search Warrant*, 367 U.S. 717 (1961); *Jacobellis* v. *Ohio*, 378 U.S. 184 (1964); *Mishkin* v. *New York*, 383 U.S. 502 (1966); *A Book Named "John Cleland's Memoir's of a Woman of Pleasure"* v. *Attorney General of Massachusetts*, 383 U.S. 913 (1966); *Keyishian* v. *Board of Regents*, 385 U.S. 589 (1967); *Ginsberg* v. *New York*, 390 U.S. 629 (1968) (majority opinions). *Manual* v. *Day*, 370 U.S. 478 (1962) (concurring opinion). *Kingsley Books, Inc.* v. *Brown*, 354 U.S. 436 (1957) (dissenting opinion).

153. See *Blout* v. *Rizzi*, 400 U.S. 410 (1971) and *Gooding* v. *Wilson*, 405 U.S. 518 (1972) (majority opinions); *McKinney* v. *Alabama*, 424 U.S. 669 (1976) (concurring opinion); *Calfironia* v. *LaRue*, 409 U.S. 109 (1972); *Miller* v. *California*, 413 U.S. 15 (1973); *Paris Adult Theatre I* v. *Slaton*, 413 U.S. 49 (1973); *Heller* v. *New York*, 413 U.S. 483 (1973); *United States* v. *Twelve 200-Foot Reels of Film*, 413 U.S. 123 (1973); *United States* v. *Orito*, 413 U.S. 139 (1973); *Kaplan* v. *California*, 413 U.S. 115 (1973); *Hamling* v. *United States*, 418 U.S. 87 (1974); *Jenkins* v. *Georgia*, 418 U.S. 153 (1974); *Splawn* v. *California*, 97 S.Ct. 1987 (1977); *Federal Communications Commission* v. *Pacifica Foundation*, 99 S.Ct. 3026 (1978) (dissenting opinions).

154. *Miller* v. *California*, 413 U.S. 15 (1973).

155. See, for example, *Paris Adult Theatre I* v. *Slaton*, 413 U.S. 49 (1973); *United States* v. *Reidel*, 402 U.S. 351 (1971); *United States* v. *Orito*, 413 U.S. 139 (1973); *United States* v. *Twelve 200-Foot Reels of Super 8mm Film*, 413 U.S. 123 (1973); *Marks* v. *United States*, 97 S.Ct. 990 (1977). See also *Federal Communications Commission* v. *Pacifica Foundation*, 98 S.Ct. 3026 (1978) and *Young* v. *American Mini Theatres*, 427 U.S. 50 (1976); and compare

Cohen v. *California*, 403 U.S. 15 (1971) and *Erzonznik* v. *City of Jacksonville*, 422 U.S. 205 (1975). For further dicussion of the cases see O'Brien, *Privacy, Law, and Public Policy* at 149–55.

156. See *Novick, Haim and Unique Specialities Inc.* v. *U.S. District Court*, 423 U.S. 911 (1975).

157. See *Jenkins* v. *Georgia*, 418 U.S. 153 (1974).

158. *Young* v. *American Mini Theatres*, 427 U.S. 50, 63–73 (1976). See also *Federal Communications Commission* v. *Pacifica Foundation*, 98 S.Ct. 3026 (1978).

159. See, for example, *Paris Adult Theatre I.* v. *Slaton*, 413 U.S. 49, 73 (1973) (Brennan, J., dis. op.).

160. *Hamling* v. *United States*, 418 U.S. 87, 141 (1974) (Douglas, J., dis. op.).

161. *Bigelow* v. *Virginia*, 421 U.S. 809, 822 (1976). See also *Pittsburg Press Co.* v. *Pittsburg Commission on Human Relations*, 413 U.S. 376 (1973).

162. *Virginia State Board of Pharmacy* v. *Virginia Citizens Consumer Council*, 425 U.S. 748, 765 (1976).

163. Ibid., at 785, 787 (Rehnquist, J., dis. op.).

164. See *Friedman* v. *Rogers*, 99 S.Ct. 887, 894 (1979). See also *Bates* v. *State Bar of Arizona*, 433 U.S. 350 (1977) (upholding lawyers' advertisements for basic services and prices). For critical discussions of the Burger Court's treatment of "commercial speech" see Note, "The Consumers Right to Know," 12 *New England Law Review* 991 (1977); Comment, "A Step Forward For The Consumer: A Constitutional Right-to-Know In Prescription Drug Price Advertising," 13 *Urban Law Annual* 179 (1977); C. Edwin Baker, "Commercial Speech: A Problem in the Theory of Freedom," 62 *Iowa Law Review* 1 (1976); and Thomas H. Jackson and John Calvin Jeffries, Jr., "Commercial Speech: Economic Due Process and the First Amendment," 65 *Virginia Law Review* 1 (1979).

165. See *New York Times* v. *Sullivan*, 376 U.S. 254 (1964) (newspapers); *Garrison* v. *Louisiana*, 379 U.S. 64 (1964) (district attorney); *Henry* v. *Collins*, 380 U.S. 356 (1965) (individual arrested for disturbing the peace); and *Linn* v. *Plant Guard Workers Local 114*, 383 U.S. 53 (1966) (publishers of union leaflets).

166. *First National Bank of Boston* v. *Bellotti*, 435 U.S. 765, 782 (1978).

167. See *Lewis Publishing Company* v. *Morgan*, 299 U.S. 288, 304 (1913) and *United States ex rel. Milwaukee Social Democratic Publishing Company* v. *Burleson*, 255 U.S. 407 (1921). See also *Ex parte Jackson*, 96 S.Ct. 767, 736 (1879) and *In re Rapier*, 143 U.S. 110, 134–35 (1892) (permitting censorship of the mails).

168. See *Toledo Newspaper Company* v. *United States*, 247 U.S. 402 (1918) (no immunity for contempt of court); *Peck* v. *Tribune Company*, 213 U.S. 185 (1909) and *White* v. *Nicholls*, 3 How. 266 (1845) (no exemption from libel law); and *United States* v. *Dickey*, 268 U.S. 378 (1925) (right to publish personal income tax returns, which at the time Congress required to be posted in a public place).

169. See, for example, *Lovell* v. *City of Griffin*, 303 U.S. 444, 452 (1938); *Schneider* v. *New Jersey*, 308 U.S. 147 (1949); *Thomas* v. *Collins*, 323 U.S. 516, 530 (1945); and *Prince* v. *Massachusetts*, 321 U.S. 158, 164 (1944).

170. *Grosjean* v. *American Press Association Company*, 297 U.S. 233, 247, 250 (1936).

171. *Associated Press* v. *United States*, 326 U.S. 1, 20 (1945) (upholding antitrust laws). See also *Mabee* v. *White Plains Publishing Company*, 327 U.S. 178 (1946) and *Oklahoma Press Publishing Company* v. *Walling*, 327 U.S. 186 (1946) (upholding application of Fair Labor Standards Act to newspapers).

172. See *Bridges* v. *California*, 314 U.S. 252, 265 (1941); *Pennekamp* v. *Florida*, 328 U.S. 331 (1946); and *Craig* v. *Harney*, 331 U.S. 367 (1947).

173. *Mills* v. *Alabama*, 384 U.S. 214, 219 (1966).

174. See *Columbia Broadcasting System* v. *Democratic National Committee*, 412 U.S. 94 (1973) and *Miami Herald Publishing Company* v. *Tornillo*, 418 U.S. 241 (1974).

175. See *Federal Communications Commission* v. *National Citizens Consumer Com-*

mittee for Broadcasting, 98 S.Ct. 2096 (1978) (upholding FCC rules on cross-ownership of broadcast media and newspapers).

176. *Branzburg* v. *Hayes*, 408 U.S. 665 (1972).

177. *Zurcher* v. *Stanford Daily*, 436 U.S. 547 (1978).

178. See *Saxbe* v. *Washington Post*, 417 U.S. 843 (1974); *Pell* v. *Procunier*, 417 U.S. 817 (1974); and *Houchins* v. *KQED*, 98 S.Ct. 2588 (1978).

179. *Cox Broadcasting Corporation* v. *Cohn*, 420 U.S. 469, 491–92 (1975). See also Warren E. Burger, "The Interdependence of Judicial and Journalistic Independence," 63 *Georgetown Law Journal* 1195 (1975); Stewart, "Or of the Press"; and John Paul Stevens, "Some Thoughts About A General Rule," 21 *Arizona Law Review* 599 (1979).

180. *Nixon* v. *Warner Communications*, 435 U.S. 589, 609 (1978). See also Presidential Recordings and Materials Preservation Act, 88 Stat. 1695 (1974) and *Nixon* v. *Administrator of General Services*, 433 U.S. 425 (1977) (upholding the constitutionality of the Act).

181. On the suggestion of a fiduciary duty see *Nebraska Press Association* v. *Stuart*, 427 U.S. 539, 560 (1976).

182. *Branzburg* v. *Hayes*, 408 U.S. 665, 703–4 (1972).

183. See, for example, *Davis* v. *Beason*, 133 U.S. 333, 342 (1890); *Reynolds* v. *United States*, 98 U.S. 145, 161–64 (1878); *United States* v. *Seeger*, 380 U.S. 163 (1965); and *Welsh* v. *United States*, 398 U.S. 333 (1970).

184. Trial transcript, *Branzburg* v. *Hayes*, No. 70–85, United States Supreme Court, October Term, 1971, at 13.

185. Office of Media Liaison, White House Press Office, *Carter Administration Stanford Daily Announcement*, December 13, 1978, at 3–4. See also 125 *Congressional Record* H1866, S3771 (daily ed., April 2, 1979). For discussions of the different kinds and obstacles to adopting federal and state shield laws see Sam J. Ervin, Jr., "In Pursuit of A Press Privilege," 11 *Harvard Journal on Legislation* 233 (1974); Note, "Shield Statutes: A Changing Problem in Light of Branzburg," 25 *Wayne Law Review* 1381 (1979); and Cohen, *Journalists' Privilege To Withhold Information in Judicial and Legislative Proceedings* at 9–31.

186. *Branzburg* v. *Hayes*, 408 U.S. 665, 703, 706 (1972). On the practical problems for journalists without a guaranteed privilege of confidentiality see Walter Cronkite, *Brief amicus curiae*, The New York Times Company, *Branzburg* v. *Hayes* at 18–19; James Goodale, "Branzburg v. Hayes and the Developing Qualified Privilege for Newmen," 26 *Hastings Law Journal* 709 (1975); and Vince Blasi, "The Newsman's Privilege: An Empirical Study," 70 *Michigan Law Review* 229 (1971). See also Note, "The Rights of Sources—The Critical Element in the Clash over Reporter's Privilege," 88 *Yale Law Journal* 1202 (1979).

187. Ibid. at 721, 725, 726, n.2 (Douglas, and Stewart, JJ., dis. ops.).

188. Ibid. at 703 (White, J., majority opinion).

CHAPTER 4

FIRST AMENDMENT AFFIRMATIVE ACTION

[T]here is no First Amendment right of access in the public or the press to judicial or other governmental proceedings.
Justice William Rehnquist, *Gannett Co.* v. *DePasquale* (1979)

These expressly guaranteed [First Amendment] freedoms share a common core purpose of assuring freedom of communication on matters relating to the functioning of government.
Chief Justice Warren E. Burger, *Richmond Newspapers, Inc.* v. *Virginia* (1980)

"There remain after nearly two hundred years unresolved questions on where the boundaries of these [First Amendment] rights shall be drawn." So concluded Justice William H. Rehnquist on the occasion of delivering the 1976 William O. Douglas Lecture at Gonzaga University School of Law, Spokane, Washington.[1] A degree of uncertainty in constitutional line drawing inescapably arises from the irrepressible human element in judicial decision making and the inexorably changing political circumstances surrounding the Court.[2]

In the twentieth century, the Court's interpretation of the First Amendment remained remarkably coherent in two fundamental respects. As the last chapter showed, on the one hand, the speech and press clauses were historically deemed constitutionally redundant, and a structuralist analysis *cum* preferred status for the institutional press was steadfastly repudiated. The scope of the First Amendment, on the other hand, was construed to guarantee the freedom from impermissible restraints on communications, but not the right of the public to demand and obtain information from the government. Traditionally, the amendment fell short of constitutionally mandating affirmative governmental action to either inform citizens about or grant their access to policy-making materials and institutions.

Constitutional history establishes, in Justice John Paul Stevens's words, the "general rule" that affirmative rights to receive, gather, and demand access to government information are outside the boundaries of First Amendment guarantees. During his address in September 1979, at the University of Arizona College of Law dedication ceremony, after quoting Justice Blackmun's observation that "this Court heretofore has not found . . . any First Amendment right of access to judicial or other governmental proceedings," he proposed that "[t]hat statement fairly identifies what one might characterize as a 'general rule' that is now on the firing line." According to Justice Stevens, "[t]he rule draws a sharp distinction between the dissemination of information and ideas, on the one hand, and the acquisition of newsworthy matter on the other." Concluding, he added: "Whereas the Court has accorded virtually absolute protection to the former, it has never squarely held that the latter is entitled to any constitutional protection whatsoever."[3]

In the 1970s that general rule was indeed on the firing line, with members of the press increasingly contending that the First Amendment grants the public and the press affirmative constitutional rights to receive, gather, or obtain access to government information and facilities. In short, the First Amendment embodies a directly enforceable public's right to know. Litigation over First Amendment affirmative rights, like that over press exceptionalism, represents nothing less than a demand for a constitutional revolution. Unlike litigation over special press privileges, however, claims to First Amendment affirmative rights are based on the Court's own functional analysis of the amendment as indirectly ensuring the public's informational interests.

Thus, although the amendment traditionally comprehended only individuals' freedom from restraints on their communications, members of the press and some constitutional scholars argue that affirmative rights to acquire information exist as a corollary of First Amendment freedoms. Thomas Emerson, for example, explains: "Reduced to its simplest terms [the public's right to know] includes two closely related features: first, the right to read, to listen, to see, and to otherwise receive communications; and, second, the right to obtain information as a basis for transmitting ideas or facts to others. Together these constitute the reverse side of a coin from the right to communicate. But the coin is one piece, namely, the system of freedom of expression." He further argues that "the right to know serves much the same function in our society as the right to communicate. It is essential to personal self-fulfillment. It is a significant method for seeking the truth, or at least for seeking the better answer. It is necessary for collective decision-making in a democratic society."[4] Justice Thurgood Marshall likewise observed:

[I]n a variety of contexts this Court has held that the First Amendment protects the right to receive information and ideas, the freedom to hear as well as the freedom to speak. The reason for this is that the First

Amendment protects a process . . . and the right to speak and hear—including the right to inform others and to be informed about public issues—are inextricably part of that process. The freedom to speak and the freedom to hear are inseparable; they are two sides of the same coin. But the coin itself is the process of thought and discussion.[5]

First Amendment freedoms, according to Emerson and Justice Marshall, are to be comprehended with the metaphor of a coin. The amendment connotes on the one side a guarantee for the freedom from restraints on the dissemination of information and on the other side a guarantee for affirmative rights to receive or acquire access to information.

The simplicity of the coin metaphor is deceptively appealing. Constitutional developments under the First Amendment established by the 1970s extensive protection for individuals' freedom from restraints on their communications, but the Court's underlying jurisprudence neither mandated nor required enforceable constitutional rights to receive information. Although Justice Marshall understood that "[t]he First Amendment means that Government has no power to thwart the process of free discussion, to 'abridge' the freedoms necessary to make the process work," neither constitutional history nor prevailing judicial politics support claims to independent First Amendment affirmative rights. Before the 1970s, members of the Court on occasion did acknowledge the amendment's embodiment of affirmative rights, such as the right to receive and gather or obtain information, but only in *dicta* and dissenting opinions. Furthermore, throughout the 1950s and 1960s affirmative rights to acquire information were recognized only as reciprocal or corollary rights, not independently assertable constitutional rights.

Litigation over First Amendment affirmative rights therefore poses the dilemma of constitutional common law and brings to bear the fundamental issue in judicial line drawing; namely, the legitimate scope of judicial creativity in constitutional interpretation.[6] Unlike common law judges, who may expand the scope of legal rights, justices of the Supreme Court are, as Thomas Jefferson said, "bound down by the chains of the Constitution." Accordingly, judicial creativity in constitutional interpretation is constrained in theory, if not always in practice, by parchment guarantees. Judicial creativity differs not only in degree but in kind when used to expand the scope of constitutional rights by broadly construing enumerated guarantees and when used to construct new "constitutional rights." The difference between *construing* constitutional provisions and the *construction* of new constitutional rights is largely what distinguishes legitimate and illegitimate exercises of judicial review. The difference between permissible judicial creativity and extraconstitutional judicial ingenuity in fashioning constitutional rights from within the "shadows"[7] of the Constitution often becomes obscured, and perhaps thereby rendered more palatable, but no less crucial, by the incremental process of constitutional adjudication.

RIGHTS TO RECEIVE AND GATHER INFORMATION

Dictum in a 1943 Jehovah's Witness case, *Martin* v. *City of Struthers*, that "freedom [of speech and press] necessarily protects the right to receive," provided the genesis for litigation over First Amendment affirmative rights.[8] In subsequent *dicta* the Court elaborated the right to receive as a corollary of the First Amendment applicable to disseminating materials about organized labor;[9] religious, educational, and political matters;[10] and commercial speech[11] as well as personal correspondence.[12] In these cases, however, the Court comprehended an affirmative right to receive to exist as a corollary of the enumerated rights in the First Amendment. For example, when invalidating a statute empowering the postmaster to detain any unsealed foreign mailings of communist political propaganda until obtaining the addressee's notification to deliver the mailings, Justice Douglas, writing for the Court in *Lamont* v. *Postmaster General*, explained: "We rest on the narrow ground that the addressee in order to receive his mail must request in writing that it be delivered. This amounts in our judgment to an unconstitutional abridgment of the addressee's First Amendment rights."[13] Here, Justice Douglas understood the right to receive as a reciprocal, rather than an independent, right with respect to the express guarantees of the First Amendment. Justice Brennan, concurring in *Lamont*, was willing to go further, observing:

> It is true that the First Amendment contains no specific guarantee of access to publications. However, the protection of the Bill of Rights goes beyond the specific guarantees to protect from congressional abridgment those equally fundamental personal rights necessary to make the express guarantees fully meaningful. . . . I think the right to receive publications is such a fundamental right.[14]

Justice Brennan's broad interpretation of the First Amendment as legitimating an independent right to receive failed to win acceptance with his colleagues. Majorities of both the Warren and Burger Courts later affirmed that any constitutionally protected right to receive exists only concomitantly with enumerated First Amendment rights in holding that individuals have the right not to receive information.[15]

The import of litigation over First Amendment affirmative rights lies in securing a independent constitutional right that gives standing to individuals to challenge governmental withholding of information. Affirmative rights appear compelling in those situations where "the speaker, who is normally the party most likely to seek vindication of the right to free expression, may not be in a position to assert that, and the listener or reader may find it necessary to defend the right of expression by invoking the constitutional right to know."[16] Yet, because the Court acknowledges a First Amendment right to receive as only a coordinate with each individual's right to free speech and press, individuals may claim a right to receive only after another individual seeks unsuccessfully to exercise the First Amendment guarantee to disseminate information. In other words, the Court's recognition of the right to receive extends to only protect the intended recipients of information from governmental interference with the voluntary dissemination of information, not to entitle public access to confidential governmental information.[17]

In 1972 the Burger Court encountered in *Kliendienst* v. *Mandel* its first opportunity to consider the merits of claims to an independent right to receive. The case arose when the U.S. attorney general refused to grant a temporary nonimmigrant visa to a Belgian journalist and Marxian theoretician whom American organizers had invited to participate in academic conferences and discussions. The majority found that the First Amendment guarantees no such independent and enforceable right against the government. Indeed, any infringement of First Amendment rights was not to be balanced against the government's bona fide exercise of discretion in the exclusion of aliens. In framing the issue for the six-member majority Justice Blackmun wrote: "The case, therefore, comes down to the narrow issue whether the First Amendment confers upon the appellee professors, because they wish to hear, speak, and debate with Mandel in person, the ability to determine that Mandel should be permitted to enter the country or, in other words, to compel the Attorney General to allow Mandel's admission."[18] After acknowledging previous cases citing a First Amendment right to receive, the Court ruled that when the attorney general decides for a legitimate reason to refuse to grant a visa to an alien, as authorized by Congress, courts may not weigh that decision against the First Amendment interests of those desiring to communicate with the alien. The majority thus rejected the broad interpretation that "[t]he First Amendment involves not only the right to speak and publish but also the right to hear, to learn, to know," advocated by dissenting Justices Douglas, Marshall, and Brennan.[19] The dissenters had argued that the First Amendment embodies affirmative constitutional rights of the public. Justice Douglas would have permitted discretionary exclusion of aliens only where there were issues of "national security, importation of drugs, and the like"; Justice Marshall would have required the showing of a compelling governmental interest outweighing the infringement of First Amendment affirmative rights of the public to be informed.

Kleindienst v. *Mandel* complemented the Warren Court's decision seven years earlier in *Zemel* v. *Rusk*, upholding the secretary of state's passport restrictions on travel to Cuba as authorized by the Passport Act of 1926 and the Immigration and Nationality Act of 1952. In *Zemel*, Chief Justice Warren, writing for the Court, acknowledged that the restriction "renders less than wholly free the free flow of information concerning that country," but pointed to the dangers of constructing a directly enforceable public's right to know:

There are few restrictions on action which could not be clothed by ingenious argument in the garb of decreased data flow. For example, the prohibition on unauthorized entry into the White House diminishes the citizen's opportunities to gather information he might find relevant to his opinion of the way the country is being run, but that does not make entry into the White House a First Amendment right. The right to speak and publish does not carry with it the unrestricted right to gather information.[20]

The majority in *Zemel*, as in *Kleindienst*, comprehended that the First Amendment does not confer on the public an independent and unqualified affirmative right to demand information from the government.

Kleindienst and *Zemel*, along with rulings upholding time, place, and manner restrictions on the dissemination of communications, render incontrovertible the fundamental point that the First Amendment does not convey an affirmative right to receive that outweighs governmental interests in imposing reasonable limits on the free flow of information. The two cases emphasize that restrictions on the free flow of information are permissible under the First Amendment when Congress has enacted legislation and where governmental officials exercise their discretion under that legislation even-handedly.

ACCESS TO GOVERNMENT FACILITIES

Two years after *Kleindienst*, members of the press pushed for First Amendment affirmative rights when challenging policies imposing blanket prohibitions of personal interviews between reporters and individually designated inmates in state and federal prisons. Writing for bare majorities in *Pell* v. *Procunier* and *Saxbe* v. *Washington Post*, Justice Stewart reaffirmed that "the First Amendment does not guarantee the press a constitutional right of special access to information not available to the public generally."[21] Hence, the Court found it "unnecessary to engage in a delicate balancing of . . . penal considerations against the legitimate demands of the First Amendment."

Justice Douglas, in dissent, joined by Justices Marshall and Brennan, again argued that the First Amendment embodies an affirmative right to know and confers special privileges on the press so it may vindicate the public's interests in information about the operation of government. Here, he found the prison regulations on press interviews to be "far broader than is necessary to protect any legitimate governmental interests and . . . an unconstitutional infringement on the public's right to know protected by the free press guarantee of the First Amendment." He thought, moreover, that special privileges for the press to receive information and acquire access to facilities not open to the public defensible because "prohibition of visits by the public has no practical effect upon their right to know beyond that achieved by the exclusion of the press. The average citizen is most unlikely to inform himself about the operation of the prison system by requesting an interview with a particular inmate with whom he has no prior relationship. He is likely instead, in a society which values a free press, to rely upon the media for information."[22]

Justice Powell also dissented in *Pell* and *Saxbe*, finding that the absolute prohibition on prisoner-press interviews "significantly impairs the right of the people to a free flow of information and ideas on the conduct of the Government." Agreeing with Justice Douglas, he further explained that "[t]he underlying right is the right of the public generally. The press is the necessary representative of the public's interests in this context and the instrumentality which effects the public's right." Justice Powell, however, emphasized that "governmental regulations should not be policed in the name of a 'right to know' unless they significantly affect the societal function of the First Amendment." He indicated that he would uphold press interview policies that accommodate both governmental and First Amendment interests, and cautioned against excessive claims to a First Amendment right to know: "Common sense and proper respect for the constitutional commitment of the affairs of state to the Legislative and Executive Branches should deter the Judiciary from chasing the right-of-access rainbows that an advocate's eye can spot in virtually all governmental actions."[23]

Pell and *Saxbe* demonstrate the appeal of the political ideal of an informed public and highlight the divisions within the Burger Court over interpreting that ideal and the First Amendment. Those divisions emerged four years later, in 1978, with a bare majority again rejecting claims by the media for a right of access to prison facilities in *Houchins* v. *KQED. KQED,* a broadcasting station, challenged as a denial of First Amendment rights the refusal by the Alameda County jail to permit access to a portion of the jail where a prisoner's suicide had occurred and was reportedly a result of the conditions of the prison. Chief Justice Burger, in an opinion joined by Justices White and Rehnquist, examined prior rulings in rejecting any claim that the press is entitled to special privileges because of the role the press plays in providing information to the public. He emphasized that "an analysis of those cases reveals that the Court was concerned with the freedom of the media to *communicate* information once it is obtained, [the cases do not intimate] that the Constitution compels the government to provide the media with information or access to it on demand." He therefore concluded:

> [KQED's] argument is flawed, not only because it lacks precedential support and is contrary to statements in this Court's opinions, but also because it invites the Court to involve itself in what is clearly a legislative task which the Constitution has left to the political process. Whether the

government should open penal institutions in the manner sought by [KQED] is a question of policy which a legislative body might appropriately resolve one way or the other.[24]

The plurality opinion in *Houchins* reaffirmed the Court's position in *Pell* and *Saxbe* that the First Amendment neither entails special rights of access to the press nor the legitimacy of a directly enforceable constitutional right to know. The author of *Pell* and *Saxbe*, Justice Stewart, wrote a concurring opinion in *Houchins* to underscore that "[t]he First and Fourteenth Amendments do not guarantee the public a right of access to information generated or controlled by government, nor do they guarantee the press any basic right of access superior to that of the public generally." After considering the importance of the press to society, however, he added that "terms of access that are reasonably imposed on individual members of the public may, if they impede effective reporting without sufficient justification, be unreasonable as applied to journalists who are there to convey to the general public what the visitors see."[25] In other words, although neither the public nor the press has a First Amendment right of access per se, on Justice Stewart's structuralist theory, once access to government facilities is granted to the public generally, the press may be able to gain access on more favorable terms so it can report adequately upon the conditions and activities in the accessible areas.

Justice Stevens, having assumed Justice Douglas's seat on the high bench, maintained with slight modification his predecessor's position expressed in *Pell* and *Saxbe*. In *Houchins* Justice Stevens wrote the dissenting opinion joined by Justices Brennan and Powell. In their view the basic question was whether the Alameda County jail's "policies, which cut off the flow of information at its source, abridged the public's right to be informed about [the jail's] conditions." Justice Stevens assumed an activist posture toward the First Amendment because "[w]ithout some protection for the acquisition of information about the operation of public institutions . . . by the public the process of self-governance contemplated by the framers would be stripped of its substance."[26]

By 1978 the Burger Court was ostensibly divided between the chief justice and Justices Rehnquist, Blackmun, White, and Stewart on the one hand and Justices Stevens, Powell, Brennan, and Marshall on the other hand. The division arose because of the latter justices' willingness to pursue judicial creativity in fashioning a limited but constitutionally enforceable right to know by extending previous *dicta* on First Amendment affirmative rights. The latter, unlike the former, bloc of justices were furthermore willing to concede special privileges for the press so journalists may inform the public of vital issues and current events. They were thus willing to substitute their judgments for those of legislatures in deciding what and how much the public is or is not entitled to know. In contrast, the chief justice and his colleagues found First Amendment affirmative rights illegitimate in terms of the historical background of, and developing case law under, the amendment as well as pernicious inasmuch as denomination of such affirmative rights would expand the Court's supervisory role and promote entanglement with legislative and administrative policy-making.

POPULAR INFORMATION, TRIALS, AND PUBLIC FORUMS

Unlike prison facilities, courtrooms and trials have historically been open to members of the public and press both at common law and under the Sixth Amendment's provision that "In all criminal prosecutions the accused shall enjoy the right to a speedy and public trial." Yet, before *Richmond Newspapers, Inc.* v. *Virginia* in 1980, the Supreme Court never squarely addressed the question of whether the public and the press possess a constitutional right of access to compel open trials.[27] The Court's seven to one decision, with Justice Powell not participating, was particularly remarkable because a year earlier, in *Gannett Co.* v. *DePasquale*, a bare majority ruled that neither members of the public nor the press may constitutionally claim access to attend pretrial hearings.[28] The plurality opinions in both cases, moreover, illustrate the extent to which litigation over First Amendment affirmative rights fragmented the Burger Court.

A presumption of openness rooted in the common law background of the Sixth Amendment underlies a defendant's right to a speedy and public trial. Open judicial proceedings were established by the seventeenth century in common law practice, stemming from earlier Anglo-Saxon customs. In 1612, Lord Edward Coke emphasized the "great importance" of the principle that "all causes ought be heard, ordered and determined . . . openly,"[29] and the seventeenth and eighteenth centuries commentators, such as Jeremy Bentham and Sir William Blackstone, on English common law practice acknowledged both the tradition and salutary effects of publicity.[30] As with the First Amendment, the Sixth Amendment was thought to incorporate common law practice. As Joseph Story noted, "in declaring that the accused shall enjoy the right to a speedy and public trial [the Sixth Amendment] does not but follow out the established course of the common law in all trials for crimes. The trial is always public."[31] Commentators such as Thomas Cooley and John Wigmore in the nineteenth and twentieth centuries likewise affirmed the tradition and auspicious policies underlying public trials.[32] In addition, while all states recognize the right to a public trial, 41 states acknowledge that right in their constitutions, in 7 states public trials are considered part of the common law tradition, and only in Massachusetts and Virginia does a statute provide the basis for the right.

The policy considerations underlying common law practice and state and federal constitutional provisions for public trials are numerous. The publicity of trials is principally viewed as deterring judicial arbitrariness, thereby ensuring the accused a right to a fair trial. In 1827, for example, Bentham observed: "[t]he knowledge that every criminal trial is subject to contemporaneous review in the forum of public opinion is an effective restraint on possible abuse of judicial power."[33] The presence of members of the public is also thought to reduce the possibility of a witness's perjury while at the same time encouraging individuals who possess relevant information to come forth and testify. Finally, open trials serve important public interests, as Lord Campbell proclaimed in 1857: "It is of great consequence that the public should know what takes place in Court."[34] Publicity both educates people about the operation of the judiciary and provides an opportunity for members of the public to scrutinize the administration of justice.

Although state and federal courts were generally open to the public and recognized the necessity for publicity, members of the public and the press never possessed an unqualified legal right—regardless of whether that right was claimed as a common law, statutory, or constitutional right—to attend criminal trials. While courts recognized, as the Ohio State Supreme Court put it in 1906, that "the people have the right to know what is being done in their court,"[35] fundamentally, the right to a public trial remained that of defendants, not the public. That is, the "universal rule against secret trials"[36] primarily guarantees procedural fairness and only derivatively the public's interests in judicial proceedings. At common law and under the Sixth Amendment, access to judicial proceedings may be restricted and neither the public nor the press could compel openness. In the late nineteenth century, Thomas Cooley, for example, observed:

> By this [provision that trials be public] is not meant that every person who sees fit shall in all cases be permitted to attend criminal trials; because there are many cases where, from the character of the charge, and the nature of the evidence by which it is to be supported, the motives to attend the trial on the part of portions of the community would be of the worst character, and where a regard to public morals and public decency would require that at least the young be excluded from hearing and witnessing the evidence of human depravity which the trial must necessarily bring to light. The requirement for a public trial is for the benefit of the accused; that the public may see he is fairly dealt with and not unjustly condemned.[37]

Public and press access remains at the control of the court, and judges may limit access to perserve the decorum of the courtroom or prevent prejudicial publicity. Additionally, under state statutes and common law some limitations on public and press access are permitted per se. Several states for example, permit judges to exclude journalists from juvenile courts and to exclude both minors and journalists from trials concerning matters thought to be scandalous or obscene.[38]

Before *Gannett* and *Richmond Newspapers* the Supreme Court never directly ruled on the public's right to attend judicial proceedings. The Court's rulings on courtroom secrecy, however, did closely follow common law practice and policies recognizing the auspicious consequences of publicity. In the 1940s, when the Court first turned to the issue of courtroom secrecy, it acknowledged the interests of both defendants and the public in open trials: "In view of this nation's historic distrust of secret proceedings, their inherent dangers to freedom, and the universal requirement of our federal and state governments that criminal trials be public, the Fifth Amendment's guarantee that no one shall be deprived of his liberty without due process of law means at least that an accused cannot be thus sentenced to prison." The Court added, nonetheless, that "[w]hatever other benefits the guarantee to an accused that his trial be conducted in public may confer upon our society, the guarantee has always been recognized as a safeguard against any attempt to employ our courts as instruments of persecution."[39] Subsequently, the Court affirmed the public's interests in open trials,[40] but ruled that the Sixth Amendment guarantees only the rights of the accused, not the public. The Court, however, also noted that "although a defendant can, under some circumstances, waive his constitutional right to a public trial, he has no absolute right to compel a private trial."[41] Under the Sixth Amendment, members of the public and press therefore have no constitutional right to compel open trials, but neither do defendants have a right to a closed trial. Yet, because the Sixth Amendment guarantees an accused person's rights, and only derivatively the public's interests, judges may restrict public access and publicity to ensure due process and procedural fairness.[42]

When judges restrict or constrain publicity about trials the press may still assert its interests by relying on the First Amendment. Under the First Amendment the interests of the public and press are distinguishable from those interests in publicity recognized by the Sixth Amendment. First Amendment claims to open trials are grounded on individuals' right of free speech and press and the public's interests in freedom of information, rather than on a particular concern about criminal justice. In 1946 Justice Frankfurter, for example, declared that "trials must be public and the public have a deep interest in trials."[43] A year later, his frequent interlocutor Justice Douglas likewise observed: "The trial is a public event. What transpires in the court room is public property."[44] Some years later Justice Frankfurter echoed Justice Douglas's sentiments, when protesting the Court's denial of a writ of *certarori*: "One of the demands of a democratic society is that the public should know what goes on in courts by being told by the press what happens there, to the end that the public may judge whether our system of criminal justice is fair and right."[45] Precisely because the First Amendment, not the Sixth Amendment, comprehends the public's broader interests in freedom of information, that amendment provides a basis for challenging restraints on publicity or access to trials even when defendants find secrecy benign or demand trial closure to guard against adverse publicity—publicity that might prove prejudicial or merely reveal personally embarrassing facts or other sensitive information such as the identity of witnesses or confidential governmental information.[46]

By the 1960s the competing interests of defendants and the public gave rise to the "fair trial/free press" controversy.[47] Sensational murder trials such as those of Dr. Sam Sheppard and Charles Simants necessitated judicial accommodation of the Sixth Amendment right of defendants to a fair trial with the First Amendment interests of the public in obtaining information. Actually, since constitutional rights are assertable only against the government, not other individuals, the fair trial/free press controversy demanded that the Court reconcile the government's actions in limiting publicity or access to trials with the First Amendment's rights of the public and the press. Accordingly, in 1965 the president of the American Bar Association, Lewis Powell, not yet on the high bench, cautioned that,

> [W]e must avoid being confused by generalizations and slogans . . . some persons have talked about "a public right to know" as if it were a constitutional right. These generalizations miss the point. . . . We must bear in mind that the primary purpose of a public trial and of the media's right as a part of the public to attend and report what occurs there is to protect the accused. . . . The ultimate public concern is not the satisfaction of curiosity or an abstract "right to know." Rather it is the assurance that trials are in fact fair and according to law.[48]

Even though the constitutional issues do not involve balancing of the First and Sixth Amendments per se, the consequence of the fair trial/free press controversy was to heighten the press's concern over the public's right to know and the availability of information about trials.

The fair trial/free press controversy turned the Court's attention to the constitutional rights of the public and press to attend and disseminate information about trials. Before the 1960s the Court generally overturned contempt charges of the press for editorials and publicity concerning judicial proceedings, appearing reluctant to sanction restraints on the press.[49] But extensive publicity occasionally proved prejudicial, and the Court eventually was forced to insist that judges exercise their responsibilities and powers to ensure fair trials.[50]

The Warren Court was particularly sensitive to the public's First Amendment interests and the availability of information about the conduct of trials. In *Estes* v. *Texas* (1965), while holding that television broadcasting of criminal trials inherently violates due process and the defendant's right to a fair trial, the Court noted that "the public has a right to be informed as to what occurs in its courts."[51] Justice Stewart, the author of *Pell* and *Saxbe*, wrote in a dissenting opinion in *Estes* that "[t]he suggestion that there are limits upon the public's right to know what goes on in courts causes me deep concern." [52] The following year, when overturning the conviction of Sam Sheppard for the murder of his wife, the Warren Court again reiterated: "The press does not simply publish information about trials but guards against the miscarriage of justice by subjecting the police, prosecutors, and judicial processes to extensive public scrutiny and criticism." [53] In both cases there was nationwide publicity, and the problem was that lower courts failed to ensure the decorum essential to a fair trial. In the Sheppard case the press had a Roman holiday with the live broadcasting of the coroner's inquest from a school gymnasium. At the trial the judge reserved three of the four rows of benches in the courtroom for news reporters and permitted the erection of a press table inside the bar of the court, which allowed journalists to overhear all of Sheppard's conversations with his attorneys! Accordingly, Justice Clark, for the Court, suggested that in such sensational trials judges may adopt rules governing reporters' access to the courtroom and insulating witnesses from journalists as well as barring police, witnesses, and counsel from talking about trial proceedings.

The Warren Court's ruling in *Sheppard* v. *Maxwell* intensified the fair trial/free press controversy. Immediately, the American Bar Association adopted as part of its Canons of Professional Ethics the Reardon Report's proposal of rules limiting attorneys' permissible statements about pending trials and recommendation that judges use their contempt power to inhibit prejudicial publicity. The American Newspapers Publishers Association (ANPA) responded by contending that such interference with news reporting thwarted First Amendment freedoms and the public's right to know and that publicity before and during a trial contributed to fair trial procedures and results. [54] The ANPA's opposition to limitations on reporting of judicial proceedings notwithstanding, *Sheppard* and the Reardon Report encouraged judges to issue "gag orders" on counsel, witnesses, and jurors in sensational trials.

In the 1970s the press vigorously contested judicially imposed gag orders as a denial of the First Amendment rights of the public and press. Although declining to review several highly controversial gag orders, [55] The Burger Court did recognize the important and interdependent interests of defendants and the public. In the Burger Court's major treatment of the fair trial/free press convroversy in 1976, the chief justice reaffirmed that "prior restraints on speech and publications are the most serious and least tolerable infringement of First Amendment rights." Here, the Nebraska Press Association challenged a trial judge's especially severe gag order. The press was forbidden to report the existence or content of a confession, made during an open-court arraignment of Charles Simants, concerning the sexual assault and murder of six members of a family in a small Nebraska farm town, and forbidden to publicize any other statements that Simants might have made to police or counsel, the identity of the victims, and certain aspects of medical testimony presented at an open preliminary hearing. In striking down the gag order, Chief Justice Burger suggested that judges employ other devices to guard against prejudicial publicity. He specifically listed as alternatives: change of venue (that is, moving the trial to another locality where there is less public interest in or publicity about the trial), postponing the trial to permit adverse publicity to die down, permitting rigorous voir dire examination of potential jurors to check against prejudice, instructing juries emphatically of their responsibility to consider admitted evidence only, and sequestering the jury.[56] In addition, mistrials for adverse publicity may be granted and convictions can be reversed on appeal.

Because the Court did not strike down gag orders per se, Justice Brennan, joined by Justices Stewart and Marshall, wrote a concurring opinion indicating that all gag orders are constitutionally impermissible. However, none of the devices outlined by the Court seriously interferes with the public's right to know. The crucial remaining issue was whether the use of these devices would indeed ensure fair trials. The difficulties of controlling prejudicial publicity nevertheless encouraged judges to not only continue the use of gag orders but to simply close pretrial hearing and trials.

In 1978 the Court refused to hear three trial secrecy cases,[57] but granted *certariori* in *Gannett Co.* v. *DePasquale*, presenting a challenge to the closure of a pretrial hearing. The case originated when, at a preliminary hearing on the suppression of allegedly involuntary confessions and certain physical evidence, the defendants requested that the public and the press be excluded on the grounds that adverse pretrial publicity would jeopardize their ability to receive a fair trial. The district attorney did not oppose the motion for closure, nor did a reporter who was employed by Gannett Publishing Company and present at the hearing offer any objection, and the trial judge granted the motion. The following day the reporter requested a copy of the trial transcript and claimed a constitutional right to cover the proceeding, which the judge denied. On appeal, the newspaper successfully challenged the closure on the First, Sixth, and Fourteenth Amendments, but the New York Court of Appeals reversed. Gannett Publishing Company then petitioned the Supreme Court to recognize an independent right of access to pretrial proceedings for reporters under the First, Sixth, and Fourteenth Amendments. Attorneys for Gannett urged the Court to narrow its holdings in *Pell, Saxbe,* and *Houchins* to the extent of acknowledging under the First and Fourteenth Amendments an enforceable constitutional right of access to pretrial hearings, and argued that the Sixth Amendment conferred a right of access on the public and press to attend pretrial proceedings as well as trials.

Divided over the issues, the Court's opinion was so broadly framed to not only invite criticisms from the Court's commentators but prompt no fewer than five justices later publicly to discuss the ruling.[58] As in *Pell* and *Saxbe,* Justice Stewart wrote the opinion for a bare majority; however, Justices Stevens and Powell now joined the chief justice and Justice Rehnquist, with the latter three writing concurring opinions. Justices

Blackmun and White joined Justices Brennan and Marshall, the staunchest supporters of a constitutional right to know, and a dissenting opinion written by Justice Blackmun. The alignment of the justices resulted from their giving precedence to the Sixth Amendment claim, rather than to the claim for a First Amendment right of access.

Turning first to the Sixth Amendment claim, Justice Stewart noted that "[t]he Constitution nowhere mentions any right of access to a criminal trial on the part of the public; its guarantee, like the others enumerated, is personal to the accused." He then formulated the issue posed in *Gannett* as "whether members of the public have an enforceable right to a public trial that can be asserted independently of the parties in the litigation." Acknowledging that "there is a strong societal interest in public trials," he emphasized that "[r]ecognition of an independent public interest in the enforcement of Sixth Amendment guarantees is a far cry . . . from the creation of a constitutional right on the part of the public." Under the Sixth Amendment, any public interest involved is protected by the participants in the litigation because the amendment is fundamentally "a 'guarantee of an accused.'" [59] Justice Stewart expressly rejected the argument that the Sixth Amendment embodies the historical common law right of the public to attend criminal trials, but, then, qualified his statement by adding:

> [E]ven if the Sixth and Fourteenth Amendments could properly be viewed as embodying the common-law right of the public to attend criminal trials, it would not necessarily follow that the petitioner would have a right of access under the circumstances of this case. For there exists no persuasive evidence that common law members of the public had any right to attend *pretrial* proceedings.[60]

Considering the First Amendment claim to a right of access, Justice Stewart's opinion for the Court hedged: "We need not decide in the abstract, however, whether there is any such constitutional right. For even assuming, *arguendo*, that the First and Fourteenth Amendments may guarantee such access in some situations, a question we do not decide, this putative right was given all appropriate deference by the state *nisi prius* court in the present case."[61] Justice Stewart found significant that the trial judge entertained the press's objections to closure, and, in any event, the denial of access was only temporary, since after the defendants pleaded guilty the press was permitted to a copy of the suppressed hearing transcript.

Because in the course of his opinion Justice Stewart stated no less than 12 times that the public and press have no constitutional right of access to either pretrials or trials, his opinion reached issues not raised by *Gannett* and invited confusion over the Court's ruling. Chief Justice Burger thus added a concurring opinion to underline that the case dealt only with pretrial hearings and to clarify the nature of such proceedings and their contemporary importance as the result of the exclusionary rule and motions to suppress evidence. He also reserved comment on whether the public and press may claim a right under the First and Fourteenth Amendments to attend trials.[62]

Although Justice Powell joined the opinion of the Court on the Sixth Amendment issue, his concurring opinion addressed the First Amendment issues that Justice Stewart avoided. Justice Powell emphasized "the importance of the public's having accurate information concerning the operation of its criminal justice system," and therefore would have held explicitly that the reporter had an interest protected by the First and Fourteenth Amendments.[63] Remaining consistent with his concurring opinion in *Branzburg*, he thought that the Court should reach an accommodation of the First Amendment rights of the public and press with those of the criminal defendant. Here, the public's right of access, he noted, was "limited both by the constitutional right of the defendants to a fair trial . . . and by the needs of government to obtain just convictions and to preserve the confidentiality of sensitive information and the identity of informants." Justice Powell nonetheless remained willing to legitimate the public's right to know as a limited but enforceable right in some circumstances. Justice Powell abandoned in *Gannett* those justices with whom he had dissented in *Pell*, *Saxbe*, and *Houchins* because here he found the trial judge's balancing of First Amendment interests of the public against those of the defendants acceptable.

Justice Rehnquist continued the dialogue with his concurrence, stressing that "the public does not have *any* Sixth Amendment right of access to such proceedings," and addressing Justice Powell's understanding of the First Amendment. Justice Rehnquist's observations were prompted by Justice Stewart's reservations on the First Amendment claims, which had in turn been required to win the votes of Justices Stevens and Powell. These latter votes were necessary because Justices Blackmun and White dissented over the Sixth Amendment issue. Arguing that the Court's reservations on claims to a First Amendment right of access were more apparent than real, he pointed out that "this Court repeatedly has held that there is no First Amendment right of access in the public or the press to judicial or other governmental proceedings." Justice Rehnquist thereupon underscored Justice Stewart's opposition to denominating any First Amendment affirmative rights by quoting from his concurring opinion in *Houchins*: "The First and Fourteenth Amendments do not guarantee the public a right of access to information generated or controlled by the government, nor do they guarantee the press any basic right of access superior to that of the public generally." Justice Rehnquist thus concluded that "this Court has emphatically rejected the proposition that . . . the First Amendment is some sort of constitutional 'sunshine law' that requires notice, an opportunity to be heard and subsequent reasons before a government proceeding may be closed to the public and press."[64]

Justice Blackmun's opinion for the dissenters quarreled only with the majority's understanding of the Sixth Amendment. He contended that the amendment establishes the public's right of access to a criminal trial and a pretrial proceeding. With regard to the First Amendment, Justice Blackmun commented simply that "[t]o the extent the Court protects a right of public access to the proceeding, the standards enunciated under the Sixth Amendment suffice to protect that right."[65] That the dissenters also declined the address the First Amendment issue is understandable because Justices Blackmun and White previously voted against denomination of First Amendment affirmative rights. Justices Brennan and Marshall, in contrast, earlier expressed their support for First Amendment rights of access in dissenting opinions in *Pell* and *Saxbe*.

Inasmuch as *Gannett* turned on the Sixth Amendment, the exclusion of public and press from pretrial hearings did not deny any previously recognized constitutional right under the First or Sixth Amendment. Moreover, *Gannett* complemented *Nebraska Press Association* by sanctioning another means of guarding against adverse pretrial publicity and enhancing the prospects for fair trial.

Justice Stewart's opinion for the Court nevertheless raised more questions than it answered. The lack of judicial craftsmanship in failing to narrowly formulate the ruling perpetuated confusion about the Court's decision, invited further litigation and thwarted the possibility of lower court compliance. No less than a dozen times, Justice Stewart intermittently suggested that the ruling applied to both pretrial hearings and trials. Yet, in approving the lower court's treatment of First Amendment interests under a hypothetical right of access, Justice Stewart severely undercut the effect of his statement that the Court had never recognized such a right of access. His ambiguous treatment of the Sixth Amendment further frustrated lower courts' compliance in two important ways. First, it remained unclear whether *Gannett* applied only to pretrial hearings or, as Justice Stewart suggested, to trials as well. Second, lower courts construing the Court's opinion as implying an as yet undefined right of access were left without a standard by which to apply that right against competing interests of defendants.

Not without precedent, but rather improperly, members of the Burger Court sought extrajudicially to clarify, explain, and defend *Gannett*. Despite the justices' public disclaimers, the Court's commentators found the decision "cloudy," "confused," "mushy," and a "muddle." As James Goodale summed it up: "Gannett Means What it Says: But Who Knows What it Says?"[66] The Reporters Committee for Freedom of the Press, a nonprofit legal research and defense organization, instituted a "Court-Watch" project to monitor lower courts' response to *Gannett* and declared that "Court Secrecy Is Spreading."[67] The American Society of Newspaper Editors (ASNE) issued a *Media Alert* urging editors and publishers to challenge closures of preliminary hearings and trials, and suggesting that reporters carry wallet-sized, Miranda-type cards to be used in the event that they were excluded from judicial proceedings. Warning that "[u]ntil and unless the *Gannett* decision is modified [the cards] will probably be needed," ASNE proposed that the cards read:

> Your honor, I am _____, a reporter for the _____. I respectfully request the opportunity to register on the record an objection to the motion to close this proceeding to the public, including the press. Our legal counsel advises me that standards set forth in some recent federal and state court decisions require a hearing before the courtroom can be closed. Accordingly, I respectfully request such a hearing and a temporary recess so that I can report to my editor and so that our counsel can be present to make the appropriate arguments. Thank you.

The ambiguity of *Gannett* had considerable effect on public and press access to judicial proceedings. Within 52 weeks following the decision, defendants, prosecutors, witnesses, and judges sought to close proceedings in no less than 13 federal courts and 259 state courts. Table 4.1 summarizes the post-*Gannett* closure actions reported by newspapers to the Reporters Committee for Freedom of the Press. Motions for closure were introduced in 214 preindictment and pretrial proceedings and in no less than 47 trials and 11 post-trial proceedings. Significantly, motions for closure were successful in 122 preindictment and pretrial hearings and resulted in 33 closed trials and 5 closed post-trial arraignments. Defendants overwhelmingly initiated motions for closure in 220 cases, whereas prosecutors sought closure in only 18 instances and joined defendants in nine other motions. Judges instigated closure in 23 cases, and in two sodomy cases witnesses unsuccessfully endeavored to close proceedings.

Although all closures explicitly or implicitly deny claims to the public's right to know, in more than half of the cases (149) judges did not even record their reasons for approving or denying closure motions. When judges did publicly justify their actions the primary reason for closure was to prevent prejudicial publicity and ensure a fair trial. Still, though the demands of securing a fair trial and impartial jury justified closure in 122 incidents, judges also entertained as grounds for closure considerations such as personal privacy and embarrassment of defendants, witnesses, and even counsel. The reason for these latter considerations becomes clear, if no more appropriate, in terms of the kinds of cases in which parties sought courtroom secrecy. The majority of cases involved prosecutions for attempted murder or murder (150 cases); followed by cases involving rapes or other sexually related crimes (38); and then violent crimes such as assault, battery, and kidnapping (22); and, finally, the possession or sale of illegal drugs (15). The remaining 49 cases involved a variety of crimes ranging from embezzle-

TABLE 4.1

Post-*Gannett* Closure Actions

Motions Made and Appealed*		Reversed
Closure motions initiated, in force, and/or upheld on appeal	146	14
Closure motions denied or withdrawn	112	1
Direct prior restraint on publications	14	6
Total	272	21

	Result of Motions		
Type of Proceeding*	Open	Closed	Total
Preindictment	18	24	42
Pretrial	74	98	172
Trials	14	33	47
Post-trial	6	5	11
Total	112	160	272*

Party Initiating Closure Motions**	Number
Defendant	220
Prosecution	18
Defendant and prosecution	9
Witnesses	2
Judges	23
Total	272

Reason for Closure**	Number
No reason given	149
Prejudice to jurors	112
Jeopardize fair trial	10
Protection of witnesses	3
Statutory basis	4
Embarrassment	22
Victims	8
Witnesses	7
Defendants	2
Others	5

*"Court Watch-Summary," Reporters Committee for Freedom of the Press, August, 1980.

**Compiled by author from records of the Reporters Committee for Freedom of the Press.

ment, bank fraud, and counterfeiting, to possession of firearms, extortion, and terrorism, to medical fraud, malpractice, and abortion/manslaughter.

Gannett appeared to substantially undermine the traditional presumption and practice of open court proceedings. The ambiguity of the ruling's applicability to preliminary hearings and trials, as much as the absence of constitutional standards for permissible closures, inevitably perpetuated litigation over closed judicial proceedings and necessitated that the Supreme Court eventually clarify the ruling. Sensitive both to the problematic nature and impact of *Gannett*, the Court agreed on October 9, 1980, to hear a challenge to the closure of a trial in *Richmond Newspapers, Inc.* v. *Virginia*. The case originated several years earlier, before *Gannett*, but involved the first constitutional challenge to the complete closure of a criminal trial.

The circumstances of the *Richmond Newspapers* case illustrate some of the problems of securing a fair trial. Here, closure was requested by defense counsel in the fourth trial of John Paul Stevenson for the stabbing and murder of a hotel manager in 1975. Initially, in 1976, Stevenson was promptly tried and convicted of second-degree murder in the circuit court of Hanover County, Virginia. A year later, however, the Virginia State Surpeme Court reversed his conviction, finding that a bloodstained shirt purportedly belonging to Stevenson had been improperly admitted as evidence at his trial. Retried the following year, his second trial in the same court ended in mistrial when one of the jurors asked to be excused after the trial had begun and there was no available alternative juror. The third trial, in 1978, also ended in a mistrial because a prospective juror had read about Stevenson's previous trials and told the other jurors about the case before the retrial had begun. At the outset of Stevenson's fourth trial his attorneys requested, and the prosecution did not object to, a closed trial on the grounds that they did not "want any information being shuffled back and forth when we have a recess as to what—who testified to what." On the bench barely a year and presiding over two of the earlier mistrials, Judge Richard Henry Caldwell Taylor agreed to closure. Judge Taylor found his authority to close the trial in the Virginia state code and justified it by the previous mistrials and the particularly small Hanover courtroom. Under Virginia law judges may close a criminal trial or exclude "from the trial any person whose presence would impair the conduct of a fair trial, provided that the right of the accused to a public trial shall not be violated."

Ironies abound in this rather routine murder trial that gave rise to the Supreme Court's watershed decision. Judge Taylor's unprecedented closure occurred in a 200-year-old courthouse where Patrick Henry once orated on First Amendment freedoms. Yet the closed trial that prompted the Richmond Newspapers' appeal to the Supreme Court had not even attracted the attention of the local weekly newspaper in Hanover County. Moreover, Stevenson was found not guilty, but not as the consequence of the jury's verdict. Instead, Judge Taylor affirmed a motion by defense counsel for a mistrial because the case against Stevenson, without the evidence of the bloodstained shirt, was only circumstantial. Still, the details of both the evidence against Stevenson and the basis for his acquittal remain obscure because the trial was closed, no trial transcript was made, and a tape recording of the trial and Judge Taylor's ruling is largely inaudable.

On appeal to the Supreme Court, Harvard law professor Laurence Tribe argued for the appellants that the First Amendment and the Sixth Amendment independently and interdependently guarantee a constitutional right to attend trials. The First Amendment secures a right of access, he argued, because trial secrecy deprives citizens of information vital to their self-governance. The Sixth Amendment establishes a norm of openness and gives the public standing to challenge closure of trials because, until the Stevenson case, trials were traditionally open to the public and the press. A right of access, Tribe further argued, was implicit in the interdependence of the First and Sixth Amendments:

> The First Amendment . . . opens a constitutional window into a proceeding already identified by the Sixth Amendment as beyond such control—assuring that, even with the connivances of the accused, the state may not bar members of the public and press from a criminal trial without compelling justification. . . . The proceedings of criminal trials are the quintessential subjects of First Amendment protection against government interference with public access: public by tradition, public by function, and public as a matter of constitutional text and structure.[68]

Significantly, rather than imploring the Court to reconsider the line of cases running from *Pell* to *Gannett*, Tribe distinguished those cases on the ground that there access had been denied to places not traditionally or constitutionally recognized as public places or proceedings. Hence, he argued that although *Branzburg* had noted that the public and press have no constitutional right of access to "grand jury proceedings, [the Supreme Court's] conferences, the meetings of other official bodies gathered in executive session, and the meetings of private organizations,"[69] the Court's former rulings never implied that the public and the press are excluded from historically public places and proceedings.

Relying on *Gannett*, Virginia attorney general Marshall Coleman defended closure of the trial, arguing that neither the Sixth Amendment nor common law practices justify a constitutional right of access to criminal trials. Considering the First Amendment claim, he emphasized that, "[t]he common thread of this Court's First Amendment decisions is the notion that freedom to *disseminate* ideas and information about public affairs is central to the purpose of the First Amendment." He conceded that "[t]he free flow of information concerning our courts of justice is undoubtedly a vital concern in our system of democratic self-governance." "But it is a wholly different proposition," Coleman insisted, "to suggest that the First

Amendment guarantees access to all sources of information that may be beneficial to informed public opinion."[70]

No majority supported an opinion for the Court's decision in *Richmond Newspapers*. A majority of the justices did embrace Tribe's argument that the public and the press are constitutionally entitled to attend criminal trials because trials traditionally and under the Constitution constitute a public forum.[71] For over 40 years when elaborating a functional analysis of the First Amendment, the Court acknowledged protection for public forums as essential to each individual's right to speak, distribute publications, or assemble in public places such as streets, sidewalks, and parks. Accordingly, Chief Justice Burger's plurality opinion, joined only by Justices White and Stevens, found trials tantamount to a constitutionally protected public forum under the First and Sixth Amendments. Justice Stewart likewise found the nexus between the amendments to create a constitutionally protected public forum, and thereby endeavored to distinguish the decision here from his opinion for the Court in *Gannett*. Justice Brennan's concurring opinion, joined by Justice Marshall, elaborated a more extensive theory of First Amendment protection for the public. Justices Stevens, White, and Blackmun added brief concurrences celebrating the Court's decision because, in Justice Blackmun's words, it was gratifying "to see the Court wash away at least some of the graffiti that marred the prevailing opinions in *Gannett*." The sole dissenter, Justice Rehnquist, lamented the Court's incursion on states' rights.

Chief Justice Burger began by clarifying that *Gannett* applied to only pretrial hearings, dismissing Justice Stewart's earlier assertions as pure *dicta*. Since the issue of public access to trials had not been previously decided, he turned to the history of the Sixth Amendment, surveying the "prophylactic purpose[s]" and "therapeutic value" of open trials. Reiterating that openness serves to ensure fair proceedings and "satisfies the appearance of justice,"[72] he reasserted that the Sixth Amendment's provision for public trials guarantees only the right of defendants. However, the chief justice interpreted the presumption of openness in the Sixth Amendment as connoting that "the people retained a 'right of visitation' which enabled them to satisfy themselves that justice was in fact being done." In other words, although the Sixth Amendment does not guarantee an enforceable right of the public to attend trials, it conveys to the public a right of visitation. Turning then to the First Amendment, Chief Justice Burger reasserted the Court's broad functional analysis of freedoms of speech, press, and assembly: "[E]xpressly guaranteed freedoms share a common core purpose of assuring freedom of communication on matters relating to the functioning of government." He argued, moreover, that "[i]t is not crucial whether we describe this right to attend criminal trials to hear, see, and communicate observations concerning them as a 'right of access,' . . . or a 'right to gather information,' for we have recognized that 'without some protection for seeking out the news, freedom of the press could be eviscerated.'" He thereupon concluded that central to the First Amendment's protection for freedom of information is the concept of a public forum or arena in which individuals may collectively and freely discuss matters of personal and public interest. Chief Justice Burger thus found trials analogous to other public forums in which members of the public and press historically enjoyed access, and distinguishable from places not generally recognized as open to the public (for example, prisons, jails, and military bases).[73]

Significantly, Chief Justice Burger's opinion did not turn on a reassessment of previous rulings in *Pell, Saxbe, Houchins*, and *Gannett* denying the constitutionality of First Amendment affirmative rights. Instead, the chief justice expanded, as it were, the concept of a public forum to include trials and thereby recognized the public's right to attend criminal trials as protected by the First Amendment. He did not denominate a First Amendment affirmative right of access per se, but, rather, acknowledged the enforceability of First Amendment claims as contingent on the place or forum to which access is demanded. Underscoring this point by expressly denying that the public possesses an unconditional right to open trials, the chief justice emphasized that "[j]ust as a government may impose reasonable time, place, and manner restrictions upon the use of its streets in the interests of such objectives as the free flow of traffic . . . so may a trial judge, in the interest of the fair administration of justice, impose reasonable limitations on access to a trial."[74] Public forums, of course, differ as much as city streets and courtrooms differ, and therefore the restrictions imposed on the public and press may vary from one forum to another. As Justice Frankfurter once eloquently pointed out:

> A trial is not a "free trade in ideas," nor is the best test of truth in a courtroom "the power of the thought to get itself accepted in the competition of the market," . . . A court is a forum with strictly defined limits for discussion. It is circumscribed in the range of its inquiry and in its methods by the Constitution, by laws, and by age-old traditions. . . . Of course freedom of speech and press are essential to the enlightenment of a free people and in restraining those who wield power. Particularly should this freedom be employed in comment upon the work of courts, who are without many influences ordinarily making for humor and humility, twin antidotes to the corrosion of power. But the Bill of Rights is not self-destructive. Freedom of expression can hardly carry implications that nullify the guarantee of impartial trials.[75]

Likewise, Chief Justice Burger recognized that public access may be limited since judges must control the decorum of courtrooms: "the question in a particular case is whether that control is exerted so as not to deny or unwarrantedly abridge . . . the opportunities for the communication of thought and the discussion of public questions immemoriably associated with resort to public places."[76]

The chief justice was obviously troubled by a declaration of unenumerated constitutional rights. Yet, by grounding the Court's decision on the First Amendment's protection for public forums, Chief Justice Burger assiduously and creatively justified the constitutionality of open trials without committing the Court to an independent First Amendment affirmative right of access per se. In other words, as much as Chief Justice Burger exercised judicial creativity in extending First Amendment protection and the concept of a public forum to criminal trials, he cautiously eschewed impermissible judicial creativity and construction of a broad and undefined affirmative right of access.

The chief justice's deliberate and careful exercise of judicial creativity was not entirely appreciated by his colleagues. In Justice Stevens's view, *Richmond Newspapers* stands as "a watershed case" because previous cases "never before . . . squarely held that the acquisition of newsworthy matter is entitled to any constitutional protection whatsoever." Concurring, Justice White pointed out that "[t]his case would have been unnecessary had *Gannett* . . . construed the Sixth Amendment to forbid excluding the public from criminal proceedings except in narrowly defined circumstances."[77] Likewise, Justice Blackmun remained convinced that the decision could have simply rested on the Sixth Amendment without invoking a "veritable potpourri" of amendments. Their broad interpretation of the Sixth Amendment, however, was not acceptable to a majority of the Court. And Chief Justice Burger's opinion therefore crucially turned on the juxtaposition of the First and Sixth Amendments to both extend the concept of public forums to criminal trials and preclude further claims to a right of access to other governmental facilities and proceedings not traditionally open to the public. Justice Stevens's concurrence thus mistakenly found it "somewhat ironic that the Court should find more reason to recognize a right of access today than it did in *Houchins*."[78] For the chief justice and Justices White, Blackmun, and Stewart there was no irony, because the touchstone for the Court's holding was that the First and Sixth Amendment run together in safeguarding access of members of the public and the press to criminal trials. The irony for Justice Stevens arose because of his willingness to make exceptions to the general rule that the amendment protects only freedom from restraints on the dissemination of information.

Justice Stevens, like Justices Powell, Brennan, and Marshall, remained prepared to recognize First Amendment affirmative action. Here, Justice Powell, the Virginian on the Court, did not participate in the decision; but Justice Brennan, joined by Justice Marshall, wrote a concurring opinion to emphasize their divergence from the majority when interpreting the First Amendment. Whereas the chief justice endeavored to narrowly define the Court's decision, Justice Brennan gave a broad jurisprudential basis for *Richmond Newspapers*, stressing that "the Court has not ruled out a public access component to the First Amendment in every circumstance." He argued: "Read with care and in context, our decisions must therefore be understood as holding only that any privilege of access to governmental information is subject to a degree of restraint dictated by the nature of the information and countervailing interests in security or confidentiality." In Justice Brennan's view, the Court's functional analysis of the First Amendment is tantamount to a structuralist interpretation of the amendment. Unlike Justice Stewart's structuralist theory of press exceptionalism, however, Justice Brennan interpreted the amendment itself to have a structural role in securing freedom of information and the public's right to know. The amendment "embodies more than a commitment to free expression and communicative interchange for their own sakes; it has a *structural* role to play in securing and fostering our republican system of self-government." For Justice Brennan the Court's articulation of a broad functional analysis of the First Amendment and the public's interests in freedom of information ultimately leads to a structuralist view: "The structural model links the First Amendment to that process of communication necessary for a democracy to survive, and thus entails solicitude not only for communication itself, but for the indispensable conditions of meaningful communications."[79] Thus, unlike the majority of the Burger Court, Justice Brennan would go beyond recognizing access to public forums and expressly denominate First Amendment affirmative rights and a directly enforceable public's right to know.

THE FIRST AMENDMENT IS NOT A FREEDOM OF INFORMATION ACT

Constitutional adjudication in the 1970s repeatedly tested the general rule that the scope of the First Amendment falls short of guaranteeing independent and enforceable rights to receive, gather, and obtain access to government information or facilities. Litigation over First Amendment affirmative rights forced the Court to reassess its functional analysis of the amendment in terms of the public's interests in freedom of information and the limits of judicial intervention. Although the Court recognized First Amendment affirmative rights as coordinate with expressly guaranteed freedoms and extended the concept of public forums to trials, a majority of the Court persistently refused to recognize independent and directly enforceable First Amendment affirmative rights against the government.

The divisions within the Burger Court over fashioning unenumerated First Amendment rights reflect the perennial dilemmas of judicial craftsmanship. In a profound sense, the foundations of our constitutional and political system inevitably depend on the tenuous and delicate balance drawn by the Court between broadly construing the requisite latitude of enumerated guarantees and extraconstitutionally constructing novel, unenumerated rights. Thus, litigation over First Amendment rights sharply divided the

Burger Court not only over the scope of the amendment but also with respect to the justices' political perceptions of the proper role of judicial review.

Chief Justice Burger and Justices Stewart and Rehnquist remained steadfast in their denial of the constitutional legitimacy of directly enforceable affirmative rights under the First Amendment. Justices Blackmun and White also rather consistently agreed with them. These justices construe the amendment as only ensuring the conditions for freedom of information and an informed public, rather than mandating First Amendment affirmative action. They maintain that premissible judicial review precludes both articulation of unenumerated rights and prescriptive policy making, since the Court thereby substitutes its wisdom for legislative determinations of governmental information policies. Hence, the majority of the Burger Court on the one hand continues to employ a broad functional analysis of enumerated guarantees: "[T]he First Amendment goes beyond protection of the press and the self-expression of individuals to prohibit government from limiting the stock of information from which members of the public may draw."[80] On the other hand they understand constitutional history and principle to preclude First Amendment affirmative rights, regardless of the rights' anticipated utility for contributing to an informed public and governmental openness. The First Amendment secures only the conditions for an informed public by guaranteeing freedom of speech and press in the absence of impermissible restraints. The amendment does not mandate a constitutional right to acquire information or obtain access to government materials and facilities not generally open to the public. Accordingly, for a majority of the Burger Court, the propriety of governmental openness presents issues of public policy reserved for the legislative and executive branches of government. As Justice Stewart succinctly put it: "The Constitution itself is neither a Freedom of Information Act nor an Official Secrets Act."[81] In sum, the First Amendment neither requires nor permits judicial formulation of information policies by the denomination of novel, unenumerated constitutional rights.

In contrast, Justices Brennan and Marshall endorsed First Amendment affirmative action because they hold that the amendment does not prohibit what it does not require and that judicially created affirmative rights serve the important policy objective of enhancing the free flow of information. While Justices Powell and Stevens agreed that a right of the public to know about government operations is defensible in terms of vindicating the interests of an informed citizenry, they disagreed with Justices Brennan and Marshall on the scope of judicial creativity and First Amendment protection. Justices Powell and Stevens, thus abandoned Justices Brennan and Marshall in *Gannett* because they found that the government had in a reasonable manner considered the interests of an informed public when denying access to judicial proceedings.

In *Richmond Newspapers*, Justice Brennan insisted that the Court's functionalist analysis of the First Amendment amounted to a structuralist theory of the amendment. He did so both to justify First Amendment affirmative rights and to explain why he, along with Justices Marshall, Powell, and Stevens, at times differ with the majority when interpreting the First Amendment. He further elaborated his interpretation during an address at the dedication of the Samuel I. Newhouse Law Center at Rutgers University on October 17, 1979.[82] There, he suggested that First Amendment litigation in the 1970s in important ways challenged the Court's interpretation of the First Amendment. He proposed two "models" of the First Amendment: first, a "speech model," the prevailing approach to the amendment, based on a functionalist analysis and definitional balancing of freedom of speech and press; second, what he called a "structural model," extending the umbrella of the First Amendment to affirmative rights to "protect the structure of communication necessary for the existence of our democracy." Fundamentally, what First Amendment litigation in the 1970s demanded and what a majority of the Burger Court repeatedly denied was a structuralist theory of the amendment. In Justice Brennan's view: "It is a mistake to suppose that the First Amendment protects only self-expression, only the right to speak out. I believe that the First Amendment in addition fosters the values of democratic self-government. The amendment also forbids the government from interfering with the communicative processes through which we citizens exercise and prepare to exercise our rights of self-government." The First Amendment plays a structural role in our constitutional and political system because the amendment's provisions for speech and press function to safeguard the public's interests in freedom of information and self-governance.

Justice Brennan echoed his earlier lecture dedicated to Alexander Meiklejohn at Brown University in 1965, in which he discussed the impact of Meiklejohn's theory of the First Amendment on his own thinking and, more generally, on the Supreme Court's approach to the amendment since the 1950s.[83] The absolutist theory of the First Amendment advanced by Meiklejohn, a philosopher and educator, was indeed a powerful influence on Justice Brennan and the Warren Court when repudiating ad hoc balancing and developing a definitional balancing approach to the First Amendment. Even in *Richmond Newspapers* the opinions of Chief Justice Burger and Justice Brennan duly credit Meiklejohn's work. The Court's commentators likewise frequently embrace Meiklejohn's interpretation of the First Amendment in support of the legitimacy of a constitutionally enforceable public's right to know. Yet, Meiklejohn's admirers, including Justices Brennan and Douglas, often misunderstand his thesis and its significance for comprehending the public's right to know.* A brief discussion of Meiklejohn's theory is

---

*For example, Justice Douglas, an admirer of Meiklejohn and an advocate of a broad construction of the First Amendment, in recognition of a directly enforceable right to know, misunderstood or, at best, significantly modified the philosopher's thesis. Justice Douglas,

beneficial for illuminating further the import of litigation over First Amendment affirmative rights and the divisions within the Burger Court.[84]

Meiklejohn argues that "the First Amendment is an absolute,"[85] but he neither shares Justice Black's absolutism nor remains absolute about his own version of absolutism.* For Meiklejohn, the First Amendment is an absolute because "[i]t is concerned, not with a private right, but with a public power, a governmental responsibility." The amendment does not guarantee rights of individuals, but, rather, embodies a basic structural principle of popular sovereignty. The First Amendment, like the preamble to the Constitution, Article I, Section 2 of the Constitution, and the Tenth Amendment,† recognizes the authority and power of citizens to enjoy self-government and therefore protects "the 'governing powers' of the people from abridgement by the agencies which are established as their servants."[86] By contrast, the Second through the Ninth Amendments, he argues, recognize that individuals are also governed by "the agencies which are established as [the people's] servants," and hence "limit the powers of the subordinate agencies in order that due regard shall be paid to the private 'rights of the governed.'" In Meiklejohn's view the First Amendment establishes not a right of individuals but a regulatory (or, in Justice Brennan's view, a structural) principle. That is, the amendment was not designed to guarantee individual self-expression or, as Meiklejohn says, an "unlimited license to talk." Instead, the amendment prohibits restrictions on speech and press so citizens may freely engage in the deliberation and debate of public issues that are essential to their electoral powers and self-government. As Meiklejohn concludes: "The First Amendment does not protect a 'freedom to speak.' It protects the freedom of those activities of thought and communication by which we 'govern.'"

---

dissenting in *Branzburg* v. *Hayes*, 408 U.S. 665, 721 (1972), claimed that "[t]he press has a preferred position in our constitutional scheme, not to enable it to make money, not to set newsmen apart as a favored class, but to bring fulfillment to the public's right to know. The right to know is crucial to the governing powers of the people, to paraphrase Alexander Meiklejohn. Knowledge is essential to informed decisions." Meiklejohn, however, made a radical and rigid distinction between the constitutional right to speak in the Fifth Amendment—a right of the governed—and the people's power to hear and debate—or, as it were, a "right" of the governors—guaranteed by the First Amendment.

*Justice Black's interpretation was absolute only with respect to speech. He, like Meiklejohn, maintained that the government may regulate conduct. But Justice Black also held defamatory publications to be absolutely privileged, whereas Meiklejohn believed that the First Amendment only prohibits prosecutions for seditious libel and therefore would premit actions for libel and pornography based on publications having no relation to citizens' governing powers.

†The principle of self-government is proclaimed in the Preamble to the Constitution, which states in part: "We the People of the United States . . . do ordain and establish this Constitution for the United States of America." Meiklejohn finds further support for the principle of self-governance in Article I, Section 2, Clause 1 of the Constitution and the Tenth Amendment. Article 1 provides that, "The House of Representatives shall be composed of

Because the First Amendment is viewed as a regulatory or structural provision of the Constitution, Meiklejohn's interpretation has appeal for proponents of affirmative rights of the public to compel governmental openness. Still, Meiklejohn's analysis does not imply or justify First Amendment affirmative rights. In the first place, he expressly denies that the First Amendment confers rights per se, so on his theory it is inconsistent to suggest that the amendment grants any affirmative right of the public to compel access to government materials or facilities. Instead, the First Amendment only—albeit absolutely—prohibits the government from restricting the freedom of citizens to communicate information that pertains to their self-governance. Meiklejohn's primary concern was to justify broad protection for political communications and to defend free speech interests at a time (during the 1950s) when the government prosecuted expressions of unpopular political doctrines and the Court upheld those actions by ad hoc balancing. In the second place, the First Amendment, as Meiklejohn recognizes, is not unconditional since citizens' freedom and governmental regulation are not antithetical. Freedom and restraint are constituents of self-government. "A citizen may be told when and where and in what manner he may or may not speak, write, assemble, and so on," Meiklejohn observes. "On the other hand, he may not be told what he shall or shall not believe. In that realm each citizen is sovereign." Meiklejohn's theory thus buttresses the Supreme Court's protection for public forums and upholding of reasonable time, place, and manner regulations on public assemblies. As *Richmond Newspapers* and the prison access cases illustrate, time, place, and manner regulations frequently restrict public access to government facilities even though an individual or segment of the public deems such access important to the governing powers of citizens. Meiklejohn, like the Supreme Court, maintains that "[t]o interpret the First Amendment as forbidding such regulation is to so misconceive its meaning as to reduce it to nonsense."[87] Just as Congress or the states may permissibly regulate the time, place, and manner of individual or group access to public forums, so too they may regulate, under Meikelejohn's analysis and the Supreme Court's interpretation of the First Amendment, access to government facilities.

Meiklejohn's theory illuminates the Supreme Court's interpretation of the First Amendment and the political ideal of the public's right to know as an important abstract right. The freedoms of speech and press ensure the availability of information and promote debate concerning the operations of representative government, and thereby indirectly contribute to the political ideal of the public's right to know. As judicially enforced, individuals' First

---

Members chosen every second Year by the People of the several States." The Tenth Amendment specifies that: "The powers not delegated to the United States by the Constitution, nor prohibited by it to the States, are reserved to the States respectively, or to the people."

Amendment rights to free speech and press promote the conditions for an informed public by safeguarding the dissemination of information, but "[t]here [exists] no constitutional right to have access to particular government information, or to require openness from the bureaucracy."[88] *Richmond Newspapers*, no less than rulings on commerical speech discussed in the last chapter, underscores the important ways in which the political ideal of freedom of information and an informed public remains integral to the Court's interpretation of the First Amendment. The Court's rebuff of litigation over First Amendment affirmative rights does not reflect insensitivity to the political ideal of the public's right to know. Instead, it registers the refusal to extraconstitutionally expand the boundaries of the First Amendment and supervise government information policies.

NOTES

1. William H. Rehnquist, "The First Amendment: Freedom, Philosophy, and the Law," 12 *Gonzaga Law Review* 1, 18 (1976).

2. *Brown* v. *Allen*, 344 U.S. 443, 540 (1953) (Jackson, J., con. op.).

3. John Paul Stevens, "Some Thoughts About A General Rule," 21 *Arizona Law Review* 559, 602 (1979), quoting *Gannett Co.* v. *DePasquale*, 99 S.Ct. 2898, 2922 (1979) (Blackmun, J., dis. op.).

4. See Thomas I. Emerson, "Legal Foundations of the Right to Know," 1976 *Washington Law Quarterly* 1.

5. *Kleindienst* v. *Mandel*, 408 U.S. 753, 775 (1972) (Marshall, J., dis. op.).

6. See, generally, David M. O'Brien, "The Seduction of the Judiciary: Social Science and the Courts," 64 *Judiciature* 8 (1980).

7. *Whalen* v. *Roe*, 97 S.Ct. 869, 876 n.23 (1977) (Justice Stevens referring to Justice Douglas's "penumbra" theory of the constitutional right of privacy). See, generally, David M. O'Brien, *Privacy, Law, and Public Policy* (New York: Praeger 1979) 177–94.

8. *Martin* v. *City of Struthers*, 319 U.S. 141, 143 (1943).

9. *Thomas* v. *Collins*, 323 U.S. 516, 534 (1945) (recognizing labor organizer's right to speak and the rights of workers "to hear what he had to say" and therupon striking down a statute requiring labor organizations to obtain a certificate before soliciting workers).

10. See *Martin* v. *City of Struthers*, 319 U.S. 141 (1943) and *Marsh* v. *Alabama*, 326 U.S. 501 (1946) (invalidating company town's prohibition of distributing religious literature on city streets without permission); *Sweez* v. *New Hampshire* , 354 U.S. 234 (1957) (investigating teacher's beliefs and political associations was held to violate First Amendment rights); and *Lamont* v. *Postmaster General*, 381 U.S. 301 (1965) (procedure withholding delivery of political propaganda sent through the mails pending addresses' notification of desire to receive held unconstitutional).

11. See, for example, *Virginia State Borad of Pharmacy* v. *Virginia Citizens Consumer Council*, 425 U.S. 748 (1976) (discussed in Chapter 3).

12. *Procunier* v. *Martinez*, 416 U.S. 396 (1974) (invalidating prisoner mail censorship regulations). See also *Wolff* v. *McDonnell*, 418 U.S. 539 (1974).

13. *Lamont* v. *Postmaster General*, 381 U.S. 301, 307 (1965).

14. Ibid., at 308 (Brennan, J., con. op.).

15. See *Kovacs* v. *Cooper*, 336 U.S. 77, 87–89 (1949) (right not to listen to noises of sound trucks); *Roman* v. *Post Office*, 397 U.S. 728, 738–39 (1970) (right of householders to request post office to order any mailer to stop sending advertisements that the householder finds "erotically arousing").

16. Thomas I. Emerson, "Colonial Intentions and Current Ralities of the First Amendment," 125 *Univeristy of Pennsylvania Law Review* 737, 755 (1977).

17. See, for example, *Virginia State Boardof Pharmacy* v. *Virginia Citizens Consumer Council*, 425 U.S. 748, 756–57 (1976); *Procunier* v. *Martinez*, 416 U.S. 396, 407–9 (1974).

18. *Kleindienst* v. *Mandel*, 408 U.S. 753, 762 (1972).

19. Ibid., at 771 (Douglas, J., dis. op.).

20. See *Zemel* v. *Rusk*, 381 U.S. 1, 16–17 (1965), ruling on the Passport Act of 1926, 22 U.S.C. 211a (1976) and the Immigration and Nationality Act of 1952, 8 U.S.C. 215 (1976).

21. *Pell* v. *Procunier*, 417 U.S. 817, 829 (1974), quoting *Branzburg* v. *Hayes*, 408 U.S. 665, 684 (1972); *Saxbe* v. *Washington Post*, 417 U.S. 843 (1974).

22. Ibid., at 841 (Douglas, J., dis. op.).

23. *Saxbe* v. *Washington Post*, 417 U.S. 843, 872 (1974) (Powell, J., dis. op.).

24. *Houchins* v. *KQED*, 438 U.S. 1, 9, 12 (1978) (Chief Justice Burger wrote the majority opinion, which Justice Stewart joined with a concurring opinion. Justice Stevens penned the dissenting opinion that Justices Brennan and Powell joined. Justices Marshall and Blackmun did not participate).

25. Ibid., at 16–17.

26. Ibid., at 32, 34 (Stevens, J., dis. op.).

27. *Richmond Newspapers, Inc.* v. *Virginia*, 100 S.Ct. 2814 (1980).

28. *Gannett Co.* v. *DePasquale*, 99 S.Ct. 2898 (1979).

29. Lord Edward Coke, *Second Institutes of the Laws of England* 6th ed. (1681) 103.

30. See Jeremy Bentham, *Treatise on Judicial Evidence* (London, 1827) 67–68; and Sir William Blackstone, *Commentaries on the Laws of England* 4 vols. (Oxford: Clarendon Press, 1766) 372–373.

31. Joseph Story, *Commentaries on the Constitution of the United States* 5th ed. (Boston: Little, Brown, 1891) 662.

32. Thomas Cooley, *A Treatise on Constitutional Limitations* 8th ed. (Boston: Little, Brown, 1927) 312; John Wigmore, *Evidence* 3d ed. (Mineola; Foundation Press, 1940) 1834.

33. Bentham, *Treatise on Judicial Evidence* at 69.

34. *Davison* v. *Duncan*, 7 El. & Bl. 229, 231, 110 Rev. R. 572, 572 (Q. B. 1857).

35. *State* v. *Hensley*, 75 Ohio St. 255, 257, 79 N.E. 462, 463–64 (1906).

36. *In re Oliver*, 333 U.S. 257, 266 (1948).

37. Cooley, *A Treatise on Constitutional Limitations* at 312.

38. See Wigmore, *Evidence*, § 1835, at 449–50; and Fredrick Seaton Siebert, *The Rights and Privileges of the Press* (New York: D. Appleton-Century, 1934) 38–45.

39. *In re Oliver*, 333 U.S. 257 (1948).

40. See for example, *Baker* v. *Wingo*, 407 U.S. 514, 519 (1972) (right to speedy trial involves societal interests).

41. *Singer* v. *United States*, 380 U.S. 24, 25 (1965) (dictum) (holding that criminal defendant has no federally recognized right to be tried before judge instead of jury).

42. *Illinois* v. *Allen*, 397 U.S. 337, 343 (1970).

43. *Pennekamp* v. *Florida*. 328 U.S. 331, 361 (1946) (Frankfurter, J., con. op.).

44. *Craig* v. *Harney*, 331 U.S. 367, 374 (1947) (Douglas, J.).

45. *Maryland* v. *Baltimore Radio Show, Inc.*, 338 U.S. 912, 920 (1950) (Frankfurter, J., dis. from denial of certariori).

46. See Siebert, *The Rights and Privileges of the Press* at 38–45.

47. See, generally, Report of the Twentieth Century Fund Task Force on Justice, Publicity and the First Amendment, *Rights in Conflict* (New York: McGraw-Hill, 1976); Chilton R. Bush, ed., *Free Press and Fair Trial* (Athens: University of Georgia, 1970).

48. Lewis F. Powell, Jr., "The Right To A Fair Trial," 51 *American Bar Association Journal* 534, 538 (1965).

49. See, for example, *Pennekamp* v. *Florida*, 328 U.S. 331 (1946); *Craig* v. *Harney*, 331 U.S. 367 (1947); and *Sheppard* v. *Florida*, 341 U.S. 50 (1951).

50. See, for example, *Irvin* v. *Dowd*, 366 U.S. 717 (1961); *Rideau* v. *Louisiana*, 373 U.S. 723 (1963).

51. *Estes* v. *Texas*, 381 U.S. 532, 541 (1965).

52. Ibid., at 615 (Stewart, J., dis. op.).

53. *Sheppard* v. *Maxwell*, 341 U.S. 350 (1951).

54. See, generally, Alfred Friendly and Ronald L. Goldfarb, *Crime and Publicity: The Impact of News on the Administration of Justice* (New York: Twentieth Century Fund, 1967).

55. See, for example, *Farr* v. *Pitchess*, 96 S.Ct. 3200 (1976); *Rosato* v. *Superior Court*, 427 U.S. 912 (1976); and *Evans* v. *Fromme*, 425 U.S. 934 (1976).

56. *Nebraska Press Association* v. *Stuart*, 427 U.S. 539, 563–64 (1976). See also *Oklahoma Press Publishing Co.* v. *District Court*, 430 U.S. 308 (1977).

57. See, for example, *United States* v. *Gurney*, 558 F.2d 1202 (5th Cir. 1977) (suppression of information during trial), cert. denied 98 S.Ct. 1606 (1978); *Central South Carolina Chapter, Society of Professional Journalists* v. *Martin*, 556 F.2d 706 (4th Cir. 1977) (gag order on trial participants), cert. denied 434 U.S. 1022 (1978); add *State ex rel. Learch* v. *Sawicki*, No. 77–368 (Ohio, June 3, 1977) cert. denied, 434, U.S. 1014 (1978).

58. See, for example, "Brennan Assails Media Criticisms of Court Decisions," *Washington Post*, A12, col. 1; "Justice Marshall Hits Colleagues on Rights," Seattle *Post-Intelligencer*, June 3, 1979, at B2; Stevens, "Some Thoughts on a General Rule"; and New York *Times*, September 9, 1979, at Sec. 1, 14, col. 1 (quoting Justice Stevens's view that "members of the general public, including the press, could not assert rights guaranteed to the accused by the Sixth Amendment"), New York *Times*, August 9, 1979, at A17, col. 1 (quoting Chief Justice Burger "that the opinion referred to pretrial proceedings only"); New York *Times*, August 14, 1979, at A13, col. 1 (reporting Justice Powell's address to a panel at the annual meeting of the American Bar Association and explanation that *Gannett* was based only on the Sixth Amendment); New York *Times*, September 4, 1979 at A15, col. 1 (reporting Justice Blackmun's view that after *Gannett* closure of trials is permissible).

59. *Gannett Co.* v. *DePasquale*, 99 S.Ct. 2898, 2901–5 (1979).

60. Ibid., at 2909.

61. Ibid., at 2912.

62. Ibid., at 2913–14 (Burger, C.J., con. op.).

63. Ibid., at 2914 (Powell, J., con. op.).

64. Ibid., at 2918 (Rehnquist, J., con. op.), quoting *Houchins* v. *KQED*, 438 U.S. 1, 16 (1978) (Stewart, J., con. op.).

65. Ibid., at 2940 (Blackmun, J., dis. op.).

66. See *The News Media and the Law* (November/December, 1979).

67. See, for example, James Goodale, "Gannett Means What it Says; But Who Knows What it Says?" *National Law Journal* (October, 15, 1979) 15; The Supreme Court, 1978 Term, 93 *Harvard Law Review* 60, 65 (1979); Birmingham *Post-Herald*, August 21, 1979, at A4; Chicago *Sun-Times*, September 20, 1979, at 56; Baltimore *Sun*, September 22, 1979, at A14; *Washington Post*, August 10, 1979 at A15; *Time*, September 17, 1979; and *Newsweek*, August 27, 1979, at 69.

68. See Brief for Appellants, *Richmond Newspapers, Inc.* v. *Virginia*, Supreme Court of the United States, October Term, 1979, No. 79–243, at 5–9, and 44 n.37.

69. Ibid., at 31, quoting *Branzburg* v. *Hayes*, 408 U.S. 665, 684 (1972).

70. Brief for Appellees, *Richmond Newspapers, Inc.* v. *Virginia*, Supreme Court of the United States, October Term, 1979, No. 79–243, at 20–22.

71. The concept of a "public forum" was initially articulated by Justice Roberts in *Hague* v. *C.I.O.*, 307 U.S. 496, 515–16 (1937), wherein he observed: "Wherever the title of streets and parks may rest, they have immemorially been held in trust for the use of the public and, time out of mind, have been used for purposes of assembly, communicating thoughts between citizens, and discussing public questions. Such use of the streets and public places has, from ancient times, been a part of the privileges, immunities, rights and liberties of citizens. The

privilege of a citizen of the United States to use the streets and parks for communication of views on national questions may be regulated in the interest of all; it is not absolute, but relative, and must be exercised in consonance with peace and good order; but it must not, in the guise of regulation, be abridged or denied." The Court has extended the concept of a public forum in *Thomas* v. *Collins*, 323 U.S. 516 (1945); *Niemotko* v. *Maryland*, 340 U.S. 268 (1951) (public parks); *Cox* v. *New Hampshire*, 312 U.S. 569 (1941); and *Cox* v. *Louisiana*, 379 U.S. 536 (1965) (public passages); and *Amalgamated Food Employees Union* v. *Logan Valley Plaza, Inc.*, 391 U.S. 308 (1968) (shopping centers). In other cases the Court has refused to extend the concept; see *Adderly* v. *Florida*, 385 U.S. 39 (1967) (jails) and *Lehman* v. *City of Shaker Heights*, 418 U.S. 298 (1974) (bus placards).

72. *Offutt* v. *United States*, 348 U.S. 11, 14 (1954).

73. *Richmond Newspapers, Inc.* v. *Virginia*, 100 S.Ct. 2814, 2826–27 (1980).

74. Ibid., at 2830 n.18.

75. *Bridges* v. *California*, 314 U.S. 252, 283 (1941) (Frankfurter, J., dis. op.).

76. *Richmond Newspapers, Inc.* v. *Virginia*, 100 S.Ct. 2814, 2830 n.18 (1980), quoting *Cox* v. *New Hampshire*, 312 U.S. 569, 574 (1941).

77. Ibid., at 2830 (White, J., con. op.).

78. Ibid., at 2831 (Stevens, J., con. op.).

79. Ibid., at 2833 (Brennan, J., con. op.).

80. *First National Bank of Boston* v. *Bellotti*, 435 U.S. 765, 783 (1978).

81. Potter Stewart, "Or of the Press," 26 *Hastings Law Journal* 631, 636 (1975).

82. William Brennan, "Address," 32 *Rutgers Law Review* (1979).

83. William Brennan, Jr., "The Supreme Court and the Meiklejohn Interpretation of the First Amendment," 79 *Harvard Law Review* 1 (1965).

84. See, for example, Edward Bloustein, "The First Amendment and Privacy: The Supreme Court Justice and the Philosopher," 28 *Rutgers Law Review* 41 (1974); and William O. Bertelsman, "The First Amendment and Protection of Reputation and Privacy," 56 *Kentucky Law Journal* 718 (1968).

85. Alexander Meiklejohn, "The First Amendment Is An Absolute," in *The Supreme Court Review*, ed. Philip Kurland (Chicago: University of Chicago Press, 1961) 245. See also Meiklejohn, *Political Freedom* (New York: Oxford University Press, 1965).

86. Ibid., at 254–55.

87. Ibid., at 257, 252.

88. Stewart, "Or of the Press," at 636.

CHAPTER 5

THE FIRST AMENDMENT, THE SUPREME COURT, AND GOVERNMENTAL SECRECY

> Adjustment of the inevitable conflict between [First Amendment freedoms] and other interests is a problem as persistent as it is perplexing.
> Justice Felix Frankfurter, *Niemotko* v. *Maryland* (1950)

> The Constitution itself is neither a Freedom of Information nor an Official Secrets Act.
> Justice Potter Stewart, Speech, 1974

In American politics the public's right to know became increasingly important with the enactment of freedom óf information laws and constitutional adjudication aimed, as it were, at transforming the First Amendment into a Freedom of Information Act. Inasmuch as in the 1970s the public's right to know became more prominent in the grammar of developing constitutional law under the First Amendment, the right to know does, as Thomas Emerson claims, appear to be "an emerging constitutional right."[1] Still, as much as judicial construction of a concrete constitutional right to know appears salutory with regard to political controversies over bureaucratic secrecy versus democratic governance, it invites the no less perennial debate over reconciling judicial review with a representative democracy. Inexorably, litigation over translating the political ideal of the public's right to know into the language of constitutional rights raises the persistent concerns about the legitimacy of judicial articulation of unenumerated rights.

Since the 1930s the predominant pattern of the Supreme Court's treatment of the First Amendment manifests neither complete self-restraint nor uninhibited judicial activism, but, rather, modest intervention. Although doctrinal evolution was forged by competing judicial approaches to the First Amendment, as Chapter 3 showed, in historical perspective as the Court elaborated a broad functionalist view of the First Amendment as essential to individuals' freedom of expression and to an informed public and self-governing electorate. Shifting majorities of the Court rather consistently apprehended the limitations of the First Amendment and the limited role of judicial review under the Constitution. The Court in an activist fashion abandoned deference to legislative determinations of what constitutes permissible or pernicious communications, and gradually articulated constitutional principles designed broadly to ensure First Amendment freedoms. The Court's activist posture, however, was moderated by the ubiquitous demands for judicial craftsmanship and a collective approach (or a composite posture forged by individual justices' competing judicial philosophies) to the exercise judicial review. Thus, in enlarging First Amendment freedoms the Court delimited the scope of the amendment by developing a two-level theory of First Amendment protection, adhering to the constitutional redundancy of the speech and press clauses, and declining to mandate affirmative constitutional rights to compel governmental openness. The First Amendment as judicially enforced, therefore, indirectly, derivatively ensures the political ideal of the public's right to know.

The Supreme Court's posture of modest intervention when interpreting the First Amendment to indirectly safeguard the public's right to know is underscored by its policy against prior restraints. Even more than litigation in the 1970s over First Amendment affirmative rights, the prior restraint controversies over *New York Times Co.* v. *United States*[2] (the Pentagon Papers case) and *United States* v. *The Progressive, Inc.*[3] are a measure of the complexity of accommodating First Amendment freedoms with other governmental interests and reconciling judicial review with the principle of separation of powers. These cases are particularly illuminating both because the information suppressed by the government did not fall within a category of unprotected speech and because the restraints threatened to diminish the public's interests in political communications more directly than would time, place, and manner regulations. Yet, as much as the Pentagon Papers and *The Progressive* cases exemplify the import of the judicial policy against prior restraints and its bearing on the public's right to know, they underscore the limitations of the First Amendment and of the Supreme Court's role in enhancing the political ideal of the public's right to know.

THE FIRST AMENDMENT AND THE POLICY AGAINST PRIOR RESTRAINTS

In construing the elimination of prior restraints on publications as the "leading purpose"[4] of the First Amendment, the Supreme Court ensured the constitutional bulwark for the political ideal of freedom of information and an informed public.[5] The doctrine of no prior restraints, as Chapter 2 showed, was firmly rooted in the Blackstonian-common law understanding of the freedom of speech and press. In one of the Supreme Court's earliest First Amendment rulings, Justice Holmes perceptively observed: "The main purpose of such constitutional provisions is to prevent all such previous restraints upon publications as had been practiced by other governments, and they do not prevent the subsequent punishment of speech as may be deemed contrary to the public welfare."[6]

The policy against prior restraints crosscuts the Court's two-level theory of First Amendment protection inasmuch as prior restraints are nullified without deciding whether the communication may be constitutionally subject to subsequent punishment. Like the common law doctrine, the judicial policy against prior restraints focuses principally on the form or method of governmental restraints on communications. Prior governmental restraints on the dissemination of information are subject to exacting judicial scrutiny because, as Justice Blackmun comments, "a free society prefers to punish the few who abuse rights of speech *after* they break the law than to throttle them and all others beforehand."[7] Similarly, Alexander Bickel in his typically eloquent way observed:

> Prior restraints fall on speech with a brutality and a finality all their own. Even if they are ultimately lifted they cause irremediable loss—a loss in the immediacy, the impact, of speech. They differ from the imposition of criminal liability in significant procedural respects as well, which in turn have their substantive consequences. The violator of a prior restraint may be assured of being held in contempt; the violator of a statute punishing speech criminally knows that he will go before a jury, and may be willing to take his chance, counting on a possible acquittal. A prior restraint, therefore, stops speech more effectively. A criminal statute chills, prior restraint freezes. Indeed it is the hypothesis of the First Amendment that injury is inflicted on our society when we stifle the immediacy of speech."[8]

Prior restraints are egregious because of their deterrent effect on the freedom of distributing and debating information and ideas. *Ex parte* injunctions, for example, not only restrain publications—therewith potentially diminishing the value of disseminating the information—but also fail to afford an adversary hearing wherein individuals may defend their First Amendment claims.[9] Since injunctions against publications, even with expedited proceedings,[10] thwart the dissemination of information to the public, they carry a "heavy burden of showing justification for the imposition of such a restraint."[11]

The presumption against prior restraints nevertheless remains rebuttable; indeed "prior restraints are not unconstitutional *per se*."[12] In *Kingsley Books, Inc.* v. *Brown*, Justice Frankfurter, writing for the Warren Court, cautioned against concluding that the policy against prior restraints is absolute: "The phrase 'prior restraint' is not a self-wielding sword. Nor can it serve as a talismanic test."[13] Quoting law professor Paul A. Freund, he emphasized that "[w]hat is needed is a pragmatic assessment of its operation in the particular circumstances. The generalization that prior restraint is particularly obnoxious in civil liberties cases must yield to more particularistic analysis."[14] In other words, the Supreme Court may neither invalidate all governmental restraints on the dissemination of information nor idly permit governmental suppression and dilution of First Amendment freedoms. Instead of either unleashed judicial activism or impotent self-restraint, the Court must attend to the particular case or controversy with a posture of moderate intervention, safeguarding essential First Amendment interests while respecting the principle of separation of powers and reasonable legislative or executive branch determinations that inhibit the free flow of information.

Illustrating the Supreme Court's posture of moderate intervention when implementing the policy against governmental censorship of communications is *Near* v. *Minnesota* (1931). In the Court's initial and major treatment of prior restraints it struck down an abatement statute for newspapers that created a public nuisance by "malicious, scandalous and defamatory" publications. In elevating the common law doctrine to the status of constitutional law, Chief Justice Hughes observed: "The objection has also been made that the principle as to immunity from previous restraint is stated too broadly, if every such restraint is deemed to be prohibited. That is undoubtedly true; the protection even as to previous restraint is not absolutely unlimited."[15] The chief justice thereupon articulated certain exceptions to the policy against prior restraints.

First, when the nation is at war the government may permissibly restrict the dissemination of information that might hinder the war effort. Recalling *Schenck*, Chief Justice Hughes observed that no one would gainsay that "a government might prevent actual obstruction of the sailing dates of transports or the number or location of troops." "On similar grounds," he also thought that "the primary requirements of decency may be enforced against obscene publications" and that "[t]he security of the community life may be protected against incitements to acts of violence and the overthrow by force of orderly government."[16] Hence, in addition to information pertaining to national security interests, communications that serve "no essential part of any exposition of ideas[17] receive no exemption from the judicial policy against prior restraints any more than they receive First Amendment protection against subsequent punishment.

Chief Justice Hughes's understanding of the First Amendment and prior restraints remains instructive. As initially enunciated the policy against prior restraints comprehended both procedural safeguards for the public's First Amendment interests and the scope of protected communications. The chief justice recognized that the First Amendment, like English and colonial common law, does not provide immunity for particular categories of speech—for example, fighting words, the libelous, and the obscene—but, more important, indicated that the amendment also does not guarantee exculpability for disseminating information that endangers national security interests. More significant, then, than the anticipation of the Court's later articulation of a definitional balancing approach to the First Amendment, is *Near*'s suggestion that matters related to national security and national defense—matters clearly political and of interest to an informed public and electorate—might be susceptible to prior restraints.

Not until 1971 and the Pentagon Papers case did the Supreme Court consider the policy of no prior restraints with regard to competing First Amendment and national security interests. In the intervening 40 years, however, the Court did enforce its policy against prior restraints in three other areas, elaborating flexible standards for determining the permissibility of prior restraints.

First Amendment protection against prior restraints was primarily asserted in cases striking down systems of administrative censorship erected by licensing or tax schemes bearing a resemblance to those traditional censorial practices that gave rise to the common law prohibition of prior restraints.[18] More problematic were challenges to administrative systems designed to determine the alleged obscenity of books, plays, and films[19] or to regulate access to public forums.[20] In *Southeastern Promotions* v. *Conrad*, for instance, the Burger Court required the municipal board of Chattanooga, Tennessee, to make its city Memorial Auditorium available for the stage production of *Hair*, a theatrical performance that includes nudity, simulated sex, and vulgar language. Over Justice Rehnquist's biting dissent that there was no real issue of prior restraint (since scheduling limitations for the auditorium precluded the presentation of every production), the majority ruled that withholding the use of the facility constituted prior restraint and that the state in regulating access to the public facility failed to provide procedural safeguards for First Amendment interests. In reaffirming that "a system of prior restraint 'avoids constitutional infirmity only if it takes place under procedural safeguards designed to obviate the dangers of a censorship system,'"[21] the Court indicated that prior restraints do not run afoul of the First Amendment when the burden of instituting judicial proceedings and of proving that the material is unprotected is placed on the government, not the individual; and restraint prior to judicial determinations is imposed for only a brief period of time; and "a prompt final determination [is] assured" by the regulatory scheme.[22] Prior restraints in the form of authorized administrative systems or regulations are permissible only if the government ensures procedural safeguards for First Amendment interests.

By the 1970s the Supreme Court had also applied its policy against prior restraints with respect to the judicial imposition of gag orders on pretrial and intrial publicity.[23] The most difficult and unsettled problems still remain in the final area of judicial assertion of the policy against prior restraints—namely, where the government requests the judiciary to enjoin the publication of information in the interest of national security.[24]

SEPARATION OF POWERS AND GOVERNMENT SECRECY

The complex and myriad issues of accommodating claims to the First Amendment and the public's right to know with governmental withholding of information pertaining to national security have infrequently risen to the level of constitutional adjudication. Indeed, as the Pentagon Papers and *The Progressive* cases illustrate, there persists serious issues in constitutional politics as to what the First Amendment requires and permits. The Supreme Court, on the one hand, has affirmed the necessity and permissibility of governmental secrecy with regard to technological materials related to defense strategy and national security, and in the conduct of diplomatic and foreign affairs in times of war and international crisis.[25] Accordingly, the First Amendment does not protect individuals who pass classified defense information to enemy agents[26] nor does it prohibit injunctions forbidding government contractors from disclosing technical information about conventional weaponry to potential customers.[27] The First Amendment, on the other hand, ensures the vital interests of the public in knowing about government operations.[28] The dilemma of reconciling the First Amendment with competing national security interests is becoming salient because of the increasingly frequent confrontations over challenges to government regulations restricting the dissemination of technical and political information relating to national defense,[29] requiring secrecy agreements of government employees,[30] and imposing limitations on the political activities of some government employees.[31]

The Pentagon Papers and *The Progressive* cases posed and left unresolved basic issues in constitutional politics. In the Pentagon Papers case the Court's brief *per curiam* opinion did not address the merits of the case. *The Progressive* case never reached the Court's docket, because the government abandoned its efforts to enjoin publication after the publication of similar material on the construction of hydrogen bombs by another source,* and because of the traditional rule of equity that injunctions may not perform a futile act.[32] Nonetheless, the cases dovetail in illuminating the

---

*Independent of Howard Morland's research and article for *The Progressive* magazine, which prompted the government to seek an injunction against publication of the article, Charles Hansen, a computer programmer in California, prepared a similar 18-page story *a la* letter on the construction of H-bombs. *The Press Connection*, a small and now defunct newspaper in Madison, Wisconsin, published his letter on September 16, 1979. The Chicago *Tribune* subsequently also published Hansen's letter. As a consequence the government abandoned its efforts to enjoin *The Progressive* magazine's publication of the Morland article.

vexatiousness of implementing the policy against prior restraints. The two cases, moreover, underscore the import of the principle of separate but shared powers, which both invites constitutional and political conflicts and constrains the Court's interpretation of the First Amendment and the public's right to know. The Pentagon Papers case raised the question of whether the executive branch possesses the inherent power to seek an injunction against publication of materials that it deems in the interests of national security; whereas *The Progressive* raised the question of whether injunctions may be issued against publication of technical materials that Congress specifically defined in the Atomic Energy Act as "restricted data" and empowered the courts to issue injunctions against the publication of such material.

In 1971 the government sought to enjoin the New York *Times* and the *Washington Post* from publishing a series of articles based on a 47-volume study, *History of U.S. Decision Making Process on Vietnam Policy*. The study, examining government involvement in Vietnam between 1945 and 1968, was prepared in 1968 under the direction of Secretary of Defense Robert McNamara and was classified "Top Secret—Sensitive," the highest authorized classification for material the disclosure of "which could result in exceptionally grave damage to the Nation."[33] The New York *Times* received copies of the study from Daniel Ellsberg, who had secretly copied them while working for Rand Corporation and after his unsuccessful efforts to persuade leading political figures (he had approached Senators Edward Kennedy and William Fulbright) to publicize the study.

After several months of reviewing the documents and bitter debates over whether to publish portions of the study,[34] the New York *Times* commenced publication of selected items on June 13, 1971. After the third installment the Department of Justice sought an injunction against publication of the balance of the series, and on June 15 obtained a temporary restraining order prohibiting further publication until June 19. On June 18 the *Washington Post* also printed two articles based on the study and by 5 o'clock that day the government had filed a similar suit against its further publication of the material.

The following morning a district court denied the government's request for a preliminary injunction, but later in the day a circuit court judge extended the temporary restraining order until noon, June 21, to give a panel of the circuit court the opportunity to consider the government's application. Following an en banc hearing on June 22 the circuit court remanded the case to the district court to determine whether any of the other materials posed "such grave and immediate danger" to the security of the country as to warrant prior restraint and continued the stay on publication until June 25. On June 24 the New York *Times* appealed to the Supreme Court to vacate the stay on publication and to expedite consideration of the case. On June 25 the Court granted *certiorari* and heard oral arguments the following day.

Remarkably, within four days, on June 30, the Supreme Court issued no less than ten opinions: one brief *per curiam* opinion simply stating that the government had not met the "heavy burden of showing justification for the imposition of such a restraint" on the press, and six concurring and three dissenting opinions! Dissenting Chief Justice Burger and Justices Harlan and Blackmun were especially critical of the "frenzied" process of rendering the decision. The chief justice, in particular, criticized the New York *Times* for its unauthorized possession of the documents for three months, during which time its reporters studied them, and then pressure on the courts for an immediate decision when the government sought to enjoin publication of the material. Pointing to the dilemma (discussed in the first chapter) of the press claiming the public's right to know or the public's "right immediately to know" he observed: "[T]he *Times*, presumably in its capacity as trustee of the public's 'right to know,' . . . held up publication for purposes it considered proper and thus public knowledge was delayed."[35]

That the New York *Times* proceeded with publication of the classified study reflects both the institutional independence of the press and the perception of the political role of the press as a guardian of the public's right to know. Indeed, the Supreme Court has often been spared the task of deciding such "hard" cases because the government and the press reached agreement on the self-censorship of highly sensitive national security and defense matters. During World War II the press generally complied with the Office of Censorship's "Code of Wartime Practices for the American Press."[36] After the war the press exercised a good deal of self-imposed censorship either by delaying publication of information or minimizing its reporting of matters potentially damaging to national security and defense. The New York *Times*, for example, possessed information for over a year that the government was flying high-altitude U-2 missions over the Soviet Union from a base in Pakistan to photograph military and missile installations but did not publish the facts until one of the planes was shot down.[37] It also considerably played down its information about the CIA's preparations for the Bay of Pigs invasion and the Cuban missile crisis.[38]

The Pentagon Papers controversy epitomizes more than the institutional independence of the press. It also reflects the growing opposition to bureaucratic secrecy after World War II. While the press's relations with Congress and the president waxed and waned during the Korean conflict and the Vietnam war, the press increasingly criticized administrative agencies for withholding too much information.[39] In addition to the problems arising under the Administrative Procedure Act discussed in Chapter 1, the development of an executive classification system greatly promoted administrative secrecy and precipitated the Pentagon Papers controversy.

The executive branch's security classification system was established during the Korean conflict by President Harry Truman.[40] All federal agencies were authorized to mark sensitive material "Top Secret," "Secret," "Confidential," or "Restricted." The order was vague and sweeping, permitting covering up personal and political mistakes. Opposition led in 1953 to President Dwight D. Eisenhower's order eliminating the latter category of "restricted" materials, curtailing the number of agencies authorized to classify information, and limiting an agency heads' power to delegate authority to classify materials.[41] Not until after the Pentagon Papers controversy was the classification process further clarified. Then, President Richard Nixon's executive order in 1972 actually produced more, rather than less, classification, with even greater dispersal of classification authority spread throughout federal agencies.[42] President Nixon's directive encouraged increased classification by reverting to the language of the original Truman order in authorizing the classification of materials related to national security, rather than national defense or foreign policy, and by leaving undefined the nature and scope of national security. Further compounding the problems of governmental secrecy federal agencies adopted the practice of inventing and affixing their own classification labels to documents.* On June 28, 1978, President James Carter issued a new executive order "to balance the public's interests in access to Government information with the need to protect certain national security information from disclosure," once again limiting the number of agencies and agency officials authorized to classify documents, and speeding up the declassification and downgrading process.[45]

In political perspective the Pentagon Papers controversy reflects the gradual extension of a system of classification to matters often outside the scope of national security and national defense, and the growing concern in the 1960s and 1970s by members of the press and Congress with the public's right to know.[46] Even on the day of oral arguments before the Supreme Court the Department of Justice conceded the excesses of administrative secrecy, agreeing that 43 volumes of the 47-volume study could without damaging national security be released to the public. Joining Alexander Bickel, who argued the case for the New York Times Company, Bob Eckhart and Thomas Emerson filed an *amici curiae* (friends of the court) brief for 27 members of Congress, arguing that here the government suppression of a historical and political study profoundly violated the public's right to know:

> The precise degree of protection afforded by the doctrine of the right to know, as embodied in the First Amendment, has not yet been fully developed. It may be some years before the specific rules can be

---

*In 1977, for example, the Interagency Classification Review Committee, established to monitor and recommend changes in the classification system, uncovered widespread "unauthorized classification markings" and that agencies continued to overclassify documents.[43] The Federal Commission on Paperwork found that the Departments of State and Defense alone had more than 60 unauthorized additional classified categories, for example, "special intelligence."[44]

worked out. Yet the starting point is clear. It is that members of the public have, as a general proposition, the right to know all information upon which decisions that affect their lives and property are based. This is the fundamental premise of a democratic system. Exceptions to the general rule must be narrow and specific. They would be recognized only in such special areas as military weapons and operations, current negotiations with a foreign country, or damage to individual reputation by premature disclosure of investigative data.[47]

Likewise, in another *amicus curaie* brief the American Civil Liberties Union (ACLU) insisted that "[t]he right of the people to know, and the right of the press to be free, are the real interests of national security which are at stake."[48]

Although the New York Times Company, the congressmen, and the ACLU attacked the government's claim of an inherent power to enjoin publication of materials in the interests of national security, they conceded that the government might suppress technical information pertaining to present or future military operations, blueprints for military equipment, and secret codes. Here, the case involved a political-historical study of interest to the electorate, not sensitive technical information relating to national defense. In opposing the inherent power of the president to enjoin publications under the label of national security, the New York *Times* agreed that the government might suppress technical information where Congress had specifically authorized the withholding, enjoining, and punishment of publishing that information. In particular it noted that the Atomic Energy Act authorizes the Atomic Energy Commission to classify and declassify "Restricted Data," and provides penalties for an individual who "communicates, transmits, or discloses [restricted data] to any individual or person, or attempts or conspires to do any of the foregoing, with intent to injure the United States or with intent to secure an advantage to any foreign nation." The Atomic Energy Act defines "Restricted Data" as all data "concerning (1) design, manufacture, or utilization of atomic weapons; (2) the production of special nuclear material; or (3) the use of special nuclear material in the production of energy." Section 2280 of the Act, furthermore, authorizes the government to obtain from the judiciary "a permanent or temporary injunction, restraining order, or other order" to prevent the dissemination of restricted data.[49]

Thus there was agreement between the New York Times Company and Solicitor General Erwin Griswold that when authorized by Congress the executive branch could possibly enjoin and punish the publication of sensitive national security information. The fundamental disagreement was over whether, consistent with the First Amendment and the principle of separation powers, the president has an inherent power to seek injunctions against the publication of materials relating to both public affairs and

national security interests; and whether, in Solicitor General Erwin Griswold's words, "the First Amendment bars a court from prohibiting a news
paper from publishing material whose disclosure would pose a 'grave and
immediate danger to the security of the United States.'"[50]

In conceding that the government might enjoin dissemination of
information where specifically authorized by Congress, as under the Atomic
Energy Act, the participants in the Pentagon Papers case anticipated *The
Progressive* case—they also apprehended the crucial import of the principle
of separation of powers in constitutionally prescribing the appropriate
political arenas for vindicating of the political ideal of the public's right to
know. Under the Constitution, only Congress, and neither the president nor
the judiciary, has the power to make law and thus enact legislation designed
to enhance the political ideal of the public's right to know, as with, for
instance, the passage of the Freedom of Information Act.[51]

The salience of the public's right to know in the post-World War II era
arose not only because of the expansion of an elaborate, all-too-often
ambiguous and unwieldy classification system or simply because of syndromes of bureaucratic secrecy.[52] Over the last 30 years Congress promulgated more than 200 statutes regulating agencies' use of specific kinds of
confidential information. In addition to the Atomic Energy Act, regulations
cover information pertaining to national defense or foreign policy,[53] classified materials under executive orders,[54] diplomatic codes,[55] intelligence
sources and methods,[56] law enforcement investigatory files,[57] trade secrets,[58]
commercial or financial information,[59] and personal privacy.[60] These statutes, as implemented by administrative agencies and enforced by the
judiciary, largely define the legal contours of the political ideal of the public's
right to know. Yet the disjointed process of legislation perpetuates syndromes of administrative secrecy and frustrates demands for governmental
openness by providing overlapping and at times conflicting laws as well as
"no uniform or even consistent policy at the Federal level of regulating the
dissemination of 'confidential' data."[61]

The complexity of governmental secrecy as authorized by legislation,
typically encouraged by executive officials and established in bureaucratic
routines and standard operating procedures, requires, as numerous study
commissions have recommended,[62] comprehensive legislation and greater
cooperation between the congressional and executive branches. Within our
constitutional system of separate but shared powers Congress and the
president possess the responsibility and power to minimize unnecessary
secrecy and maximize governmental accountability and openness. Thus, as
the Pentagon Papers case illustrates, the judiciary plays an important but
essentially limited role when vindicating the political ideal of the public's
right to know.

Although the Supreme Court refused to enjoin the publication of the
Pentagon Papers, the case does not establish a precedent forbidding the
government from enjoining publication of classified or confidential materi-

als. That is so not because of the Court's *per curiam* ruling *cum* nine separate concurring and dissenting opinions. Instead, or in spite of, its *per curiam* decision, a majority of the Court indicated acceptance of two fundamental principles: first, five justices (Brennan, Stewart, White, Blackmun, and Chief Justice Burger) acknowledged that the First Amendment neither provides absolute, unconditional protection nor mandates impunity for dissemination of all information;[63] second, a majority of the justices (Black, Douglas, Stewart, White, and Marshall) concluded that the executive branch possesses no inherent power to impose a prior restraint on publications. Only the chief justice and Justice Harlan embraced the proposition that the executive branch has an unqualified inherent power to maintain secrecy.[64] Justices Brennan and Blackmun also recognized a limited but inherent power to enjoin publication of sensitive information.[65] By contrast, Justices Black, Douglas, Stewart, White, and Marshall rejected the president's possession of such inherent power.[66]

Justice Marshall's concurring opinion remains the most instructive for illuminating the constitutional and political issues in the Pentagon Papers and *The Progressive* cases. Justice Marshall found the Pentagon Papers case to turn not on the First Amendment per se but on the principle of separation of powers since the ultimate issue was "whether this Court or the Congress has the power to make law."[67] He affirmed that the president has the power, as authorized by Congress, to classify documents,[68] and the power, as chief executive and commander in chief,[69] to ensure national security and discipline employees who disclose confidential or classified information.[70] The critical question in the Pentagon Papers case was whether the president possesses inherent authority to invoke the equity powers of the courts to protect what the president perceives to be in the interests of national security. Here, for Justice Marshall the reasoning in *Youngstown Sheet & Tube Co.* v. *Sawyer* was controlling.[71]

In *Youngstown*, although a nationwide steel strike was imminent and potentially would jeopardize the national defense and war efforts in Korea, the Court struck down an executive order from President Harry Truman directing the secretary of commerce to seize and operate steel mills. While a majority of the Court concluded that here the president had no constitutional authority to issue the order in the absence of a congressional mandate, Justices Black and Douglas specifically contended that the president does not have any such inherent power.[72] Justice Marshall interpreted their understanding to be determinative of the Court's holding. As Justice Black explained in *Youngstown*: "The President's power if any, to issue the order must stem either from an act of Congress or from the Constitution itself."[73] Likewise, Justice Marshall observed:

> It would . . . be utterly inconsistent with the concept of separation of powers for this Court to use its power of contempt to prevent behavior that Congress has specifically declined to prohibit. There

would be a similar damage to the basic concept of these co-equal branches of Government if when the Executive Branch has adequate authority granted by Congress to protect "national security" it can choose instead to invoke the contempt power of a court to enjoin the threatened conduct. The Constitution provides that Congress shall make laws, the President execute laws, and courts interpret laws.[74]

In the absence of authorization by Congress the judiciary may not legitimately enforce prior restraints on the dissemination of information. As Justice Marshall poignantly noted: "It is not for this Court to fling itself into every breach perceived by some Government official nor is it for this Court to take on itself the burden of enacting law, especially law that Congress has refused to pass."[75]

Justice Marshall's view that the executive branch has no inherent power to invoke the equity jurisdiction of the judiciary is buttressed by *In re Debs* (1895). There, a unanimous Court upheld the contempt conviction of Eugene Debs for violating an injunction (although issued without express statutory authority) restraining a labor boycott designed to prevent the operations of certain railroads. Justice David Brewer upheld the convictions and the permissibility of the injunction, however, solely because the executive branch had broad congressional authority to regulate interstate commerce: "The national government, given by the Constitution power to regulate interstate commerce, has by express statute assumed jurisdiction over such commerce when carried on railroads. It is charged, therefore, with the duty of keeping those highways of interstate commerce free from obstruction. . . ."[76] *Debs* and *Youngstown* thus are complementary in supporting the view that the executive branch must receive specific authorization from Congress to seek injunctions and hence impose prior restraints on publications.

In both the Pentagon Papers and *The Progressive* cases the government improperly claimed an inherent power to restrain the publication of materials.[77] But the Pentagon Papers and *The Progressive* cases are distinguishable in that in the latter case the government sought an injunction pursuant to a specific authorization in the Atomic Energy Act. While acknowledging that the article on the construction of thermonuclear weapons contained restricted data that might prove beneficial to foreign nations in developing thermonuclear arsenals, the appellees defended the publication on the grounds that the information for the article was gathered from data within the public domain, that the article was an essential part of the exposition of ideas, and that publication would not result in direct immediate and irreparable damage to national security.[78] Although raising a number of unsettled constitutional issues, the fundamental question in *The Progressive* was whether the government may permissibly rely on the judiciary to enjoin publication of materials that Congress specifically defines as restricted data and authorizes the government to seek and the courts to provide injunctions against the dissemination of that information.[79]

Justice Marshall prophetically addressed that issue in the Pentagon Papers case when he found that the executive branch improperly sought an injunction against publication of materials that Congress had not expressly restricted by statute or empowered the courts to enjoin. Justice Marshall emphasized that the executive branch and the judiciary may constitutiohally restrain publications that threaten national security interests only when Congress has given its express authorization. With virtual clairvoyance he suggested that the government and the courts might enjoin publications when authorized by Congress, as under the Atomic Energy Act.[80] Accordingly, in *United States* v. *The Progressive, Inc.*, after district court judge Robert Warren wrestled with the claim of a First Amendment public's right to know, concluding that he could "find no plausible reason why the public needs to know the technical details about hydrogen bomb construction," the court rested with the preliminary finding that the injunction was appropriate as provided by Congress.[81]

Congressional authorization of the withholding and enjoining of publications in the interest of national security, however, does not immunize prior restraints or preclude judicial review. As the Burger Court emphasized in *Landmark Communications* v. *Virginia*: "Deference to a legislative finding cannot limit judicial inquiry when First Amendment rights are at stake."[82] Moreover, although several members of the Court anticipated in the Pentagon Papers case the *Progressive* controversy, a majority agreed that the government may enjoin publication only when authorized by a *narrowly drawn statute*. Justice White, in his concurring opinion, underscored that the problem in the Pentagon Papers case was that "[t]o sustain the Government [when claiming an inherent power to enjoin publications] . . . would start the courts down a long and hazardous road that I am not willing to travel, at least without congressional guidance and direction."[83] Congress is the appropriate institution for either mandating prohibitions of the disclosure of information or vindicating the public's interests in governmental openness. But where Congress authorizes the withholding, enjoining, and punishment of dissemination of information the judiciary has a crucial role in ensuring that statutory regulations are neither overbroad[84] nor vague[85] and thus impermissibly restrictive of First Amendment freedoms. "Faced with a clear conflict between a federal statute enacted in the interests of national security and an individual's exercise of his First Amendment rights," the Warren Court stressed in *United States* v. *Robel*, judicial "analysis [must focus on] whether Congress has adopted a constitutional means in achieving its concededly legitimate legislative goal." Legislative or executive branch claims of national security do not "justify any exercise of legislative power designed to promote such a goal."[86] In *The Progressive* the injunction issued under the Atomic Energy Act might have been found improper since the Act is overbroad when applied to *any* information, regardless of its origins, about atomic weapons. As *The Progressive*'s attorney, Gordon Sinykin, argued: "A journalist's idle musing about the nature or use of nuclear weapons or the operation and development of nuclear power facilities ... fits the category [of "restricted data"]."[87]

In constitutional politics reconciliation of the First Amendment with national security interests remains an unsettled, perplexing issue. The Pentagon Papers and *The Progressive* controversies dramatically illustrate the problem of bureaucratic secrecy and the significant if limited role of the judiciary in vindicating the public's right to know. As a practical matter, both cases underscore the futility of government attempts to enjoin publication of sensitive information no longer in its control: "To put it colloquially, a cat in the bag cannot be treated the same way as a cat outside the bag."[88]

In the future the Supreme Court may be forced to establish a standard for accommodating First Amendment and national security interests. Dissenting in the Pentagon Papers case, Justice Blackmun urged the necessity for such a standard: "What is needed here is a weighing, upon properly developed standards, of the broad right of the press to print and the very narrow right of the Government to prevent. Such standards are not yet developed."[89] The alternatives to the unenviable judicial task of articulating constitutional standards appear unacceptable: on the one hand, the First Amendment renders the government powerless to punish the disclosure of any secrets; and, on the other hand, that the classification of information precludes First Amendment claims and judicial inquiry. Thus, in reconciling the First Amendment with competing national security interests the Court will be faced with a vexing line-drawing problem in distinguishing between protected and unprotected communications concerning national security matters, as, analogously, when it applied its definitional balancing approach to libel and obscenity.

The Pentagon Papers case, furthermore, indicates that any national security exception to the First Amendment and the policy against prior restraints is extremely narrow. Governmental interference "in advance of "publication must inevitably, directly, and immediately cause the occurrence barrier."[90] Although in the Pentagon Papers case only Justices Black and Douglas would not countenance any prior restraints, the remaining concurring justices indicated that any national security exception is limited to situations where the alleged harm from publication would, in Justice Stewart's words, "surely result in direct, immediate, and irreparable damage to our Nation or its people."[91] Justice Brennan further underlined that a "publication must inevitably, directly, and immediately cause the occurence of an event kindred to imperiling the safety of a transport already at sea."[92]

Incontrovertibly, the *onus probandi* is on the government to justify its suppression of materials, and warrant judical creation of a national security exception to First Amendment protection. In this regard *United States* v. *Nixon* (1974) remains instructive. There, a unanimous Court (with Justice

Rehnquist not participating) recognized the presidential claim of executive privilege[93] as "fundamental to the operation of government and inextricably rooted in the separation of powers under the Constitution."[94] Writing for the Court, Chief Justice Burger, however, rejected President Nixon's assertion of an absolute privilege and the right to make a final, unreviewable claim of executive privilege: "Neither the doctrine of separation of powers, nor the need for confidentiality of high level communications, without more, can sustain an absolute, unqualified, presidential privilege of immunity from [the] judicial process." In the absence of a claim to the "need to protect military, diplomatic or sensitive national security secrets," the Court resolutely rejected the assertion of an executive privilege based on a generalized claim to national security. The Burger Court also unanimously agreed that an assertion of national security does not foreclose judicial review. To the contrary, as when Congress has authorized the withholding of information, presidential claims of executive privilege to protect national security are subject to exacting judicial scrutiny and an *in camera* review of the materials to determine whether the claim of national security is justified by a "demonstrated, specific need."[95]

Finally, the Pentagon Papers and *The Progressive* controversies again point out the dilemma of judicial construction of a constitutionally enforceable public's right to know. Not only does judicial creation of such a right violate the principle of separation of powers but (as Chapter 1 indicated) it actually poses an increased potential for prior restraints. Judge Warren, in *The Progressive*, for example, found "no plausible reason why the public needs to know the technical details about hydrogen bomb construction to carry on an informed debate on this issue." Judicial invention and delimitation of a constitutional right to know leads to judicial substitution of its judgments for not only legislative determinations of the wisdom, need, and propriety of governmental secrecy or openness but also editorial decisions as to what to print.[96] In the Pentagon Papers and *The Progressive* cases consideration of the public's right to know was not the crucial factor, and at best remains tangential, in the judiciary's First Amendment analysis and implementation of the policy against prior restraints. The First Amendment expressly guarantees individuals' freedom of speech and press, and only indirectly ensures the public's right to know. "The First Amendment," as Gordon Sinykin put it in his brief for *The Progressive*, "was not drafted to enable any branch of government to determine what information the public 'needs to know.' That was a responsibility left—for better or worse—to a free press and a free people."[97]

THE PUBLIC'S RIGHT TO KNOW, THE FIRST AMENDMENT, AND THE SUPREME COURT

In U.S. constitutional politics the political ideal of the public's right to know promises to remain a highly controversial issue. Politically salient, the pubic's right to know has been championed by the press and in Congress when combating bureaucratic secrecy. In the post-World War II era Congress and state legislatures enacted an impressive number of laws designed to enhance governmental openness, and constitutional adjudication has increasingly involved claims to First Amendment affirmative rights and press privileges to ensure an informed public and electorate.

In constitutional politics claims to the public's right to know nevertheless appear neither defensible nor salutory in terms of constitutional history, developing constitutional law, or considerations of public policy. A directly enforceable public's right to know has no basis in the text or historical background of either the Constitution or the First Amendment. Although the attraction of freedom of information and governmental openness has enchanted some members of both the Warren and Burger Courts to accept the constitutional legitimacy of the public's right to know, developing law under the First Amendment neither supports nor justifies claims to an independently enforceable right to know against the government. Rather, constitutional history and judicial politics demonstrate that the public's right to know is an important abstract right within the background of the Constitution and First Amendment. The First Amendment literally and as judicially enforced only indirectly, derivatively ensures the political ideal of the public's right to know. In historical perspective, the Supreme Court elaborated a broad functionalist view of First Amendment freedoms as essential to both individuals and an informed self-governing electorate. In protecting First Amendment freedoms and recognizing the public's interests in the free flow of information, the Court was characteristically modest when intervening in political controversies. In delimiting the scope of the amendment by developing a two-level theory of First Amendment protection, the Court acknowledged the public's important interests in wide-ranging information and narrowly defined those categories of unprotected speech while rigorously implementing its policy against prior restraints. The Court also steadfastly adhered to the constitutional redundancy of the speech and press clauses and declined to further extend the First Amendment by mandating affirmative rights to compel governmental openness. The Court's posture of modest intervention when interpreting the First Amendment was reinforced by considerations of public policy. The denomination of a concrete constitutional public's right to know, or press privileges and affirmative rights of access, not only commits the Court to extraconstitutional decision making and violates the principle of separation of powers. Concomitantly, the inevitability of judicial delimitation of the scope the public's right to know poses the potential for more restraints and dilution of First Amendment freedoms.

Within our constitutional and political system the political ideal of the public's right to know has been enhanced by the Supreme Court's broad interpretation of the First Amendment as securing the conditions for an informed public and electorate. Further vindication of the public's right to know requires congressional legislation and executive branch cooperation toward ensuring governmental openness and accountability as well as the continued vigilance of the institutional press, the lonely pamphleter, and the citizen-critic.

NOTES

1. Thomas I. Emerson, "Legal Foundations of the Right to Know," 1976 *Washington University Law Quarterly* 1, 23.

2. *New York Times, Col* v. *United States*, 403 U.S. 713 (1971) and *United States* v. *Washington Post Co.*, 403 U.S. 713 (1971) (companion case).

3. *United States* v. *The Progressive, Inc.*, 467 F. Supp. 990 (1979).

4. *Lovell* v. *Griffin*, 303 U.S. 444, 451 (1938).

5. See *Grosjean* v. *American Press Co.*, 297 U.S. 233, 244, 249 (1936).

6. *Patterson* v. *Colorado*, 205 U.S. 454, 462 (1907).

7. *Southeastern Promotions* v. *Conrad*, 420 U.S. 546, 559 (1975). See also *Near* v. *Minnesota*, 283 U.S. 697, 708 (1931).

8. Alexander Bickel, *The Morality of Consent* (New Haven: Yale University Press, 1975) 61.

9. *A Quantity of Books* v. *Kansas*, 378 U.S. 205, 211 (1964). See also *Marcus* v. *Search Warrant*, 367 U.S. 717, 731 (1961) (rejecting contention that *Kingsley Books, Inc.* v. *Brown*, 354 U.S. 436 [1957] supported "the proposition that the State may impose the extensive restraints imposed here on the distinction of these publications prior to an adversary proceeding on the issue of obscenity." Ibid., at 736); and *Corroll* v. *Princess Anne*, 393 U.S. 175 (1968) (setting aside a 10-day *ex parte* restraining order).

10. See *Freedman* v. *Maryland*, 380 U.S. 51, 60–61 (1965).

11. *Bantam Books, Inc.* v. *Sullivan*, 372 U.S. 58, 70 (1963). See also *Organization for a Better Austin* v. *Keefe*, 402 U.S. 415, 418–19 (1971).

12. *Southeastern Promotions* v. *Conrad*, 420 U.S. 546, 558 (1975).

13. *Kingsley Books, Inc.* v. *Brown*, 354 U.S. 436, 441 (1957).

14. Ibid., quoting Paul Freund, "The Supreme Court and Civil Liberties," 4 *Vanderbilt Law Review* 553, 539 (1952).

15. *Near* v. *Minnesota*, 283 U.S. 697 (1931).

16. Ibid., at 716. See also *Schenck* v. *United States* 249 U.S. 47, 52 (1919); *Cantwell* v. *Connecticut*, 310 U.S. 296, 398 (1940); *Milk Wagon Drivers Union* v. *Meadowmoor Dairies*, 312 U.S. 287, 294 (1941); and *Chaplinsky* v. *New Hampshire*, 315 U.S. 568, 572 (1942).

17. *Chaplinsky* v. *New Hampshire*, 315 U.S. 568, 571 (1942).

18. See, for example, *Grosjean* v. *American Press Co.*, 297 U.S. 233 (1936) and *Pittsburg Press Co.* v. *Pittsburg Commission on Human Rights*, 413 U.S. 376, 390 (1973).

19. See *Carroll* v. *Princess Anne*, 393 U.S. 175 (1968) and *Southeastern Promotions* v. *Conrad*, 420 U.S. 546, 559 (1975).

20. See, for example, *Shuttlesworth* v. *City of Birmingham*, 394 U.S. 146, 163 (1969) (Harlan, J., con. op.).

21. *Southeastern Promotions* v. *Conrad*, 420 U.S. 546, 559 (1975).

22. Ibid., at 559–60. See also *Cantwell* v. *Connecticut*, 310 U.S. 296, 305 (1940).

23. See, for example, *Nebraska Press Association* v. *Stuart*, 427 U.S. 539 (1976) and *Oklahoma Publishing Co.* v. *District Court*, 430 U.S. 308 (1977).

24. The Court has considered the issue of the First Amendment and competing national security interests with regard to its policy of no prior restraints in only two cases: *Near* v. *Minnesota*, 283 U.S. 697 (1931) and *New York Times Co.* v. *United States*, 403 U.S. 713 (1971).

25. See, for example, *Totten* v. *United States*, 92 U.S. 105 (1876); *United States* v. *Curtiss-Wright Export Corporation*, 299 U.S. 304, 320 (1936); *Chicago & S. Airlines* v. *Waterman S. S. Corporation*, 333 U.S. 103, 111 (1948); *United States* v. *Reynolds*, 345 U.S. 1

(1953); and *United States* v. *Nixon*, 418 U.S. 683 (1974).

26. See, for example, *United States* v. *Rosenberg*, 195 F.2d 583, 591–92 (2d Cir. 1952), cert. denied, 344 U.S. 838 (1953); *United States* v. *Donas-Botto*, 363 F. Supp. 191 (E. D. Mich. 1973); and *United States* v. *Van Hee*, 531 F.2d 354 (6th Cir. 1976).

27. See, for example, *E. W. Bliss Co.* v. *United States*, 248 U.S. 37 (1918) (upholding prior restraint on a government contractor from disclosing technical information on torpedo construction to a potential customer).

28. See, for example, *Garrison* v. *Louisiana*, 379 U.S. 64, 77 (1964); and *Time, Inc.* v. *Hill*, 385 U.S. 374, 389 (1967).

29. See, for example, *United States* v. *Edler Industries Incorporated*, 579 F.2d 516 (1978) (upholding restrictions on exportation of technical data under the National Security Act of 1954 against First Amendment challenge).

30. See *Alfred A. Knopf, Inc.* v. *Colby*, 509 U.S. 1362, cert. denied, 95 S.Ct. 1999 (1975); *United States* v. *Marchetti*, 466 F.2d 1309, 1313 (4th Cir. 1971), cert. denied, 409 U.S. 1063 (1972); and *United States* v. *Snepp*, 100 S.Ct. 763 (1980) (upholding CIA secrecy agreements with employees and former employees). See also Comment, "National Security and the First Amendment: The CIA In The Market-Place of Ideas," 14 *Harvard Civil Liberties-Civil Rights Law Review* 655 (1979).

31. See *United Public Workers of America* v. *Mitchell*, 330 U.S. 75, 95–103 (1947); *Pickering* v. *Board of Education*, 391 U.S. 563, 568 (1968); and *United States Civil Service Commission* v. *National Association of Letter Carriers*, 413 U.S. 548 (1973).

32. See *New York Times, Co.* v. *United States*, 403 U.S. 713, 733 (1971) (White, J., con. op.) and *Smith* v. *Daily Mail Publishing Co.*, 99 S.Ct. 2667 (1979).

33. Executive Order 10501, Code of Federal Regulations (1949–1953 Compilation) at 979.

34. See Harrison Salisbury, *Without Fear or Favor* (New York: New York Times Co., 1980). See also Sanford Ungar, *The Papers & The Papers* (New York: E. P. Dutton, 1972).

35. *New York Times, Co.* v. *United States*, 403 U.S. 713, 750 (1971) (Burger, C.J., dis. op.).

36. For a discussion see James R. Wiggins, *Freedom of Secrecy* (New York: Oxford University, 1956) 98–99.

37. See Salisbury, *Without Fear or Favor* at 512–13, 549–50, 554n.

38. Considerable disagreement exists over whether the New York *Times* completely suppressed or simply played down its information (the latter view appears the most appropriate conclusion). For discussions of the incident see Salisbury, ibid., at 137–47 and 162–63; and Ungar, *The Papers & The Papers* at 99–100.

39. See Chapter 1. See also Miles Johnson, *The Government Secrecy Controversy* (New York: Vantage Press, 1967) and Norman Dorsen and Stephen Gillers, eds., *None Of Your Business* (New York: Viking 1974).

40. See Executive Order 10290. On the development of the classification system see Carol M. Barker and matthew H. Fox, *Classified Files: Yellowing Pages* (New York: Twentieth Century Fund, 1972); Tryus Fain, ed. and compiler, *The Intelligence Community* (New York: R. R. Brower, 1977) 3–23, 459–662; and Morton Halperin, *National Security Policy-Making* (Lexington, Mass.: Lexington, 1975).

41. See Executive Order 10501 (President Eisenhower, November 5, 1953).

42. Executive Order 11652 (President Nixon, March 8, 1972).

43. Interagency Classification Review Committee, *1976 Progress Report* (Washington, D.C.: Government Printing Office, 1977) 30.

44. Federal Commission on Paperwork, *Confidentiality and Privacy* (Washington, D.C.: Government Printing Office, 1977).

45. Executive Order 12065 (President Carter, June 28, 1978). The Information Security Oversight Office found that the Carter executive order had generally encouraged federal agencies to promote openness in the handling of government information. The General

Accounting Office, however, found problems with the classification of 49 percent of the records at 23 Defense Department installations. See, Information Security Oversight Office, *Annual Report to the President* (Washington, D.C.: Government Printing Office, 1980); General Accounting Office, *Continuing Problems in DOD's Classification of National Security Information, Report to Congress* (Washington, D.C.: Government Printing Office, 1979); and General Accounting Office, *Improved Executive Branch Oversight Needed for the Government's National Security Information Classification Program, Report to Congress* (Washington, D.C.: Government Printing Office, 1979).

46. See Chapter 1 and accompanying notes.

47. Brief for 27 Members of Congress Amici Curiae, *New York Times, Co.* v. *United States* and *United States* v. *Washington Post*, Supreme Court of the United States, October Term 1970, No. 1873, at 12.

48. Brief of the American Civil Liberties Union, Amicus Curiae *New York Times, Co.* v. *United States*, Supreme Court of the United States, October Term 1970, No. 1873, at 4.

49. Atomic Energy Act of 1954, 42 U.S.C. §§ 2014(y)-2162, 2274, 2280.

50. Brief for the United States, *New York Times, Co.* v. *United States*, Supreme Court of the United States, October Term 1970, No. 1873, at 7.

51. Freedom of Information Act, 5 U.S.C. § 552 (1975). See also Government in the Sunshine Act, 5 U.S.C. § 552b (1976) and the Federal Advisory Committee Act, 5 U.S.C. App. 1 (1973).

52. See, generally, Baker and Fox, *Classified Files* and Francis Rourke, *Secrecy & Publicity: Dilemmas of Democracy* (Baltimore: Johns Hopkins, 1966).

53. See, for example, Freedom of Information Act, 5 U.S.C. 552(b) (1) (exemption for matters pertaining to national defense or foreign affairs).

54. See, for example, 18 U.S.C. § 798 (disclosure of classified information).

55. See for example, 18 U.S.C. § 952 (diplomatic codes and correspondence).

56. See, for example, 50 U.S.C. § 403 (d) (3).

57. See, for example, 5 U.S.C. § 552 (b) (7) (exemption for investigatory files).

58. Trade Secrets Act, 18 U.S.C. § 1905.

59. See, for example, Fair Credit Reporting Act, 15 U.S.C. § 1681.

60. See, for example, Privacy Act, 5 U.S.C. § 552a.

61. Federal Commission on Paperwork, *Confidentiality and Privacy*, at 2.

62. See ibid.; Domestic Committee on the Right of Privacy, *National Information Policy* Report to the President of the United States (Washington, D.C.: 1976); and David M. O'Brien, "Freedom of Information, Privacy and Information Control: A Contemporary Administrative Dilemma," 39 *Public Administration Review* 323 (1979).

63. *New York Times, Co.* v. *United States*, 403 U.S. 713 (1971) (Brennan, J., con. op.) at 726; (Stewart, J., con. op.) at 730; (White J., con. op.) at 740; (Burger, C.J., dis. op.) at 749-50; and (Blackmun, J., dis. op.) at 761. See also Peter Junger, "Down Memory Lane: The Case of the Pentagon Papers," 23 *Case Western Reserve Law Review* 3 (1971).

64. Ibid., at 749-51 (Burger, C.J., dis. op.) and at 755-58 (Harlan, J., dis. op.).

65. Ibid., at 726 (Brennan, J., con. op.) (wherein he points out that "there is a single, extremely narrow class of cases in which the First Amendment's ban on prior restraint may be overriden"); and at 761 (Blackmun, J., dis. op.) (wherein he states that "what is needed here is a weighing upon properly developed standards, of the broad right of the press to print and of the very narrow right of the Government to prevent").

66. Ibid., at 718-19 (Black, J., con. op.); at 723 (Douglas, J., con. op.); at 728 (Stewart, J., con. op.); at 731-33 (White, J., con. op.); and at 741-47 (Marshall, J., con. op.).

67. Ibid., at 741 (Marshall, J., con. op.).

68. As discussed in Chapter 2, the only constitutional provision for government secrecy appears in Article 1, Section 5, Clause 3, with respect to congressional journals. For an excellent brief discussion of the joint constitutional responsibilities and powers of the legislative and executive branches in classification of materials see Fain, *The Intelligence Community* at 4-14.

69. U.S. Constitution, Article 2, Section 2. See also *United States* v. *Curtiss-Wright Export Corporation*, 299 U.S. 304 (1936); *Chicago & S. Air Lines, Inc.* v. *Waterman Corporation*, 333 U.S. 103 (1948); *United States* v. *Belmont*, 301 U.S. 324 (1937); and *United States* v. *Pink*, 315 203, 229 (1942).

70. See cases cited in supra note 25.

71. *Youngstown Sheet & Tube* v. *Sawyer*, 343 U.S. 579 (1952).

72. Ibid., at 582–89 (Black, J.) and at 629–34 (Douglas, J., con. op.). Compare ibid., at 593–614 (Frankfurter, J., con. op.).

73. Ibid., at 585.

74. *New York Times, Co.* v. *United States*, 403 U.S. 713, 742 (Marshall, J., con. op.).

75. Ibid., at 747.

76. *In re Debs*, 158 U.S. 564, 586 (1895).

77. See *Brief for the United States, United States* v. *The Progressive, Inc.*, United States Court of Appeals for the Seventh Circuit, October Term, 1979, Nos. 79-1428, 79-1664, at 26 and 107-114.

78. Brief for The Progressive, *United States* v. *The Progressive, Inc.*, United States Court of Appeals for the Seventh Circuit, October Term, 1979, Nos. 79-1428, 79-1664, at 11-12 and 95.

79. *United States* v. *The Progressive, Inc.*, 467 F. Supp. 990, 994 (1979). See also *United States* v. *Edler Industries Incorporated*, 579 F.2d 516 (1978) (upholding restrictions on exporting technical data under the National Security Act of 1954 against First Amendment challenge).

80. *New York Times, Co.* v. *United States*, 403 U.S. 713, 743 n.3 (1971) (Marshall, J., con. op.).

81. *United States* v. *The Progressive, Inc.*, 467 F. Supp. 990, 994, 999-1000 (1979).

82. *Landmark Communications* v. *Virginia*, 435 U.S. 829, 843 (1978).

83. *New York Times, Co.* v. *United States*, 403 U.S. 713, 733 (1971) (White, J., con. op.).

84. See, for example, *Shelton* v. *Tucker*, 364 U.S. 479, 488 (1960); *N.A.A.C.P.* v. *Button*, 371 U.S. 415, 433 (1963); *Ashton* v. *Kentucky*, 384 U.S. 195 (1966); and *Grayned* v. *City of Rockford*, 408 U.S. 104 (1972).

85. See, for example, *Broadrick* v. *Oklahoma*, 413 U.S. 601, 611–12 (1973); and *Gooding* v. *Wilson*, 405 U.S. 518, 520 (1972).

86. *United States* v. *Robel*, 389 U.S. 258, 264 (1967).

87. Brief for the Progressive, Inc., at 8.

88. Brief for 27 Members of Congress, *Amici Curiae, New York Times, Co.* v. *United States* at 5.

89. *New York Times, Co.* v. *United States*, 403 U.S. 713, 761 (Blackmun, J., dis. op.).

90. *Miami Herald Publishing Co.* v. *Tornillo*, 418 U.S. 241, 259 (1974) White, J., con. op.).

91. *New York Times, Co.* v. *United States*, 403 U.S. 713, 730 (1971) (Stewart, J., con. op.).

92. Ibid., at 726–27 (Brennan, J., con. op.).

93. On the development and legitimacy of claims to executive privilege see Raoul Berger, *Executive Privilege: A Constitutional Myth* (Cambridge: Harvard University Press, 1974).

94. *United States* v. *Nixon*, 418 U.S. 683, 708 (1974).

95. Ibid., at 713. Congress in amending the Freedom of Information Act in 1974 overrode the Court's earlier decision in *Environmental Protection Agency* v. *Mink*, 410 U.S. 73 (1973), and authorized the judiciary to undertake *in camera* review of materials withheld under exemptions to the act.

96. On this point see Chief Justice Burger's comments in *Columbia Broadcasting System, Inc.* v. *Democratic National Committee*, 412 U.S. 94, 124–25 (1973).

97. Brief for The Progressive, at 9. See also ibid., at 48–50.

APPENDICES

APPENDIX A

The Freedom of Information Act

5 USC § 552. PUBLIC INFORMATION; AGENCY RULES, OPINIONS, ORDERS, RECORDS, AND PROCEEDINGS

(a) Each agency shall make available to the public information as follows:

(1) Each agency shall separately state and currently publish in the Federal Register for the guidance of the public—

(A) description of its central and field organization and the established places at which, the employees (and in the case of a uniformed service, the members) from whom, and the methods whereby, the public may obtain information, make submittals or requests, or obtain decisions;

(B) statements of the general course and method by which its functions are channeled and determined, including the nature and requirements of all formal and informal procedures available;

(C) rules of procedure, descriptions of forms available, or the places at which forms may be obtained, and instructions as to the scope and contents of all papers, reports, or examinations;

(D) substantive rules of general applicability adopted as authorized by law, and statements of general policy or interpretations of general applicability formulated and adopted by the agency; and

(E) each amendment, revision, or repeal of the foregoing.

Except to the extent that a person has actual and timely notice of the terms thereof, a person may not in any manner be required to resort to, or be adversely affected by, a matter required to be published in the Federal Register and not so published. For the purpose of this paragraph, matter reasonably available to the class of persons affected thereby is deemed published in the Federal Register when incorporated by reference therein with the approval of the Director of the Federal Register.

(2) Each agency, in accordance with published rules, shall make available for public inspection and copying—

(A) final opinions, including concurring and dissenting opinions, as well as orders, made in the adjudication of cases;

(B) those statements of policy and interpretations which have been adopted by the agency and are not published in the Federal Register; and

(C) administrative staff manuals and instructions to staff that affect a member of the public; unless the materials are promptly published and copies offered for sale. To the extent required to prevent a clearly unwarranted invasion of personal privacy, an agency may delete identifying details when it makes available or publishes an opinion, statement of policy, interpretation, or staff manual or instruction. However, in each case the justification for the deletion shall be explained fully in writing. Each agency shall also maintain and make available for public inspection and copying current indexes providing identifying information for the public as to any matter issued, adopted, or promulgated after July 4, 1967, and required by this paragraph to be made available or published. Each agency shall promptly publish, quarterly or more frequently, and distribute (by sale or otherwise) copies of each index or supplements thereto unless it determines by order published in the Federal Register that the publication would be unnecessary and impracticable, in which case the agency shall nonetheless provide copies of such index on request at a cost not to exceed the direct cost of duplication. A final order, opinion, statement of policy, interpretation, or staff manual or instruction that affects a member of the public may be relied on, used, or cited as precedent by an agency against a party other than an agency only if—

(i) it has been indexed and either made available or published as provided by this paragraph; or

(ii) the party has actual and timely notice of the terms thereof.

(3) Except with respect to the records made available under paragraphs (1) and (2) of this subsection, each agency, upon any request for records which (A) reasonably describes such records and (B) is made in accordance with published rules stating the time, place, fees (if any), and procedures to be followed, shall make the records promptly available to any person.

(4) (A) In order to carry out the provisions of this section, each agency shall promulgate regulations, pursuant to notice and receipt of public comment, specifying a uniform schedule of fees applicable to all constituent units of such agency. Such fees shall be limited to reasonable standard charges for document search and duplication and provide for recovery of only the direct charge or at a reduced charge where the agency determines that waiver or reduction can be considered as primarily benefiting the general public.

(B) On complaint, the district court of the United States in the district in which the complainant resides, or has his principal place of business, or in which the agency records are situated, or in the District of Columbia, has jurisdiction to enjoin the agency from withholding agency records and to order the production of any agency records improperly withheld from the complainant. In such a case the court shall determine the matter de novo, and may examine the contents of such agency records in camera to determine whether such records or any part thereof shall be withheld under any of the exemptions set forth in subsection (b) of this section, and the burden is on the agency to sustain its action.

(C) Notwithstanding any other provision of law, the defendant shall serve an answer or otherwise plead to any complaint made under this subsection within thirty days after service upon the defendant of the pleading in which such complaint is made, unless the court otherwise directs for good cause shown.

(D) Except as to cases the court considers of greater importance, proceedings before the district court, as authorized by this subsection, and appeals therefrom, take precedence on the docket over all cases and shall be assigned for hearing and trial or for argument at the earliest practicable date and expedited in every way.

(E) The court may assess against the United States reasonable attorney fees and other litigation costs reasonably incurred in any case under this section in which the complainant has substantially prevailed.

(F) Whenever the court orders the production of any agency records improperly withheld from the complainant and assesses against the United States reasonable attorney fees and other litigation costs, and the court additionally issues a written finding that the circumstances surrounding the withholding raise questions whether agency personnel acted arbitrarily or capriciously with respect to the withholding, the Civil Service Commission shall promptly initiate a proceeding to determine whether disciplinary action is warranted against the officer or employee who was primarily responsible for the withholding. The Commission, after investigation and consideration of the evidence submitted, shall submit its findings and recommendations to the administrative authority of the agency concerned and shall send copies of the findings and recommendations to the officer or employee or his representative. The administrative authority shall take the corrective action that the Commission recommends.

(G) In the event of noncompliance with the order of the court, the district court may punish for contempt the responsible employee, and in the case of a uniformed service the responsible officer.

(5) Each agency having more than one member shall maintain and make available for public inspection a record of the final votes of each member in every agency proceedings.

(6) (A) Each agency, upon any request for records made under paragraph (1), (2), or (3) of this subsection, shall—

(i) determine within ten days (excepting Saturdays, Sundays, and legal public holidays) after the receipt of any such request whether to comply with such request and shall immediately notify the person making such request of such determination and the reasons thereof, and of the right of such person to appeal to the head of the agency any adverse determination; and

(ii) make a determination with respect to any appeal within twenty days (excepting Saturdays, Sundays, and legal public holidays) after the receipt of such appeal. If on appeal the denial of the request for records is in whole or in part upheld, the agency shall notify the person making such request of the provisions for judicial review of that determination under paragraph (4) of this subsection.

(B) In unusual circumstances as specified in this subparagraph, the time limits prescribed in either clause (i) or clause (ii) of subparagraph (A) may be extended by written notice to the person making such request setting forth the reasons for such extension and the date on which a determination is expected to be dispatched. No such notice shall specify a date that would result in an extension for more than ten days. As used in this subparagraph, "unusual circumstances" means, but only to the extent reasonably necessary to the proper processing of the particular request—

(i) the need to search for and collect the requested records from field facilities or other establishments that are separate from the office processing the request;

(ii) the need to search for, collect, and appropriately examine a voluminous amount of separate and distinct records which are demanded in a single request; or

(iii) the need for consultation, which shall be conducted with all practicable speed, with another agency having a substantial interest in the determination of the request or among two or more components of the agency having substantial subject-matter interest therein.

(C) Any person making a request to any agency for records under paragraph (1), (2), or (3) of this subsection shall be deemed to have exhausted his administrative remedies with respect to such request if the agency fails to comply with the applicable time limit provisions of this paragraph. If the Government can show exceptional circumstances exist and that the agency is exercising due diligence in responding to the request, the court may retain jurisdiction and allow the agency additional time to complete its review of the records. Upon any determination by an agency to comply with a request for records, the records shall be made promptly available to such person making such request. Any notification of denial of any request for records under this subsection shall set forth the names or positions of each person responsible for the denial of such request.

(b) This section does not apply to matters that are—

(1) (A) specifically authorized under criteria established by an Executive order to be kept secret in the interest of national defense or foreign policy and (B) are in fact properly classified pursuant to such Executive order;

(2) related solely to the internal personnel rules and practices of an agency;

(3) specifically exempted from disclosure by statute (other than section 552b of this title), provided that such statute (A) requires that the matters be withheld from the public in such a manner as to leave no discretion on the issue, or (B) establishes particular criteria for withholding or refers to particular types of matters to be withheld;

(4) trade secrets and commercial or financial information obtained from a person and privileged or confidential;

(5) inter-agency or intra-agency memorandums or letters which would not be available by law ot a party other than an agency in litigation with the agency;

(6) personnel and medical files and similar files the disclosure of which would constitute a clearly unwarranted invasion of personal privacy;

(7) investigatory records compiled for law enforcement purposes, but only to the extent that the production of such records would (A) interfere with enforcement proceedings, (B) deprive a person of a right to a fair trial or an impartial adjudication, (C) constitute an unwarranted invasion of personal privacy, (D) disclose the identity of a confidential source and, in the case of a record compiled by a criminal law enforcement authority in the course of a criminal investigation, or by an agency conducting a lawful national security intelligence investigation, confidential information furnished only by the confidential source, or (F) endanger the life or physical safety of law enforcement personnel;

(8) contained in or related to examination, operating, or condition reports prepared by, on behalf of, or for the use of an agency responsible for the regulation or supervision of financial institutions; or

(9) geological and geophysical information and data, including maps concerning wells.

Any reasonably segregable portion of a record shall be provided to any person requesting such record after deletion of the portions which are exempt under this subsection.

(c) This section does not authorize withholding of information or limit the availability of records to the public, except as specifically stated in this section. This section is not authority to withhold information from Congress.

(d) On or before March 1 of each calendar year, each agency shall submit a report covering the preceding calendar year to the Speaker of the House of Representatives and President of the Senate for referral to the appropriate committees of the Congress. The report shall include—

(1) the number of determinations made by such agency not to comply with requests for records made to such agency under subsection (a) and the reasons for each such determination;

(2) the number of appeals made by persons under subsection (a) (6), the result of such appeals, and the reason for the action upon each appeal that results in a denial of information;

(3) the names and titles or positions of each person responsible

for the denial of records requested under this section, and the number of instances of participation for each;

(4) the results of each proceeding conducted pursuant to subsection (a) (4) (F), including a report of the disciplinary action taken against the officer or employee who was primarily responsible for improperly withholding records or an explanation of why disciplinary action was not taken;

(5) a copy of every rule made by such agency regarding this section;

(6) a copy of the fee schedule and the total amount of fees collected by the agency for making records available under this section; and

(7) such other information as indicates efforts to administer fully this section.

The Attorney General shall submit an annual report on or before March 1 of each calendar year which shall include for the prior calendar year a listing of the number of cases arising under this section, the exemption involved in each case, the disposition of such case, and the cost, fees, and penalities assessed under subsection (a) (4) (E), (F), and (G). Such report shall also include a description of the efforts undertaken by the Department of Justice to encourage agency compliance with this section.

(e) For purposes of this section, the term "agency" as defined in section 551(1) of this title includes any executive department, military department, Government corporation, Government controlled corporation, or other establishment in the executive branch of the Government (including the Executive Office of the President), or any independent regulatory agency.

APPENDIX B

State Open-Records and Open-Meetings Laws

State	Enacted	Amended	Statute
Alabama	(1923)	(1945)	Title 41, Secs. 145–47 (records); Title 14, Secs. 393–94 (meetings)
Alaska	(1913)	(1968)	AS 9.25.110–.125 and 11.30.245 (records); AS 44.62.310 (1975 Supp.) (meetings)
Arizona	(1901)	(1975)	Title 39, Ch. 1, Art. 2, Sec. 39-121.01–.02 (records); Sec. 38-431 (meetings)
Arkansas	(1967)		Secs. 12-2801 to -2807 (records and meetings)
California	(1872)	(1975)	G. Code 2650 to 2660 (records); Secs. 11120 and 54952 (meetings)
Colorado	(1968)	(1969)	Sec. 24-72-203 (records); Sec. 29-9-101 and 24-6-4 (meetings)
Connecticut	(1957)	(1975)	Ch. 1, Sec. 19 (records and meetings)
Delaware	(1976)		Title 29, Secs. 10002–3 (records); Sec. 10004 (meetings)
District of Columbia	(1935)	(1968)	Title 11 (records); Title 1-503a (meetings)
Florida	(1909)	(1973)	Ch. 119 (records); Ch. 286 (meetings)
Georgia	(1959)	(1972)	Sec. 40-8c and 40-2701 to -2703 (records); Sec. 23-802 (meetings)
Hawaii	(1921)	(1975)	Ch. 92, Pt. 4, Secs. 92.50–.52 (records); Ch. 92, Pt. 1 (meetings)
Idaho	(1901)	(1974)	Secs. 9-301, 59-1009, and 59-1011 (records and meetings)

APPENDIX B (continued)

State Open-Records and Open-Meetings Laws

State	Enacted	Amended	Statute
Illinois	(1957)	(1975)	Ch. 116, Sec. 43 (records); Ch. 102, Sec. 41 (meetings)
Indiana	(1953)	(1971)	Title 57-6 (records and meetings)
Iowa	(1965)	(1975)	Ch. 68A (records); Sec. 28A (meetings)
Kansas	(1957)	(1975)	Ch. 45, Secs. 201–3 (records); Secs. 75-4317 to 432 (meetings)
Kentucky	(1958)	(1976)	Ch. 61, Secs. 870–84 (records and meetings)
Louisiana	(1940)	(1976)	Title 44, Pt. 1 Secs. 31–38 (records); Secs. 42:4.1–42:10 (meetings)
Maine	(1959)	(1975)	Title 1, Ch. 13, Sec. 405 (records and meetings)
Maryland	(1970)	(1978)	Art. 76A, Sec. 1–5, amend. Ch. 1006, Art. 3, Sec. 21 (records); Art. 25, Sec. 5, Art. 23A, Sec. 8 (meetings)
Massachusetts	(1851)	(1973)	Title 10, Ch. 66 (records); Ch. 30A, Sec. 11A and B (meetings)
Michigan	(1899)	(1976)	Sec. 750.492 (records); Sec. 15.261–15.275 (meetings)
Minnesota	(1941)	(1974)	Sec. 15.17(4) (records); Sec. 471.705 (meetings)
Missouri	(1961)	(1973)	Ch. 610, Secs. 610.010–610.030 (records and meetings)
Montana	(1895)	(1977)	Title 93, Ch. 1001, Sec. 93-1001-1 to -5 (records); Title 82, Ch. 3402 (meetings)

APPENDIX B (continued)

State Open-Records and Open-Meetings Laws

State	Enacted	Amended	Statute
Nebraska	(1961)		Sec. 84-712 (records and meetings)
Nevada	(1909)	(1973)	Secs. 239.010 to .030 (records); Secs. 241.010 to .040, Secs. 244.080, 268.305, and 396.100 (meetings)
New Hampshire	(1968)	(1975)	Ch. 91-A, Sec. 4 (records and meetings)
New Jersey	(1953)	(1975)	Sec. 41:1A (records); A-1030 (meetings)
New Mexico	(1947)	(1973)	Secs. 71-5-1 to 71-5-3 (records); Secs. 5-6-23 to 5-6-26 (meetings)
New York	(1974)	(1977)	Art. 6, Secs. 84–90 (records); Art. 7, Secs. 90–101 (meetings)
North Carolina	(1935)	(1975)	Ch. 132, Secs. 132-1 to 132-9 (records); Art. 33B, Secs. 143-318.1 to .7 (meetings)
North Dakota	(1957)	(1975)	Sec. 44-04-18 (records); Sec. 44-04-19 (meetings)
Ohio	(1953)	(1975)	Sec. 149.34 (records); SB 74 (meetings)
Oklahoma	(1957)	(1972)	Title 51, Sec. 24 (records); Title 25, Secs. 201–2 (meetings)
Oregon	(1909)	(1973)	Secs. 192.610–.690 (records and meetings)
Pennsylvania	(1957)	(1978)	Secs. 66.1–66.4 and P. L. 390, No. 212 (1978) (records); Act 175 (1974) (meetings)
Rhode Island	No records law (Common law right of access)		Secs. 42-46-1 to 10 (1976) (meetings)

APPENDIX B (continued)

State Open-Records and Open-Meetings Laws

State	Enacted	Amended	Statute
South Carolina	(1954)	(1978)	Art. 1, Sec. 10 of Const. and Act 593 (1978) (records and meetings)
South Dakota	(1935)		Title 1, Ch. 27, Secs. 1–7 (records); Ch. 1–25 (meetings)
Tennessee	(1957)	(1975)	Title 15, Ch. 3, Secs. 15-304 to 15-308 (records); Title 8, Ch. 4, Sec. 8-4402 (meetings)
Texas	(1947)	(1974)	Art. 6252-17a, Sec. 1-13 (records); Art. 6252-17, Sec. 2 (meetings)
Utah	(1943)	(1951)	Secs. 78-26-1 to -8 (records); Sec. 52-4 (meetings)
Vermont	(1957)	(1978)	Secs. 315–320 (records and meetings)
Virginia	(1968)	(1979)	Secs. 2.1-340 to -346.1 (records and meetings)
Washington	(1941)	(1973)	Title 42, Ch. 17, Sec. 42, 17.250 (records); Ch. 42.30 (meetings)
West Virginia	(1964)	(1977)	Ch. 147, Secs. 29B-1-1 to -1-6 (records); Sec. 6-9A-1 (meetings)
Wisconsin	(1849)	(1976)	Secs. 19.21, 59.142, and 59.71 (records); Ch. 297, Sec. 66.77 (meetings)
Wyoming	(1959)	(1971)	Sec. 9-692.1 (records and meetings)

APPENDIX C

State Press-Shield Statutes

State	Enacted	Statute
Alabama	(1935)	Title 7, Sec. 370 (1960)
Alaska	(1967)	Stat. 9.25.250-.220 (1973)
Arizona	(1937)	Sec. 12-2237 (Supp. 1978)
Arkansas	(1936)	Sec. 43-917 (1977)
California	(1935)	Evid. Code, Sec. 1070 (1979)
Delaware	(1974)	Title 10, Secs. 4320-25 (1979)
Illinois	(1971)	Ch. 51, Secs. 111-19 (Smith-Hurd Supp. 1979)
Indiana	(1941)	Code, Sec. 34-3-5-1 (Burns Supp. 1978)
Kentucky	(1936)	Sec. 421.100 (1972)
Louisiana	(1970)	Rev. Stat., Secs. 45.1451-.1454 (West Supp. 1978)
Maryland	(1896)	Cts. & Jud. Proc. Code, Sec. 9-113 (1972)
Michigan	(1949)	Comp. Laws, Sec. 767.5a (1968)
Minnesota	(1973)	Secs. 595.021-.024 (west Supp. 1979)
Montana	(1943)	Secs. 93-1-1 to -2 (Supp. 1977)
Nebraska	(1973)	Secs. 20-144 to -147 (1974)
Nevada	(1969)	Sec. 49.275 (1975)
New Jersey	(1933)	Secs. 2A:84A-21 to -29 (Supp. 1979-1980)
New Mexico	(1953)	Sec. 20-2-12.1 (Supp. 1975)
New York	(1970)	Civ. Rights Law, Sec. 79-h (McKinney's 1976)
North Dakota	(1973)	Sec. 31-01-06.2 (1976)

APPENDIX C (continued)

State Press-Shield Statutes

State	Enacted	Statute
Ohio	(1941)	Secs. 2739.04 and 2739.12 (Supp. 1978)
Oklahoma	(1973)	Title 12, Sec. 2506 (Supp. 1978)
Oregon	(1973)	Rev. Stat., Secs. 44.510–.540 (1977)
Pennsylvania	(1937)	Title 28, Sec. 330 (Purdon Supp. 1978–1979)
Rhode Island	(1973)	Secs. 9-19.1-1 to .1-3 (Supp. 1978)
Tennessee	(1975)	Secs. 24-113 to -115 (Supp. 1978)

SELECTED BIBLIOGRAPHY

BOOKS

Abraham, Henry J. *Freedom and the Court*. 3rd. ed. New York: Oxford University Press, 1977.

Annals of Congress: First Congress, 1798–1791, vols. one and two. Washington, D.C.: Gales and Seaton, 1834.

Aronson, James. *The Press and the Cold War*. New York: Bobbs-Merrill, 1970.

Barron, Jerome. *Freedom of The Press For Whom?* Bloomington: Indiana University Press, 1973.

Berns, Walter. *Freedom, Virtue and the First Amendment*. Baton Rouge: Louisiana State University Press, 1957.

Berns, Walter. *The First Amendment and the Future of American Democracy*. New York: Basic Books, 1976.

Bickel, Alexander. *The Morality of Consent*. New Haven: Yale University Press, 1975.

Black, Hugo. *Constitutional Faith*. New York: Alfred Knopf, 1969.

Blackstone, Sir William, *Commentaries on the Laws of England*, 4 vols. Oxford: Clarendon Press, 1766.

Bollan, William. *The Freedom of Speech and Writings Upon Public Affairs, Considered, with a Historical View*. London: S. Baker, 1766.

Boyd, Julian, ed. *The Papers of Thomas Jefferson*. Princeton: Princeton University Press, 1955.

Cater, Douglass. *The Fourth Branch of Government*. Boston: Houghton Mifflin, 1959.

Chafee, Zechariah, Jr. *Free Speech in the United States*. Cambridge: Harvard University Press, 1941.

Cooley, Thomas M. *A Treatise on the Constitutional Limitations*. Boston: Little, Brown and Company, 1868.

Cooper, Kent. *The Right to Know*. New York: Farrar, Straus and Cudahy, 1956.

Cross, Harold L. *The People's Right to Know*. Morningside Heights: Columbia University Press, 1953.

Dorsen, Norman, and Gillers, Stephen, eds. *None of Your Business: Government Secrecy in America*. New York: Viking Press, 1974.

Duniway, Clyde A. *The Development of Freedom of the Press in Massachusetts*, New York: Longmans, Green and Co., 1906.

Elliot, Jonathan. *The Debates in the Several State Conventions on the Adoption of the Federal Constitution*, 5 vols. New York: Burt Franklin Reprints, 1974.

Emerson, Thomas I. *The System of Freedom of Expression*. New York: Vintage Books, 1970.

Fain, Tyrus G., with Plant, Katharine C., eds. *The Intelligence Community*. New York: R. R. Bowker, 1977.

Farrand, Max. *The Records of the Federal Convention of 1787*. New Haven: Yale University Press, 1911.

Federalist Papers. New York: Mentor Books, 1961.

Franck, Thomas M., and Weisband, Edward, eds. *Secrecy and Foreign Policy*. New York: Oxford University Press, 1974

Galnoor, Itzhak. *Government Secrecy In Democracies*. New York: New York University Press, 1977.

Halperin, Morton, and Hoffman, Daniel, eds., *National Security and the Right to Know*. Washington, D.C.: New Republic Books, 1977.

Hay, George. *An Essay on the Liberty of the Press, Respectfully Inscribed to the Republican Printers throughout the United States*. Richmond: Samuel Pleasants, Jr., 1803.

Hocking, William. *Freedom of the Press: A Framework of Principle*. Chicago: University of Chicago Press, 1947.

Hudon, Edward G., *Freedom of Speech and Press in America*. Washington, D.C.: Public Affairs Press, 1963.

Hunt, Gaillard, ed. *The Writings of James Madison*. New York: Putnam's Sons, 1910.

Jacobson, David, ed. *The English Libertarian Heritage: From the Writings of John Trenchard and Thomas Green*. Indianapolis: Bobbs-Merrill, 1965.

Johnson, Miles. *The Government Secrecy Controversy*. New York: Vantage Press, 1967.

Lee, Richard Henry. *An Additional Number of Letters from the Federal Farmer to the Republican (1788)*. Chicago: Quadrangle, 1962.

Levenson, Alan, and Pitt, Harvey L., eds. *Government Information*. New York: Practising Law Institute, 1978.

Levy, Leonard. *Legacy of Suppression*. Cambridge, Mass.: Belknap, 1960.

Levy, Leonard, ed. *Freedom of the Press from Zenger to Jefferson*. New York: Bobbs-Merrill, 1966.

Lipscomb, Andrew, and Bergh, Albert, eds. *The Writings of Thomas Jefferson*, 20 vols. Washington, D. C., 1904–5.

Liston, Robert. *The Right to Know*. New York: Franklin Watts, 1973.

Lofton, John. *The Press as Guardian of the First Amendment*. Columbia: University of South Carolina, 1980.

Marnell, William H. *The Right to Know*. New York: Seabury Press, 1973.

Marwick, Christine, ed. *The 1980 Edition of Litigation Under the Federal Freedom of Information Act and Privacy Act*. Washington, D.C.: Center for National Security Studies, 1979.

Meiklejohn, Alexander. *Political Freedom*. New York: Harper & Row, 1948.

Nelson, Harold, ed. *Freedom of the Press from Hamilton to the Warren Court*. New York: Bobbs-Merrill, 1967.

Nimmo, Dan. *Newsgathering in Washington*. New York: Atherton Press, 1964.

Nye, Russell. *Fettered Freedom*, Urbana: University of Illinois Press, 1972.

O'Brien, David M. *Privacy, Law, and Public Policy*. New York: Praeger, 1979.

O'Reilly, James. *Federal Information Disclosure: Procedures, Forms, and the Law*. Colorado: Shepard's, 1979.

Patterson, Giles, *Free Speech and A Free Press*. Boston: Little, Brown and Co., 1939.

Paul, James, and Schwartz, Murray. *Federal Censorship: Obscenity in the Mail*. New York: Free Press, 1961.

Pritchett, C. Herman. *The American Constitution*. 3d ed. New York: McGraw-Hill, 1977.

Rourke, Francis. *Secrecy & Publicity*. Baltimore: Johns Hopkins Press, 1966.

Rutherford, Livingston. *John Peter Zenger. His Papers, His Trial, and a Bibliography of Zenger Imprints*. New York: Dodd, Mead & Co., 1904.

Salisbury, Harrison. *Without Fear or Favor*. New York: New York Times Book Co., 1980.

Shapiro, Martin. *Freedom of Speech: The Supreme Court and Judicial Review*. Englewood Cliffs, N.J.: Prentice-Hall, 1966.

Siebert, Fredrick. *The Rights and Privileges of the Press*. New York: D. Appleton-Century, 1934.

Siebert, Fredrick. *Free Press and Fair Trial*. Athens: University of Georgia, 1970.

Smith, James Morton. *Freedom's Fetters: The Alien and Sedition Laws and American Civil Liberties*. Ithaca, N.Y.: Cornell University Press, 1956.

Story, Joseph. *Commentaries on the Constitution of the United States*, 3 vols. Boston: Little, Brown, 1833.

Thomson, John. *An Enquiry, Concerning the Liberty, and Licentiousness of the Press, and the Uncontrolable Nature of the Human Mind*. New York: Johnson and Styker, 1801.

Thorpe, Francis. *The Federal and State Constitutions, Colonial Charters, and Other Organic Laws*, 7 vols. Washington, D.C.: 1909.

Tucker, St. George. *Blackstone's Commentaries: With Notes of Reference to the Constitution and Laws, of the Federal Government of the United States, and the Commonwealth of Virginia*. Philadelphia: William V. Birch and Abraham Small, 1803.

Tussman, Joseph. *Government and the Mind*. New York: Oxford University Press, 1977.

Ungar, Sanford. *The Papers and The Papers*. New York: E. P. Dutton, 1972.

Van Gerpen, Maurice. *Privileged Communication and the Press*. Westport, Conn.: Greenwood Press, 1979.

Warren, Charles. *The Supreme Court in United States History*, 3 vols. Boston: Little, Brown, 1922.

Whalen, Charles, Jr. *Your Right to Know: How The Free Flow of News Depends on the Journalist's Right to Protect His Sources*. New York: Vintage Books, 1973.

Williams, Francis. *The Right to Know: The Rise of the World Press*. London: Longmans, 1969.

Wortman, Tunis. *A Treatise Concerning Political Enquiry, and the Liberty of the Press*. New York: Forman, 1800.

Wiggins, James Russell. *Freedom or Secrecy*. New York: Oxford University Press, 1956.

Wise, David, and Ross, Thomas. *The Invisible Government*. New York: Random House, 1964.

ARTICLES

Abrams, Floyd. "The Press *Is* Different: Reflections on Justice Stewart and The Autonomous Press." 7 *Hofstra Law Review* 559 (1979).

Aithchison, Bill. "The Right to Receive and The Commercial Speech Doctrine: New Constitutional Considerations." 63 *Georgetown Law Journal* 775 (1975).

Alfange, Dean, Jr. "The Balancing of Interests in Free Speech Cases: In Defense of an Abused Doctrine." 2 *Law in Transition Quarterly* 35 (1965).

Barnett, Stephen. "The Puzzle of Prior Restraint." 29 *Stanford Law Review* 539 (1977).

Barron, Jerome. "Access to the Press—A New First Amendment Right." 80 *Harvard Law Review* 1641 (1967).

Bennis, Warren. "Have We Gone Overboard on 'The Right to Know'?" 3 *Saturday Review* 18 (March 1976).

Bezanson, Randall. "The New Free Press Guarantee." 63 *Virginia Law Review* 731 (1977).

Blasi, Vincent. "The Newsman's Privilege: An Empirical Study." 70 *Michigan Law Review* 229 (1971).

Bloustein, Edward. "The First Amendment and Privacy: The Supreme Court Justice and The Philosopher." 28 *Rutgers Law Review* 41 (1974).

Brennan, William, Jr. "The Supreme Court and The Meiklejohn Interpretation of The First Amendment." 79 *Harvard Law Review* 1 (1965).

———. Address. 32 *Rutgers Law Review* 173 (1979).

Burger, Warren E. "The Interdependence of Judicial and Journalistic Independence." 63 *Georgetown Law Journal* 1195 (1975).

Cahn, Edmond. "The Firstness of The First Amendment." 65 *Yale Law Journal* 464 (1956).

Emerson, Thomas I. "Toward A General Theory of The First Amendment." *Yale Law Journal* 853 (1963).

———. "Colonial Intentions and Current Realities of The First Amendment." 125 *University of Pennsylvania Law Review* 737 (1977).

———. "Legal Foundations of The Right to Know." 1976 *Washington University Law Quarterly* 1.

———. "The Doctrine of Prior Restraint." 50 *Law & Contemporary Problems* 648 (1955).

Ervin, Sam. "In Pursuit of a Press Privilege." 11 *Harvard Journal of Legislation* 233 (1974).

Frantz, Laurent B. "The First Amendment in the Balance." 71 *Yale Law Journal* 1424 (1962).

———. "Is the First Amendment Law? A Reply To Professor Mendelson." 51 *California Law Review* 729 (1963).

Gellhorn, Walter. "The Right to Know: First Amendment Overbreadth?" 1976 *Washington University Law Quarterly* 25.

Goodale, James C. "Legal Pitfalls In the Right to Know." 1976 *Washington University Law Quarterly* 29 (1976).

———. "Branzburg v. Hayes and the Developing Qualified Privilege for Newsmen." 26 *Hastings Law Journal* 709 (1975).

Halperin, Morton, and Hoffman, Daniel. "Secrecy and The Right to Know." 40 *Law and Contemporary Problems* 132 (1976).

Henkin Louis. "The Right to Know and The Duty to Withhold: The Case of the Pentagon Papers." 120 *University of Pennsylvania Law Review* 271 (1971).

Hennings, Thomas, Jr. "The People's Right to Know." 45 American *Bar Association Journal* 667 (1959).

———. "The Executive Privilege and The Public's Right to Know." 19 *Federal Bar Journal* 1 (1959).

Horton, Frank. "The Public's Right to Know." 3 *North Carolina Central Law Journal* 123 (1972).

Ivester, David. "The Constitutional Right to Know." 4 *Hastings Constitutional Law Quarterly* 109 (1977).

Junger, Peter. "Down Memory Lane: The Case of the Pentagon Papers." 23 *Case Western Reserve Law Review* 3 (1971).

Kalven, Harry. "'Uninhibited, Robust, and Wide-Open'—A Note on Free Speech and the Warren Court." 67 *Michigan Law Review* 289 (1968).

———. "The Concept of the Public Forum." In *The Supreme Court Review*, edited by Philip Kurland, p. 1. Chicago: University of Chicago Press, 1965.

———. "The New York Times Case: A Note On 'The Central Meaning of the First Amendment.'" In *The Supreme Court Review* edited by Philip Kurland, p. 191. Chicago: University of Chicago Press, 1964.

Katz, Alan. "Government Information Leaks and the First Amendment." 64 *California Law Review* 108 (1976).

Kutner, Luis. "Freedom of Information: Due Process of the Right to Know." 18 *Catholic Lawyer* 50 (1972).

Levi, Edward. "Confidentiality and Democratic Government." 30 *Record of the Association of the Bar of the City of New York* 323 (1975).

Lewis, Anthony. "A Preferred Position For Journalism." 7 *Hofstra Law Review* 595 (1979).

McKay, Robert. "The Preference For Freedom." 34 *New York University Law Review* 1182 (1959).

Meiklejohn, Alexander. "The First Amendment Is An Absolute." *The Supreme Court Review*. edited by Philip Kurland, p. 245. Chicago: University of Chicago Press, 1961.

Mendelson, Wallace. "On the Meaning of the First Amendment: Absolutes in the Balance." 50 *California Law Review* 821 (1962).

Merrill, John. "The 'People's Right to Know' Myth." 45 *New York State Bar Journal* 461 (1973).

Moyers, Bill. "The Right and the Need to Know." 38 *Social Action* 3 (1972).

Nimmer, Melville. "The Right to Speak From *Times* to *Time*: First Amendment Theory Applied to Libel and Misapplied to Privacy." 56 *California Law Review* 935 (1968).

———. "National Security Secrets v. Free Speech: The Issues Left Undecided in the Ellsberg Case." 26 *Stanford Law Review* 311 (1974).

———. "Is Freedom of the Press A Redundancy: What Does It Add to Freedom of Speech? 26 *Hastings Law Journal* 639 (1975).

O'Brien, David M. "Privacy and the Right of Access: Purposes and Paradoxes of Information Control." 30 *Administrative Law Review* 45 (1978).

———. "Freedom of Information, Privacy, and Information Control. A Contemporary Administrative Dilemma." 39 *Public Administration Review* 323 (1979).

———. "The First Amendment and The Public's 'Right to Know.'" 7 *Hastings Constitutional Law Quarterly* 101 (1980).

———. "Reassessing the First Amendment and the Public's 'Right to Know' in Constitutional Adjudication." 25 *Villanova Law Review* (Summer, 1980).

———. "The Seduction of the Judiciary: Social Science and the Courts." 64 *Judicature* 8 (1980).

Parks, Wallace. "The Open Government Principle: Applying the Right to Know Under the Constitution." 26 *George Washington Law Review* 1 (1957).

Powell, Lewis. "The Right to A Fair Trial." 51 *American Bar Association Journal* 534 (1965).

Rau, James. "Government Secrecy Agreements and the First Amendment." 28 *American University Law Review* 395 (1979).

Rehnquist, William. "The First Amendment: Freedom, Philosophy and the Law." 12 *Gonzaga Law Review* 1 (1976).

————, and Mondello, Anthony. "Rights in Conflict—Reconciling Privacy With The Public's Right to Know." 63 *Law Library Journal* 551 (1970).

Relyea, Harold. "Freedom of Information, Privacy, and Official Secrecy: The Evolution of Federal Government Information Policy Concepts." 6 *Social Indicators Research* 1 (1979).

————. "Faithful Execution of the FOI Act: A Legislative Branch Perspective." 39 *Public Administration Review* 328 (1979).

Rockwell, Lawrence. "The Public's Right to Know." 2 *Hastings Constitutional Law Quarterly* 829 (1975).

Rogers, William. "The Right to Know Government Business From The Viewpoint of the Government Official." 40 *Marquette Law Review* 83 (1956).

Rogge, O. John. "The Right to Know." 41 *American Scholar* 648 (1972).

Sack, Robert. "Reflections on the Wrong Question: Special Constitutional Privilege for The Institutional Press." 7 *Hofstra Law Review* 629 (1979).

Seymour, Whitney. "The Public's Right to Know—Who Decides What the Public Should Be Told?" 29 *Record of the Association of the Bar of the City of New York* 625 (1974).

Stevens, John Paul. "Some Thoughts About A General Rule." 21 *Arizona Law Review* 599 (1979).

Stewart, Potter. "Or of the Press." 26 *Hastings Law Journal* 631 (1975).

Strong, Frank. "Fifty Years of 'Clear and Present Danger.'" *The Supreme Court Review*. edited by Philip Kurland, p. 41. Chicago: University of Chicago Press, 1969.

Symposium. "Administrative Secrecy: A Comparative Perspective." 35 *Public Administration Review* 1 (1975).

————. "The Freedom of Information Act a Decade Later." 39 *Public Administration Review* 310 (1979).

————. "Openness in Government—A New Era." 34 *Federal Bar Journal* 279 (1975).

————. "Openness in Government—A Continuing Era." 38 *Federal Bar Journal* 95 (1979).

————. "The People's Right to Know." 8 *Trial* 12 (1972).

Van Alstyne, William. "First Amendment and the Suppression of War Mongering Propaganda in the United States." 31 *Law & Contemporary Problems* 530 (1966).

————. "The Hazards to the Press of Claiming a 'Preferred Position.'" 26 *Hastings Law Journal* 761 (1977).

Wellington, Harry. "On Freedom of Expression." 88 *Yale Law Journal* 1105 (1979).

Wiggins, James R. "The Role of the Press in Safeguarding The People's Right to Know Government Business." 40 *Marquette Law Review* 74 (1956).

Wright, J. Skelly. "Defamation, Privacy, And The Public's Right to Know: A National Problem and A New Approach." 46 *Texas Law Review* 630 (1968).

Yankwich, Leon. "Legal Implications of, and Barriers to, The Right to Know." 40 *Marquette Law Review* 3 (1956).

GOVERNMENT PUBLICATIONS

U.S., Congress, Senate. Subcommittee on Constitutional Rights of the Committee on the Judiciary. *Freedom of the Press*, 92d Cong., 1st and 2nd Sess., 1971 and 1972.

U.S., Congress, House. Committee on the Judiciary. *Newsmen's Privilege*, 93d Cong., 1st Sess., 1973.

U.S., Congress, Senate. Committee on the Judiciary, Subcommittee on Administrative Practice and Procedure. *Freedom of Information Act*, 95th Cong., 1st Sess., 1977.

U.S., General Accounting Office. *Government Field Offices Should Better Implement the Freedom of Information Act*, 1978.

U.S., Department of Health, Education and Welfare. *Records, Computers and the Rights of Citizens*, 1973.

U.S., Congress, Senate. Committee on Government Operations, Subcommittee on Intergovernmental Relations. *Executive Privilege—Secrecy in Government*, 94th Cong., 1st Sess., 1975.

U.S., Congress, Senate. Committee on Government Operations, Subcommittee on Intergovernmental Relations and Committee on the Judiciary, Subcommittee on Separation of Powers and Administrative Practice and Procedure. *Executive Privilege, Secrecy in Government, Freedom of Information*, 93d Cong. 1st Sess., 1973.

U.S., Congress, Senate. Committee on the Judiciary, Subcommittee on Constitutional Rights. *Executive Privilege*, 86th Cong., 1st Sess., 1959.

U.S., Congress, Senate. Committee on Government Operations. *Government in the Sunshine Act—S.5. (P.L. 94-409) Source Book: Legislative History, Texts, and Other Documents*, 1976.

U.S., Congress, House. Committee on the Judiciary, Subcommittee on Administrative Law and Government Relations. *Government in The Sunshine Implementation*, 95th Cong., 1st Sess., 1977.

U.S., Congress, Senate. Committee on Governmental Affairs, Subcommittee on Federal Spending Practices and Open Government. *Oversight of the Government in the Sunshine Act*, 95th Cong., 1st and 2nd Sess., 1978.

U.S., Commission on Federal Paperwork. *Confidentiality and Privacy*, 1977.

U.S., National Study Commission on Records and Documents of Federal Officials, *Final Report*, 1977.

U.S., National Study Commission on Records and Documents of Federal Officials. *Study of the Records of Supreme Court Justices*, 1977.

U.S., Congress, Senate. Committee on the Judiciary. *Freedom of Information Act*, 95th Cong., 1st Sess, 1978.

U.S., Congress, Senate. Committee on the Judiciary, Subcommittee on Administrative Practice and Procedure. *Freedom of Information Act Source Book: Legislative Materials, Cases, Articles*, 93rd Cong., 2d Sess., 1974.

U.S., Congress, House. Committee on Government Operations, Subcommittee on Government Information and Individual Rights. *Freedom of Information Act and Amendments of 1974—Sourcebook: Legislative History, Texts and Other Documents,* 1975.

U.S., Congress, House. Committee on Government Operations, Subcommittee on Foreign Operations and Government Information. *Access to Records,* 1974.

U.S., Congress, House. Committee on Government Operations, Subcommittee on Operations and Government Information. *Security Classification Reform,* 93d Cong., 2d Sess., 1975.

U.S., Congress, House and Senate. Joint Committee on Congressional Operations. *Constitutional Immunity of Members of Congress, Legislative Role of Congress in Gathering and Disclosing Information,* 93d Cong., 1st Sess., 1973.

U.S., Congress, Senate. Committee on Government Operations, Subcommittee on Intergovernmental Relations. *Government Secrecy,* 1975.

U.S., Congress, Senate. Committee on Government Operations, Subcommittee on Intergovernmental Relations. *Legislation on Government Secrecy,* 93d Cong., 2d Sess., 1974.

U.S., Congress, House. Committee on Government Operations, Subcommittee on Government Information and Individual Rights. *Citizen's Guide on How to Use the Freedom of Information Act and the Privacy Act in Requesting Government Documents,* 95th Cong., 1st Sess., 1977.

U.S., Comptroller General. *Report to Congress: Improved Executive Branch Oversight Needed For The Government's National Security Information Classification Program,* 1979.

U.S., Congress, House. Committee on Government Operations. *Justice Department Handling of Cases Involving Classified Data and Claims of National Security,* 96th Cong., 1st Sess., 1979.

U.S., Congress, Senate. Select Committee on Intelligence, Subcommittee on Secrecy and Disclosure. *National Security Secrets and the Administration of Justice,* 95th Cong., 2d. Sess., 1978.

PERIODICALS

Access. National Citizens Committee for Broadcasting, P.O. Box 12038, Washington, D.C. 20005.

Access Reports/FOI Newsletter (biweekly). 2626 Pennsylvania Avenue, N.W., Washington, D.C. 20037.

AIM Report. Accuracy in Media, 777 14th Street, N.W., Washington, D.C. 20005.

Columbia Journalism Review. 700 Journalism Building, Columbia University, New York, New York 10027.

First Principles. Center for National Security Studies, 122 Maryland Avenue, N.W., Washington, D.C. 20002.

FoI Digest. The Freedom of Information Center, School of Journalism, University of Missouri, Columbia, Missouri 65205.

The News Media & The Law. The Reporters Committee for Freedom of the Press, 1750 Pennsylvania Avenue, N.W., Room 1112, Washington, D.C. 20006.

Washington Journalism Review. 3122 M Street, N.W., Washington, D.C. 20007.

INDEX OF COURT CASES

Freedman v. Maryland, 380 U.S. 1 (1965), 167
Friedman v. Rogers, 440 U.S. 1 (1979), 115
Frowerk v. United States, 249 U.S. 204 (1919), 75, 111

Gannett, Co. v. DePasquale, 443 U.S. 368 (1979), 19, 108–09, 117, 125, 126–27, 130–34, 137–39, 140, 142, 146, 148
Garrison v. Louisiana, 379 U.S. 64 (1964), 108, 110, 115, 167
Gertz v. Robert Welch, 418 U.S. 323 (1974), 97–98, 114
Giboney v. Empire Storage and Ice Company, 336 U.S. 409 (1949), 111
Gibson v. Florida Legislative Committee, 372 U.S. 539 (1963), 112
Gilbert v. Minnesota, 254 U.S. 325 (1920), 28, 71–72, 74–76, 110–11
Ginsberg v. New York, 390 U.S. 629 (1968), 114
Ginzburg v. United States, 383 U.S. 463 (1966), 113, 114
Gitlow v. New York, 268 U.S. 652 (1925), 58, 73–74, 76, 111
Gojack v. United States, 384 U.S. 702 (1966), 112
Gompers v. Bucks Store & R. Co., 221 U.S. 418 (1911), 25
Gompers v. United States, 233 U.S. 604 (1914), 111
Gooding v. Wilson, 405 U.S. 518 (1972), 106, 114–15
Gordon v. United States, 344 U.S. 414 (1953), 15, 26
Gravel v. United States, 408 U.S. 606 (1972), 26, 56
Grayned v. City of Rockford, 408 U.S. 104 (1972), 170
Greenbelt Cooperative Publishing Association v. Bresler, 398 U.S. 6 (1970), 108, 114
Greene v. McElroy, 360 U.S. 474 (1958), 25

Greer v. Spock, 428 U.S. 828 (1976), 113
Griswold v. Connecticut, 381 U.S. 479 (1965), 21, 22–23, 26, 27, 53
Grosjean v. American Press Association Company, 297 U.S. 233 (1936), 52–54, 58, 115, 167–68

Hague v. C.I.O., 307 U.S. 496 (1939), 148
Hamilton v. Regents of University of California, 293 U.S. 245 (1934), 58
Hamling v. United States, 418 U.S. 87 (1974), 26, 108, 114–15
Hannah v. Larche, 363 U.S. 420 (1960), 25
Heller v. New York, 413 U.S. 483 (1973), 114
Herbert v. Lando, 441 U.S. 153 (1979), 98–99, 110–114
Herndon v. Georgia, 295 U.S. 441 (1935), 111
Herndon v. Lowry, 301 U.S. 242 (1937), 111–12
Hotel and Restaurant Employees Local v. Wisconsin Employment Relations Board, 315 U.S. 437 (1942), 112
Houchins v. KQED, 438 U.S. 1 (1978), 26, 109, 123–25, 132, 138, 140, 146

Illinois v. Allen, 397 U.S. 337 (1970), 147
International Brotherhood of Teamsters v. Vogt, 354 U.S. 294 (1957), 112
International Longshoremen's Ass'n. v. Philadelphia Marine Trade Asso., 389 U.S. 64 (1967), 25, 112
Irvin v. Dowd, 366 U.S. 717 (1961), 147

Jackson, Ex parte, 96 U.S. 728 (1878), 110, 115
Jacobellis v. Ohio, 378 U.S. 184 (1964), 113, 114
Jay v. Boyd, 351 U.S. 245 (1956), 26
Jencks v. United States, 353 U.S. 657 (1957), 15–17, 23
Jenkins v. Georgia, 418 U.S. 153 (1974), 114, 115

United States Civil Service Commission v. National Association of Letter Carriers, 413 U.S. 548 (1973), 168
United States ex rel. Milwaukee Social Democratic Publishing Company v. Burleson, 255 U.S. 407 (1921), 115
United States v. Belmont, 301 U.S. 324 (1937), 169; v. Bennett, 24 Fed. Cases 1,093 (1879), 110; v. Caldwell, 408 U.S. 665 (1972), 109; v. Cruikshank, 92 U.S. 542 (1876), 25, 108; v. Curtiss-Wright Export Corporation, 299 U.S. 304 (1936), 167, 169; v. Dennis, 183 F.2d 201 (1950), 112; v. Dickey, 268 U.S. 378 (1925), 115; v. Donas-Botto, 363 F. Supp. 191 (E.D. Mich. 1974), 167; v. Edler Industries Incorporated, 579 F.2d 516 (1978), 167, 170; v. Guest, 383 U.S. 745 (1966), 26; v. Gurney, 434 U.S. 1423 (1978), 147; v. Hudson and Goodwin, 1 Cranch 32 (1812), 50, 58; v. Marchetti, 466 F.2d 1309 (4th Cir. 1972), 167; v. Mine Workers of America, 330 U.S. 258 (1947), 25; v. Nixon, 418 U.S. 683 (1974), 167; v. Orito, 413 U.S. 139 (1973), 114; v. Pink, 315 U.S. 203 (1942), 169; v. Reidel, 402 U.S. 351 (1971), 114; v. Reynolds, 345 U.S. 1 (1952), 26, 169; v. Richardson, 418 U.S. 87 (1974), 26, 56; v. Robel, 389 U.S. 258 (1967), 87, 113, 163, 170; v. Rosenberg, 195 F.2d (2d Cir. 1952), 167; v. Seeger, 380 U.S. 163 (1965), 116; v. Snepp, 100 S.Ct. 763 (1980), 167; v. Subversive Activities Control Board, 367 U.S. 1 (1961), 86-87, 112-13; v. The Progressive, Inc., 467 F. Supp. 990 (1979), 2, 16, 23, 151, 155-65, 167, 170; v. Twelve 200-Foot Reels of Film, 413 U.S. 123 (1973), 114; v. Van Hee, 531 F.2d 354 (6th Cir.

1976), 167; v. Washington Post Co., 403 U.S. 713 (1971), 167
Uphaus v. Wyman, 360 U.S. 72 (1959), 112

Valentine v. Chrestensen, 316 U.S. 52 (1942), 90, 101, 113
Van Ness v. Pacard, 2 Peters 137 (1829), 58
Virginia State Board of Pharmacy v. Virginia Citizens Consumer Council, 425 U.S. 748 (1975), 26, 101-02, 108-09, 115, 146

Watkins v. United States, 354 U.S. 178 (1957), 112
Watts v. United States, 344 U.S. 705 (1969), 114
Welsh v. United States, 398 U.S. 333 (1970), 116
West Virginia Board of Education v. Barnette, 319 U.S. 624 (1943), 27, 111
Whalen v. Roe, 97 S.Ct. 869 (1977), 26, 146
White v. Nicholls, 3 How. 266 (1845), 115
Whitney v. California, 274 U.S. 357 (1927), 76, 110, 111
Wiseman v. Massachusetts, 398 U.S. 960 (1969), 26
Wolff v. McDonnell, 418 U.S. 539 (1974), 146
Wolston v. Reader's Digest, 99 S.Ct. 2701 (1979), 114
Wood v. Georgia, 370 U.S. 375 (1962), 113

Yates v. United States, 354 U.S. 178 (1957), 83-85, 112
Yellin v. United States, 374 U.S. 109 (1963), 112
Young v. American Mini Theatres, 427 U.S. 50 (1976), 114-15

NAME AND SUBJECT INDEX

Goldberg, Arthur, 16, 85, 134
Gordon, Thomas, (*see* Cato) 33
Government in the Sunshine Act, 17, 169
gray mail, 16–17
Griswold, Erwin, 159–60

Haldeman, H. R., 105
Hamilton, Alexander, 42–43
Hamilton, Andrew, 33–35
Hancock, John, 40–42
Hand, Learned, 81–82
Hansen, Charles, 156
Harlan, John M., Jr., 19, 83, 84–86, 87, 91–92, 93, 95–96, 156, 160
Hay, George, 48
H-bomb controversy, 1, 155–65
Henkin, Louis, 5
Hennings, Thomas, 6, 28
Henry, Patrick, 38–39, 41, 136
Herndon, Angelo, 77
Hocking, William, 10
Holmes, Oliver W., 52, 71–73, 74–76, 80, 81, 85, 88, 152
Housekeeping Statute, 5, 23
House Committee on Un-American Activities, 80, 84–85, 87
Hughes, Charles Evans, 52, 71, 76–78, 103–04, 153–54

Immigration Act, 69
Immigration and Nationality Act, 121
inherent powers, 155, 159, 161–63
injunctions, 1, 152–53, 155–56
intelligence methods, 160
Interagency Classification Review Committee, 157
Iredell, James, 48

Jackson, Andrew, 68
Jackson, Robert, 14, 81, 83, 117
Jefferson, Thomas, 13, 28, 37–38, 42–45, 47, 48–50, 89, 119, 139
Jehovah's Witnesses cases, 71–79, 120
John Birch Society, 97
Johnson, Lyndon, 7, 24
judicial, activism, 62, 65–66, 71, 74, 79–80, 102–03, 124, 137, 150,

approaches to the First Amendment, 65–103, 86; craftsmanship, 21, 55, 133, 150; modest intervention, 150–51, 166; review, 7, 21–23, 78, 82; self-restraint, 65–66, 69, 70–71, 73, 79–80, 102, 150, 153

Kalven, Harry, 65
Kennedy, Edward, 156
Kentucky Resolutions, 44, 48
King, Martin Luther, Jr., 93
Korean conflict, 157, 158, 161
Ku Klux Klan, 71, 87

Labor-Management Relations Act, 80
law enforcement investigatory files, 7, 160
Lee, Richard Henry, 42
legislative investigations, 80, 84–88
Levi, Edward, 13
Lewis, Anthony, 62
libel, 29–31, 50, 69–71, 89, 90, 93–96, 96–99, 101, 103, 164
liberty of contract, 21, 71
licentiousness, 31, 45, 66
Lincoln, Abraham, 69
Livingston, Edward, 48
Livingston, William, 35
Locke, John, 33–34
Long, Edward, 6
Long, Huey, 103
Long Parliament, 31
Lord Campbell's Act, 32, 54
Lovejoy, Elijah, 68
Lucas, John R., 10

Macon, Nathan, 48
Madison, James, 13, 28, 37, 42–44, 45–47, 48–49, 50, 53, 82, 89, 139
Mansfield, Lord, 31
Marshall, John, 48, 51, 82, 107
Marshall, Thurgood, 59, 61–62, 87, 99, 100, 105, 118–19, 121, 122, 129, 130, 133, 137, 140, 142–43, 160–63
Mason, George, 38–39
Massachusetts Convention, 40

ABOUT THE AUTHOR

David M. O'Brien received his B.A. (1973), M.A. (1974), and Ph.D. (1977) from the University of California, Santa Barbara. He is an assistant professor in the Woodrow Wilson Department of Government and Foreign Affairs, University of Virginia, and previously taught at the University of California, Santa Barbara, and the University of Puget Sound, where he also served as chairman of the Department of Politics. Mr. O'Brien is the author of *Privacy, Law, and Public Policy* (1979) and numerous articles in law reviews and other professional journals. He is a recipient of awards from the National Endowment for the Humanities, the Earhart Foundation, and Project '87, which was sponsored by the American Political Science Association and the American Historical Association.